MICHELE GUINNESS

THE

RECOVER THE FUN: LIFE-CHANGING CELEBRATIONS

HEAVENLY

FOR HOME & COMMUNITY

PARTY

MONARCH
BOOKS

Oxford, UK & Grand Rapids, Michigan, USA

First published in the UK in 2007 by Monarch Books
(a publishing imprint of Lion Hudson plc),
Wilkinson House, Jordan Hill Road, Oxford OX2 8DR.
Tel: +44 (0)1865 302750   Fax: +44 (0)1865 302757
Email: monarch@lionhudson.com
www.lionhudson.com

ISBN: 978-1-85424-835-0 (UK)
ISBN: 978-0-8254-6174-3 USA)

Distributed by:
UK: Marston Book Services Ltd, PO Box 269,
Abingdon, Oxon OX14 4YN;
USA: Kregel Publications, PO Box 2607,
Grand Rapids, Michigan 49501.

British Library Cataloguing Data
A catalogue record for this book is available from
the British Library.

Printed and bound in Malta by Gutenberg Press.

Contents

For Livvy,
first of a new generation
of heavenly partygoers

Acknowledgments

The Oscars have turned giving thanks into something of a ritual, but on reflection, it is true that no one ever accomplishes anything without the intervention of others – be it through circumstances, intention or necessity. And never is that more so than with celebration – and writing about it. It isn't easy to celebrate alone. It would be impossible to describe it. I am therefore immensely grateful to the members of St Thomas' Lancaster, who have allowed my husband Peter and me to experiment, innovate, play with tradition, make mistakes, learn and change things accordingly. Few churches are as accommodating, open-minded, adventurous, forgiving, flexible and as much fun as you are. For being such gracious, supportive ecclesiastical guinea-pigs, I thank you from the bottom of my heart.

Some there have made a very special contribution to the celebratory life and culture of the community. A previous youth minister, Ruth Hassall, who now works for the Church Pastoral Aid Society, took the Tabernacles service outline and developed it further, in her own inimitable way, proving that it needed the eyes of someone who wasn't Jewish to see what I had missed, and that the rich symbolism was an object-lesson in what constituted effective all-age worship. With real imagination and ingenuity, assistant vicar Debbie Peatman, curate Sam Corley and lay reader Sue Kiernan have turned Holy Week into a spiritual banquet. Debbie's stories of the people who encountered Jesus (used as meditations throughout the year) have enriched beyond measure my understanding of his love for all of us, and I am deeply touched by her generosity in allowing me to include two of them here. Every festival at St Tees leaves our Administrator Dave Cumming and his wife Meriel, and countless unnamed helpers, the unenviable job of clearing chairs, setting tables, building a booth (Tabernacles), peeling dozens of hard-boiled eggs and chopping horseradish (at Passover), clearing away slops, and hoovering the leftovers out of the carpets. Celebration doesn't happen without a great deal of hard work. They are the real facilitators. Wendy Moore and Ceridwen Copping regularly transform the building into Bethlehem, Jerusalem, a garden, a beach, a town centre, wherever their or anyone else's imagination takes them, and I have learnt so much from them about the importance of visual stimulation in appreciating the presence of God.

I am indebted to all the others who have shared their own creative ideas for celebration with me – Kate Porteous, Christine Jenson, and all the folk at the New Wine Newark seminar on parenting in 2006. They didn't know their ruminations would be so seminal, but that's the spice of life. My gratitude too, to John and Anne Coles and Mark Melluish, who had the courage to let me loose with the idea at a New Wine evening celebration at Shepton Mallett, and coped manfully with the partying that then went on half the night.

A special thank you to the readers of *Woman Alive* magazine, who allowed me to try out on them first the recipes at the back of the book, and to the editor, Jackie Stead, for taking the culinary risk of publishing them.

Without my children, I would probably never have begun the adventure in the first place. Engaging them spiritually and supporting them financially necessitated first the experience of celebration, and then the writing about it. There hasn't been a day since they were first lent to me that their influence hasn't permeated my life with joy and laughter.

My minister, technical manager, accountant, theological adviser, plumber, electrician, cleaner, lover and husband have all been indispensable – particularly since they are all one man. Peter has always given me my head of steam. More than that, he piles on the fuel. Few men, especially church leaders, are as courageous as he, but without his constant inspiration, risk-taking, encouragement, patience, partnership and love, my celebration would have been very much the poorer.

Glossary of Hebrew Terms

Festivals

Rosh Hashanah: Jewish New Year (usually in September)
Yom Kippur: the Day of Atonement (a week after the New Year)
Succoth: the Feast of Booths or Tabernacles (a week after Yom Kippur)
Pesach: the Passover
Purim: the Feast of Esther (March)
Shevuoth: Pentecost (the Feast of Weeks, in May or June).
Hannukah: the Festival of Lights (December)

Other terms

aficomen: the middle piece of three matzos used by the leader in the
    Passover service and symbolic of the Passover lamb
bar mitzvah: literally 'blessing of the son', the coming of age of a Jewish boy
    at thirteen
bat mitzvah: literally 'blessing of the daughter', the coming of age of a
    Jewish girl at twelve
berakhot: blessings
charoseth: a mixture of apples, wine and walnuts eaten at Passover as a
    symbol of the mud that held the bricks together in Egypt
gefilte fish: chopped fish-balls
goy: a Gentile
haggadah: literally 'the telling', the Passover service book

halachah: literally 'the progress or journey', the rules of Judaism passed down
 by word of mouth that describe the proper path through life

kaddish: prayers in memory of the dead

kiddush: the traditional Friday evening Sabbath prayers

kishkas: Yiddish for 'guts'

kosher: prepared according to the dietary rules

matzah: unleavened bread

mikvot: ritual temple baths

moedim: holidays, or rehearsals

simcha: literally 'joy', celebration or party

seder: literally 'service' – the Passover service, usually in the home

siddur: the Jewish prayer book

shofar: the ram's horn

shivah: seven days of official mourning after a bereavement

shabbat: Sabbath

succah: a booth or tabernacle

taschlich: the tradition at *Yom Kippur* of using stones cast into running water as
 a symbol of throwing away our sins.

Part 1

The
Appetizer

Our Christian culture needs to cultivate an anarchic lightness, a lust for free-dom, a celebratory spirit. It needs to learn from the boom in festival cul-ture...we yearn to join a crowd that is celebrating... Christianity is meant to be a religion of celebration.   Theo Hobson, *The Guardian*, July 2005

6 'Celebration' must be one of the most devalued words in the currency of the English language. Everybody seems to be having one, in some disguise or another, but they are as different from each other as best rump steak from economy burgers. A celebration can, for example, be a full-blown banquet with ten courses and bottles of bollie, or tea and buns at the Women's Fellowship. It can be a lavish concert or ball with full orchestra and canapés in the interval, or a picnic in the rain on the school playing-field. It can be a rowdy, booze-soaked night out in the local bar, or a bring-and-share supper of cold pastry and Netto trifles. It can be a totally joyous, abandoned way of marking a special anniversary event, or, quite frankly, an awfully Anglo-Saxon, damp squib.

Churches, who seem to think they have a monopoly on the word, are often most guilty of reducing it. For Anglo-Catholics it can involve an extra-long procession, for conservative evangelicals an extra-long sermon, and for charismatics several extra songs, sung with even more gusto than usual. Celebration certainly isn't a priority in our own homes.

Like Sleeping Beauty, Christian imaginations seem to have fallen into a deep sleep in a quiet, hidden corner of our beings, hedged in by our very limited expectations of what worship is supposed to be. In the dim and distant past, in the earliest days of the church, our fingers were pricked by the bad fairy and our spirits infected with a fear of emotion and excess, with a mistrust of fun and play. We became dull and joyless, turned countless children off the very thing we most want them to enjoy, and now we wait to be kissed into wholeness again by the gentle Holy Spirit.

It is a strange state of affairs, given that Judaism, from which Christianity sprang, never lost its appetite for celebration. The Jewish teachers of old said there could be no real celebration without decent food and drink, and despite persecution, poverty and genocide, the Jews have practised and perfected the art with ever more obsessive dedication throughout the generations.

'I hear Sadie is having an affair', says one Jewish woman to another in the synagogue.

'So,' says the other, 'who's doing the catering?'

'Affairs' or 'functions' are favourite Jewish words to describe the regular, communal orgies of the palate that accompany bar mitzvahs, graduations, weddings, anniversaries and the whole gamut of life's milestones that provide so many wonderful excuses for what they call a *simcha*. The Hebrew word is actually translated 'joy' or 'enjoyment', but in common usage it has come to mean a party. There is little joy for the organizers of a *simcha*, who have the stress of making a bigger and better do than the Cohens' or the Levys', and paying the bill at the end of it. There are websites that help you find the venue, the caterer, the band, the decorations, the outfit – and even the rabbi. But for the guests, the satisfaction is immense, especially if they happen to be among the first paratroopers to fight their way through to the smoked salmon and *gefilte fish*. Food, not alcohol, is what gives Jews their fix. In all my experience of *simchas*, I never remember a rush for the bar, but at five foot nothing, trying to get anywhere near the buffet table required professional elbow- and foot-work. If I managed to get a plateful, I had the bruises to show for it.

Many years later, when the church had become my prime community, oh how I missed that all-in wrestling, not to mention the mouth-watering food, the deafening noise as everyone spoke at once and no one conversed, the flickering candles, the long and lilting grace sung after meals, and the manic dancing, *hora* style, or spinning round and round in circles like a top. Even my rather sedate church wedding, lovely as it was, felt a tad flat compared to being married under a canopy of flowers, smugly watching the scrum at the buffet table because I was there first for the only time in my life, and being carried around on a chair hoisted up on people's shoulders.

I missed the festivals celebrated round the table at home most of all – New Year and apples dipped in honey, with prayers for sweet and happy months ahead; Pentecost and Gran's baked cheesecake, pure and white like the law given to Moses on Mount Sinai; and Passover lasting late into the night because my grandfather, who led the service, had fallen asleep in the middle, and we were all so busy chatting that no one had noticed. Once Gran realized that proceedings had ground to a halt, she would temporarily interrupt her own conversation to call him to order.

All the festivals required a cooking marathon, but nothing gave her greater satisfaction than sitting down at the table, surrounded by her extended family. She looked at us fondly through glasses so smeared with the remnants of her culinary efforts that it would have been a miracle if she could have actually seen any of us. But we were there – and eating, that was all that mattered. 'I've made it specially for you,' she said, if we dared decline the tiniest mouthful. 'No pressure, then' is certainly not Jewish. None of us realized until after she died that she was actually anorexic. She was so busy serving us that we never registered the fact that she had lived on whisky and Woodbines.

I married a man, who though not Jewish, had a raft of family traditions of his own, mainly established by his mother, who came from a staunch Canadian Baptist home with strict but loving Sunday observance. For Peter's father, an Anglican clergyman, raised by a single mother after his father died when he was two and sent off to boarding school, home and family celebration provided a sense of security and stability that mattered enormously. But in the early days of our marriage, we never fully appreciated how much our inherited traditions meant to us, or thought about creating some new ones of our own. As a Jew in the church, I often felt like a guest on a cruise ship, alone in an unfamiliar and not altogether sympathetic environment. I didn't want to rock the boat by incorporating any Jewish-style rituals into our home, let alone try walking on water by suggesting them to our church. When Peter left his teaching job to become a minister, I felt I had been condemned to a life sentence of crimplene frocks and staid, sensible, Anglican behaviour. Then I had children.

When I was pregnant for the first time, a number of older folk, whose wisdom I valued, repeated knowingly, 'The family that prays together, stays together.' What a good idea, I thought – until they were born and then I didn't know how to do it. Has anyone ever successfully told their children to come in from the garden or switch off the TV for family prayers? 'Stop playing for praying' was in effect what I said. And they replied 'Oooo yes, Mummy!' No, of course they didn't. The groans of reluctance quickly convinced me that this was not the best way to encourage their spiritual development.

If prayer was to be a meaningful, lifetime's experience, I felt it should be instinctive and natural, like breathing, not a strange, dislocated activity, generated by bowed head, closed eyes and folded hands. We tried to model this kind of spirituality every morning, reading Bible stories with them both over hot drinks in our king-sized bed. At least, Peter read the stories. I was more of a sleeping partner. But later in the day, when I called them away from their fun, all I was doing was passing on the subconscious message that God is a killjoy. In fact, I was hacking off their spiritual side and putting it in a special box marked 'sacred', to be taken out on Sundays or on holy occasions, accompanied by suitably pious behaviour. My fears were not so much that they would ditch this charade as soon as they were old enough to see it for what it was, but that they would throw God out with it. In fact, within a few weeks of starting primary school, Joel began the shut-eyes, palms-together, 'God bless list' ritual, in as good a parsonical voice as any vicar, but it did wear off as our more meaningful alternatives prevailed.

We weren't at all sure how to create a spiritual environment that would nurture, not stifle a child's budding faith. All we knew for certain was that it would involve throwing out adult inconsistencies in favour of absolute integrity. 'Don't talk to me about Jesus,' my mother once said to Joel, our firstborn. 'Talk to me about Moses.' He thought long and hard, and said finally, 'Moses...was Jesus' daddy.' 'Integrity' comes from the same root as the word 'integration', and involves pulling all the bits of ourselves together – body, mind, spirit and soul – and not pandering to a religious culture that has separated them out for centuries.

As I reflected on my own childhood (which was far from perfect, or I would never have tinkered with Christianity), I realized that I was introduced, not to the Jewish faith – for Jews know they cannot force belief – but to a Jewish way of life that would provide a rich and colourful context in which faith could blossom. Christians also know that they can't make anyone believe – or do they? 'God has no grandchildren', said Corrie Ten Boom, the brave Dutch preacher who survived Ravensbruck Concentration Camp, where she had been sent for hiding Jews. We all sign up to that, yet persist, nonetheless, in trying to convince our children intellectually. Perhaps we need to concentrate instead on providing them with a feel for a 'Christian way of life' that is so full of wonder and glory that wherever they go, whatever befalls, they will associate their best, their happiest memories with the celebration of their faith. And then perhaps, if they do decide to turn away from their heritage, they'll never quite find the unalloyed joy of those magical moments in anything else, and will return to it in the end.

There was no guide or handbook, no material, prayers or liturgies, no creative ideas or suggestions to help me do that. Despite the fact that home has by far the greatest impact on the spiritual development of a child, the job tended to be devolved to the church. But since Judaism is home-based, rather than synagogue-based, and since it was all I knew, we tentatively experimented with a

Jewish *Shabbat* – a family Sabbath eve once a week with bread and wine. Bread is the symbol of work, and wine of rest and rejoicing. We lit candles, just as my mother had done when I was a child, prayed for the children and for the right spouses to make themselves known in due time, sang a few songs, gave them small presents, and reminded ourselves that Jesus had said, 'Whenever you do this, remember me.' We didn't close our eyes or introduce any other extraneous, unnecessary rituals. And sometimes it worked like a dream, sometimes it didn't. On occasions, especially during the prolonged miners' strike that drastically affected the town where we lived, with a piece of bread disintegrating in his hot little hand, six-year-old Joel prayed for people who had no food, for people who had no work, for people who were ill, sad, frightened, badly done by. On and on he prayed around the world, while the smell of the meal wafted in from the kitchen, and Peter and I did our best to stifle the demands of our bellies. On other occasions, usually when we had invited extended-family friends, both our children would play up and insist on singing 'Twinkle, twinkle little star' or some other profound, well-known spiritual song.

It was only when Joel went to university and continued the tradition in his room in hall with a motley band of friends, with beer or lemonade when he had no wine, and biscuits when he had no bread, that we realized that generally speaking, the idea seemed to have paid off.

By then we had become bolder about breaking down taboos, initiating and encouraging all kinds of celebration in our local community and church, aided and abetted by creative, adventurous colleagues and wonderful congregations who were up for anything. We discovered that though there were increasing resources for church services of every kind, especially when the internet arrived to bless us, there were still few suggestions for celebration in the home, whether in families, or in that ever more popular extended family, the house group or cell. How could they ring the changes from the pure brain activity of study and discussion every once in a while, have children present (especially if single parents had no babysitter), celebrate a festival, and invite in the neighbours to introduce them to non-institutional, no-threat church?

A host of other problems presented themselves. Early on in our marriage, when money was very tight, inviting in friends for a meal was a major test of faith. Could celebratory meals be meatless and fish-less if necessary, managed on a mortgage-reduced budget? And since levels of creativity in my childhood home began and ended with putting a pair of candles on the table, and vicar's wife or no, I have the flower-arranging skills of a donkey, how exactly did one give a very ordinary occasion a festive feel? These were difficulties others have expressed over the years: 'I can't afford it'; 'I can't cook'; or more often, 'I'm no good at that sort of thing'. Neither was I. I learnt slowly by trial and error. Where there is a will, there is a way – as long as we abandon any idea of becoming a domestic guru. These days, few things give me as much pleasure as watching the people seated around my table – whether they're engaging in excellent conversation, or simply enjoying the atmosphere, their faces in the candlelight full of wonder and worship. I must be turning into my grandmother.

In time, we summoned up enough courage to introduce our churches to relevant Judaic festivals. Passover became an integral part of Holy Week. Harvest had a decided Tabernacles feel to it, complete with a large temporary *succah* or booth. Pentecost, the birthday of the church, was a time for drama and dancing. And we didn't stop at the Hebraic festivals. An All Saints' Day party replaced Halloween. We once had a Valentine's Day dinner dance in celebration of marital romance. The journalist at the local BBC radio station couldn't believe that marriage and romance were feasible cohabitees, and came to interview us.

In fact, any and no reason is a good enough excuse for a party these days, as long as it is well and lovingly constructed by an imaginative team dedicated to avoiding the cringe factor, which continually lies in wait for the unsuspecting and unprepared. And the local community, many of whom had never darkened the door of a church for years, have welcomed the invitation, come and then come again.

This book is a reflection of that long journey of discovery, full of tentative steps, frustrating obstacles, false trails, sudden forest glades, and ultimate mountain-tops, as Peter and I pursued our mission to make celebration a way of life in home and community. At the very beginning that meant discarding false impressions of God, and replacing them with the idea of a fun- and people-loving Creator who invented so many festivals that there was one for virtually every week of the year. Then, behind the Man of Sorrows mask, we uncovered a very Jewish Jesus, a man of the party, who still likes nothing better than a night out with his friends. Finally, the last part of the adventure involved rethinking our own expression of faith, both on a personal and a shared level. How could we, as individuals, extended family and community, become more integrated, more naturally spiritual, more joyously holy?

If the basic concept of creating seasons of joy and festival, of integrating the sacred and the secular, the holy and the ordinary, is primarily Hebraic, the practical application is not necessarily or uniquely so. By 'Hebraic' I am referring to the Judaism of the Old Testament, of the period between the end of the Old and the beginning of the New Testament, and of the time of Jesus – until just after the destruction of the Second Temple in AD 70. While that kind of Judaism is still fairly recognizable in medieval and contemporary practice, it had by then acquired a host of extra-biblical regulations, alterations and rabbinic addenda that make it more like Pharisaism than anything Jesus ever knew. Meanwhile, non-orthodox Jews today might not even know what most of the symbols mean. If I had found all the answers in contemporary Judaism, if that had satisfied me completely, I would never have become a Christian. Much of the material here, borrowed from Jewish tradition, has been subject to Messianic amendment in order to make it a mine of rich and relevant celebration.

But we have also begged, borrowed and stolen suggestions and material from a wide range of cultures from all over the world and adapted them to suit our purposes. So here it is – at least, as much as can be fitted into these few pages. Any ideas contained here are what our Joel, in engineering terms, would call prototypes waiting for the creative evolutionary process! In other words, do whatever you want with them. Let them grow and develop to fit your needs and circumstances. Don't be restricted by the words on the page. Make them work for you and those you love, and as you do, let this Jewish mama imagine you all seated around her table, with her favourite festival dishes spread out before you. It is traditional on these occasions to wish you the health and happiness to enjoy many more wonderful *simchas*. I know you will, for ultimately, all our celebrations, however successful, however joyous, are but a pale reflection of the greatest party there will ever be – one that will last for all eternity. We might as well get into practice now.

Part 2

The Hors D'Oeuvres

God, the Great Party-Giver

> **God, the Father**
>
> Requests the pleasure of the company of
> **Mr and Mrs Everybody and family**
>
> at the marriage of his Son
> **Jesus**
> to
> **The Church**
>
> At: Heavenly Mansions
> On: From now to eternity
>
> RSVP before you die

An invitation from the Good-Time God

The first time I went to church, I might just as well have been on Mars. It was a totally alien environment. I remember thinking that was odd, if its founder was really Jewish. But there was nothing here that seemed even vaguely familiar. There was I, on my way to the disco at the Jewish Youth Club round the corner, in a tiny, glitzy number and a Mary Quant red PVC mac barely covering my nether regions. It had a matching PVC hat balanced on back-combed, bee-hive hair, above Dusty Springfield-style kohl-blackened eyes that were so heavy with false lashes I could barely keep them open. And here was a sparse congregation in a vast, echoing, barely-lit, barely-heated stone barn of a building, vainly trying to keep warm in drab greatcoats, while chanting fitfully, 'And make thy chosen people joyful' as if they were at a funeral. I'd seen a great deal more joy at a Jewish funeral. As I clattered my way through the middle of Evensong, down the centre aisle, negotiating the treacherous heating ducts on my dagger-sharp stilettos, I was aware from the stares that any attempt at remaining unobtrusive had failed – miserably. I felt like a pork sausage at a *Bar Mitzvah*.

Although I joined a Christian youth group, it was many years before I became a regular member of a church, and even then, there were moments of profound culture shock, akin to panic, when I looked at the bland greyness around me, and said to myself: How on earth did I get here? This isn't where I belong. Where is the crimson and damson, the velvet and silk, the glimmering and twinkling and gold and silver of the synagogue? If Jesus walked into this gloomy, austere building with its stiff observance and studied formality, would he know what it was? Whatever happened to the radical, dynamic Jewish sect that threw off the stringent shackles of religious conformity, brought the message of a loving, living, redeeming God to those who had never heard it before, and transformed the world?

I don't know whose idea it was to make Western Christianity so lifeless and dull, but it certainly didn't come from God. From the beginning of time, when he gave human beings a glorious garden setting where they could rest, play and sport to their hearts' content, through the Jewish Scriptures with their detailed instructions for festivals, pageants and lengthy extended holidays, to the Gospel parables where Jesus describes heaven as a fabulous banquet to which everyone has an invitation, it is abundantly clear that God loves nothing better than having a good time. And since no one, not even God, wants to party alone, he made human companions to share in the fun. In fact, he so enjoys our company that he regularly manages to out-party all of us.

There's a lovely Jewish explanation as to why the Feast of Tabernacles is celebrated for eight, rather than the statutory seven days in the Book of Leviticus. In ancient times it was a tradition, every night of Tabernacles, for the people to wait in the Temple courts for the high priest to return from the Pool of Siloam with the pitcher of water that would be poured out on the altar the following day amidst pleas for the later rain. His arrival would be greeted with loud shouting, and then the men would dance for joy – sometimes all night. Apparently, on one occasion, God was having such a good time that, like a child on holiday who doesn't want to go home, he begged the people to stay on in Jerusalem for an extra day's jollities. 'I'm enjoying your company so much, give me just one more day...please!' How could they refuse, even if they were on the floor with exhaustion? 'Go on, then, God, just for you – one last dance, or two, or three.'

There is a great deal of exuberance in the African church, but little competition from its Western counterpart. Despite a host of injunctions in the Psalms to celebrate God's goodness with shouts, drums, trumpets, dance, and a general, ungainly hullabaloo, we tend to be so buttoned-up and on our dignity, that the impression of God we have unwittingly conveyed is of an austere, sadistic old tyrant, who imposes a raft of boring, guilt-inducing rules and regulations on his victims. In a recent, low-budget documentary series on BBC TV called *The Meaning of Life*, with the usual, unsatisfying format where half a dozen or so third-rate celebs pontificate on something they have manifestly never experienced, they concluded that if there was a God, their behaviour ruled out any relationship with him. Who wants to spend time with a disapproving head teacher? Where's the fun in that? The only way to overcome a guilty conscience induced by the religious myths of childhood is to laugh them to scorn, and dismiss them altogether. And who can blame them? Great religious highs are reserved instead for twenty-two men in mortal combat kicking a bag of wind around a pitch.

In yet another BBC TV religious series, presented by the Olympic medalist Jonathan Edwards, where potential punters tried out a number of different religions, Christianity was portrayed as the most 'hair-shirt' option. The Jews involved the 'religion tasters' in a Sabbath meal, the Muslims whisked them off their feet in *sufi* dancing, but a woman vicar merely encouraged one of them to give up her hair straighteners for Lent. For me with my curly locks, that was a sacrifice too far. But nor is it a fair or honest reflection of the endlessly loving, abundantly generous Father we have, or of the expansive, extensive, intensive, technicolour kind of life he intends us to enjoy. It revealed instead that we humans like our religion dedicated to the mortification, rather than the enjoyments of the flesh, possibly because we don't always like ourselves very much and project onto God our worst memories of authoritarian fathers or teachers, whose sole aim was to punish us for our misdemeanours. And even if we had wonderful, affirming, encouraging fathers and teachers, excellent role models for the Father of all, we are cursed with such a contrary, innate sense of worthlessness and unworthiness, that we can still find it hard to believe we are really included in the invitation to an eternal party.

We simply cannot get our heads or our hearts around the notion that the Creator wants one thing above all else from the human beings he made with such love and excitement – companionship and enjoyment. From the very beginning, relationship was his sole intention, and when Adam and Eve and we, by association, flung his staggering generosity in his face, when we turned away from the beauty, liberty, abundance and generosity of the garden and opted instead for poverty, adversity and niggardliness, he went to the last lengths, made the ultimate sacrifice, to woo and win us back again, so that we could party with him forever and ever. Pain, weeping, disappointment and despair are peculiarly human, temporary conditions. Eternal joy is the ultimate promise for the final morning.

The invitation goes missing

Many people live their lives unaware that the invitation exists at all. I had a grandmother with a Master's in manipulation. She was never overly fond of her husband's French relatives, and the war gave her a wonderful opportunity to cut them out of her life altogether. When the fighting was over, she made sure she always got to the post first and destroyed every letter they ever sent to my grandfather. He believed that they had all perished in the Holocaust, and went to the grave grieving for them. Years after the death of both my grandparents, to our amazement, the French relatives turned up in the UK looking for their family, and told us they had been hidden in the Alps by sympathetic Italians. They had been puzzled that none of their letters ever received a reply.

I suspect that in a similar way, when the Western church became organized and institutionalized, as it did very soon after its birth, the church authorities, standing on their new dignity and position, snatched away God's party invitation before it ever reached the mass of intended guests. The Romans, under whose roof the infant church was nurtured, were the first to hide the heavenly mail. Roman culture was steeped in the classical philosophy of the

Greeks – Socrates, Plato and Aristotle, born several hundred years before the birth of Christ, but whose theories extended their tentacles for centuries after his death. Basically they believed that the world was constructed with such mathematical order that logic and deduction would enable human beings to reason their way to the truth. Rational thought, therefore, or the mind, was the most important part of a human being. The body, the senses, the imagination, intuition, every part of being human that wasn't rational or logical, was inferior and suspect. Aristotle added that since women were manifestly less reasonable than men, it followed that 'female' characteristics were of less value. 'A man's reason fits him for government, a women's reason fits her for domestic life.'

Classical thinking loved order, structure, systems. It gave the world democracy, decent roads and public conveniences, but ultimately, it tore the heart out of the church, transforming a warm, home- and community-based Jewish sect into a formidable Christian institution with sophisticated buildings, hierarchical structures and solemn, formalized services.

One of the first Jewish Christian communities sprang up in the little Galilean town of Capernaum, home of the Apostle Peter. Locals lived in something like rows of back-to-back, two-up, two-down cottages, with narrow, interconnecting alleyways and shared courtyards. When anyone was having a bad-hair day, when they yelled at the kids, rowed with the spouse, or kicked the cat, the whole neighbourhood would have been treated to the entertainment. Sabbath meals and religious feasts would have been celebrated at home in extended-family groups, or in the small, communal synagogue, where men, women and children mixed together freely.[1] Three times a year, the entire community would pack up and set off for the three-day trek to Jerusalem for the pilgrim festivals, and a week of camping, partying and grand religious celebration in the Temple. The Hebraic approach to faith was untouched by any notion that the brain was superior to the senses, and required intellectual satisfaction. In the everyday reality of work and leisure, it was as natural and as unselfconscious as breathing. Brain and bodily function were inseparable. And since sanitary provision was rudimentary and shared, 'having everything in common'[2] was presumably a way of life already. When the new Christians began to worship together, their meetings would have reflected their well-established, communal, open, joyous, very public way of life.

But time-travel twenty years with the spread of the gospel, fifty miles towards the Jordan Valley and the sophisticated Roman town of Beth Shean, or Scythopolis as the Romans called it, and the newly emergent church would have looked very different. Beth Shean was a prosperous, sophisticated trading and cultural centre, with many fine buildings, gracious architecture, wide boulevards, and – oh joy! – decent plumbing. The church here, though more fragrant, would inevitably have reflected the local culture. It would have been more formal, more solemn, more hierarchical, more intellectually rigorous, and, since most public events in Roman towns took place in amphitheatres and assembly rooms, would slowly have moved away from the home into a building deemed more suitable for worship purposes.

There really is no question about which model the Western church inherited. When the Emperor Constantine was conveniently converted to Christianity from sun-god worship, he quickly made his new religion the official religion of the Roman Empire. In AD 325 he summoned religious and secular leaders to a great council at Nicaea, set up to ensure state control over the fast-growing new faith, separate it from any Judaic association, and prevent the danger of political subversion. The Sabbath was officially moved from the Jewish Saturday to the pagan Sun Day. Easter was moved to coincide with the pagan festival of Oester, away from any possible connection with the Passover. And then, as his final *pièce de résistance*, he made the observance of Sabbath or Passover, or any Jewish festival, for that matter, an offence punishable with excommunication. With its Jewish roots hacked off, the church was firmly and finally replanted in Roman soil.

During the time of the Roman Empire any attempts to re-create a more Hebraic way of living out the Christian faith, integrating it into the daily routine of work and play, as the Celts in Britain tried to do, were annihilated by the heavily Romanized ecclesiastical machinery. Then, through the centuries, rabid anti-Semitism in the church's spiritual leaders, from the Early Church Fathers, through the medieval mystics like Mother Julian, to Luther himself, the founding father of Protestantism, blinded them to any possibility of a Jewish Jesus and wedded them to the classical, Romanized view of the church. Gradually, Christians appropriated all the Old Testament promises, left the threats, warnings and curses to the Jews, and dispensed with all the rest – festivals included.

In the thirteenth century Thomas Aquinas, probably the foremost influence on Roman Catholic doctrine, showed how Christianity could be made as reasonable and rational as the philosophy of Aristotle. The mind was the prime way to experience God, not the senses, not the imagination, and certainly not the emotions. But then, Aquinas also said, 'Woman is defective and misbegotten…biologically, spiritually and intellectually inferior', so a bias towards

Aristotle over the God of the Jews led Aquinas into some very odd thinking. Nonetheless, he was one of the single most important influences on the Western church for many centuries.

The Protestant reformers of the sixteenth century, loathing what they saw as quasi-pagan, Catholic 'jiggery-popery' – vestments, pictures, liturgies, candles, incense, crosses, and processions – became more brain-bound than ever, colder, and more subdued in the expression of their Christian faith. The unvarnished biblical word was all that really mattered. What people believed and how they explained it was more important than how they lived or experienced it.

By the seventeenth and eighteenth centuries, the emphasis on intellectual rigour and logic culminated in what came to be called the Age of Reason or the Enlightenment. Francis Bacon, Descartes, Kant and Voltaire concocted philosophical potions that included large doses of scepticism, individualism, rationalism and a firm belief in the pre-eminence of science – ideas that were largely hostile to faith and the doctrines of the church. Only knowledge based on what was measurable was reliable, they claimed. Since religious belief was unproven, and its practice unthinking, it stood in the way of intellectual, social and scientific progress. In response, Christian theologians began to dissect and explain the scriptural texts to prove that faith could be reasonable and logical, but that only served to widen further the gulf between the church and the Hebraic worldview of Jesus.

Western culture has never fully shaken off the heritage of the Enlightenment. The whole of our educational system was based on this rational approach to life. For example, when Sir John Barbirolli first became conductor in residence with the Halle Orchestra in Manchester in 1943, people were appalled by the emotional impact of his concerts, and by their own responses to the power of the music. The arts could be analysed, admired for being well crafted, but were not supposed to touch the places the brain couldn't reach, or provoke anything resembling spiritual ecstasy, for heaven's sake. Quintessential Western niceness required rational comprehension and self-control. When Daniel Goleman wrote his famous book on the importance of emotional intelligence as late as 1995, it was a revelation. We now have to be coached in it.

And so, over the years, in the name of reverence and good sense, the relationship between God and his people became somewhat constrained and formalized, and worship lost its party spirit. Not so, of course, in most of Africa, where Christianity is now growing so fast that hundreds of new churches are planted weekly. The exception is where denominationally based missionaries imported Western culture, and set up great cathedrals where the women still wear hats and gloves, and congregations sing nineteenth-century hymns.

But even in the West, the party instinct could not be eradicated altogether, and throughout history, it would burst out from time to time – in plays, pageants, festivals, revivals, and grand gatherings. The Incomprehensible still managed to break through the Western mindset – through the ministry of people such as John and Charles Wesley, Jonathan Edwards, George Whitefield, William and Catherine Booth of the Salvation Army, D. L. Moody, and perhaps John Wimber, who always maintained that the English, even more than their American or Australian cousins, were constrained in too tight an emotional straitjacket. These moments have been characterized by huge outpourings of unalloyed joy, laughter, dance, a fresh sense of community, a need to celebrate, and many new hymns and songs. Then, largely, the faithful quieten down and return to the safety of their accepted boundaries, leaving their Hebraic roots where they have always been, well buried beneath twenty centuries of classical soil.

Today, it seems, that rather than finding fun in faith, the perceived restraints of religion have to be thrown off in an alcohol-induced haze before people feel uninhibited enough to rediscover the pure, abandoned celebration they know is their birthright. The church has a great deal of ground to reclaim.

So get a bigger God

Those who forget the past are condemned to repeat it.
George Santayana

If the church lost sight of its rightful inheritance, relegating imagination and emotion to the bottom league, if the party invitation went missing and the regular cycle of exuberant celebration was lost, what implications did it have? No God of the Jews, then no God of history. No sense of history means a severely reduced sense of the immensity of God. Only a seamless narrative between Old and New Scriptures gives a true impression of the enormity of God's eternal plan for human beings, and his total control of their destiny.

In the Old Testament the New is hidden. In the New the meaning of the Hebrew Scriptures becomes clear. There is only one redemption story, encapsulated in the Book of Genesis, unfolded in the rest of the pages of the Bible, lived out by the generations of followers fortunate enough to get caught up in its narrative. The call of Abraham, the choosing of a people, the exodus from slavery in Egypt, the wilderness wanderings, the giving of the law and the land, the building of the Temple, the coming of the Messiah and the outpouring of the Holy Spirit at Pentecost, the promise of a final harvest and eternal glory are all woven into one enormous Bayeux-style tapestry that charts the story of God's love for his people from the beginning to the end of time. We are there, each one of us, in the myriad, glistening, tiny threads that make up light and shade, texture and shape in his detailed, meticulous work. Grasp that, and even in the seemingly fleeting and arbitrary nature of our own existence, we see pattern, structure and meaning. We see the significance of times, events and seasons. We see that nothing is arbitrary, nothing is futile, nothing is wasted. We find our appointed place in this vast universe.

When we stop to celebrate, we are pausing to reflect on the wonder of being a tiny part of a magnificent plan, and not simply a fluke of nature. And that is so liberating from the great angst of thinking that somehow, I am solely responsible for discovering my purpose on this earth and for giving significance to my little life. Now it's no longer, 'What is your plan for my life?' but 'What is your overall plan for humanity, and what is my part in it?' Western Christianity has always tended to emphasize the individual – belief is my decision, religion is my private business, prayer and worship are better on my own, no commitment to a church is needed. But the Scriptures are about peoples, communities and congregations, demonstrating the love and faithfulness of God in their shared interactions with him over thousands of years. In that global context, the gift of faith, of becoming part of God's people, and of being drawn into his story, becomes a mind-blowing, miraculous privilege.

People used to say to me, 'What convinced you that Jesus was the Messiah? Was it Isaiah chapter 53, the prophecy of the suffering servant who would die a horrible death in order to deal with our pain, disease and sin?' Extraordinary as that prophecy seems when I read it now, I had no knowledge of it in my pre-Christian days. It may be missed out of the weekly synagogue readings because it is too loaded. More likely it was read out in ancient Hebrew and I missed it, having a very rudimentary, read-only knowledge of the language.

What drew me, as I read the forbidden New Testament for the first time, was the disciple Philip's demand that Jesus 'show us the Father, and then we'll be satisfied.'

'Aha,' I thought, 'my question too.'

I believed in 'the Father' – or at least, a God who had enabled us to survive as a people, despite the worst efforts of a host of tyrants, from Pharaoh to Hitler. After all, had I been born a mere ten years earlier, in virtually any other European country, I might have had as much value as meatloaf. There isn't a Jew who does not look over their shoulder and say, 'By the grace of God, I was not there.' My very existence had to mean something. But what? The God who gave me life and let me live was distant, remote. I knew him much as I knew the Queen. He was a black-and-white image on the TV screen in my head. But I had no concept of what he was actually like. 'Philip,' says Jesus, 'have I been with you all this time and you still don't know me? He who has seen me has seen the Father.'

Now at last the Father became flesh and blood, muscle and sinew, love and mercy. All that I most admired and respected and loved about Jesus as I read about him for the first time, was a reflection of the God I had always known, but not with any intimacy. Now he was accessible, warm and welcoming.

But this was not the end of the mystery. As with most close relationships, it was only the beginning of the adventure. The great Jewish sage Maimonides used to say that getting to know God was a bit like walking down the street, when ahead of you, you see the back of someone you recognize. You rush up to them, tap them on the shoulder, but when they turn around – surprise, surprise – it isn't who you think it is.

Perhaps Maimonides explains why the traditional 'Enlightenment' approach to God – uneasy with mystery, dismissing the incomprehensible, hunting for logical, rational explanations of every spiritual truth – now leaves many people cold and unsatisfied. The Hebraic Old Testament approach was completely comfortable with apparent ambivalence and perplexity. In one breath the psalmist says, 'God, you are so wonderful for answering my prayers,' and in the other, 'God, why do you never answer my prayers?' In fact, there is no real conflict. Experience tells us that both can be true. As a Public Relations professional, I've often thought that if I had been hired by God, the first thing I would do would be to eradicate the Psalms from the canon of Scripture. They are far too honest – but, oh, so real. While there is access to a joyful, comforting familiarity with the Father, no relationship with God himself will ever be without awe and wonder, perplexity and surprise – at least, in this life. He will always be a little unknowable rather than remote, for if human beings could know him completely, he would no longer be God. And even if our celebrations and festivals anticipate the glorious happy ending to the eternal story, we acknowledge that for now, the tale we tell is interspersed with inexplicable pain, suffering and despair.

I once interviewed the wonderful Holocaust survivor, Rabbi Hugo Gryn, for a television documentary. I always felt that the word 'survivor' didn't do his courage justice. To live a life that enriched and enlightened thousands of others in the aftermath of such a horrendous experience reflects more than mere survival. It is a victory.

I had the naivety to ask him where God was in Auschwitz.

'Wrong question! I'll tell you a story,' he said, instantly drawing me back sixty years into that Nazi hell-hole. 'I was only around fifteen years old at the time, but on *Yom Kippur*, the Day of Atonement, I went behind the sheds and began to recite as many of the familiar prayers as I could remember. And then, as I prayed and wept, I became aware of a quiet presence with me, weeping too as if his heart would break.'

We paused to absorb the implications of this extraordinary experience.

'You ask me where God was in Auschwitz? He was there, with his people, suffering every humiliation and indignation and pain they were forced to endure. The question is not, "Where was God?" but "Where was man in Auschwitz?" As he looked at the perpetrators of such a heinous crime against humanity, didn't he ask himself, with a broken heart, how the creatures he had created with such love, such hope and such potential, could descend to this?'

The dethroning of God, the belief that man alone is responsible for history – that is man's tragedy, said Rabbi Hugo. The American theologian, Walter Breuggemann, claims in his *Theology of the Old Testament* that the Holocaust would and could never have happened at all, had the Nazis not inherited centuries of deJudaizing Christianity.

It isn't simply that we need to know history – we need to confront our place in it, as in every generation God goes out searching for his loved ones, and asks the eternal question: 'Adam, where are you?' Because of their festivals, the Jews are very familiar with their history of sin and grace, of failure and mercy, of apparent abandonment and extraordinary favour. They know that God can and does rescue, that he may or may not, but that there are always lessons to learn from the past and resolutions to make for the future. Here is the secret of the preservation of Jewish identity from one generation to another, through many persecutions in the long Diaspora.

The church, however, is often painfully unaware of its own, not-so-glorious, two-thousand-year history: the betrayals, from Judas to the ministers whose dishonesty and disgrace fill the newspapers; its anti-Semitism from medieval times to the Holocaust; its silence on injustice and the abuse of the environment. It hasn't had the regular festivals that provide an opportunity to confront its own history of failure and forgiveness. Nor the chance to acknowledge the shining examples of God's faithfulness, inspiring his followers to acts of immense courage and self-sacrifice, from Peter and the early church martyrs to those who gave their lives for the dynamic new churches in Africa and China.

Not facing up to its whole story weakens any sense of corporate identity and makes it much harder for the church to secure the commitment of future generations. Over ten years ago it was discovered that a former treasurer had been substantially defrauding our church. The congregation was divided over where the blame lay. Some thought the fault was his alone. After all, the man had a gambling problem. Others felt it was our corporate responsibility. Surely a caring community should have protected him from his folly, had they known of it or not, by putting careful checks in place? It's never wise to expose anyone to the temptation of money. Not only that, but if the press had got hold of the story, the reputation of the whole organization would have been at stake. No one could then say, 'not my problem'. He spent years washing the dishes in our coffee bar as an act of repentance, but that alone would not ensure the mistake was not repeated. The whole church had to remember, and remembering meant owning our communal responsibility to ensure that steps were taken to see that it never happened again.

To celebrate is to remember

To remember is the key to redemption.
Baal Shem Tov (Jewish sage)

A party often commemorates an important event such as a birthday, an anniversary or an achievement. But the best memorial days are not simply about nostalgia. Stories of God's intervention, recalling his faithfulness in the past, save us from a destructive disappointment or cynical negativity, and fill us instead with fresh trust, excitement and hope. That's why there is such encouragement to do it. 'I am to be remembered from generation to generation'; 'Remember that you were slaves in Egypt'; 'Remember all the ways in which the Lord led you these forty years in the wilderness'; 'Remember his wonders he has done, his miracles'.

God in turn never forgets us. He remembers his love, he remembers we are dust, he remembers his mercy, he remembers his covenant, he remembers to be gracious. When Lot was in dire straits, God remembered him and rescued him from Sodom and Gomorrah; he remembered Rachel and Hannah crying out for children; he remembered Joseph languishing in prison.

Remembering that he remembers, establishing a discipline of regular occasions when we do, carries us through the tough times, the times when it feels as if God must be forgetful, and we feel abandoned, beset by fear and anxiety. Some parts of the church suggest that God has now given up on the Jews because of their many perceived failures, and appropriate new-covenant exclusivity for themselves. It's known as 'replacement theology' – and it has a major weakness. If God does not fulfil his promises to the Jews, in whatever way he deems fit, simply because they don't deserve it, what evidence is there that he will be faithful to the undeserving likes of us? Or do we think we are somehow more worthy? Hard evidence is what we need when we are beset by the struggles of daily life – the absolute assurance of God's constant commitment and care – and a great deal of it is to be found in the Old Testament.

Holy Communion, par excellence, provides a regular opportunity to remember. Samuel Wells writes: 'This means the church's memory can never become detached from its intimate bond with the Jews, for the Last Supper is characterised by the recollection of God's saving purpose in the Exodus, his faithfulness to the Sinai covenant, and his promise to bring their long exile to an end.'[3] Communion reminds us that the promise has been finally fulfilled, and at what cost. That's why at the last Passover meal Jesus said, 'Whenever you eat together and say the appropriate blessings, as I have always done with you and especially this one last time tonight, remember me.'

The Hebrew for 'to remember' is *zakar*, which means 'to have imprinted on one's subconscious'. In other words, we need to tell the stories of our people to our children and to our children's children until they are so familiar that they are a part of our communal psyche. We must tell them the exploits of men and women of faith from the beginning of time to the present day, the saints who gave their all to follow the call of God.

We need to tell the stories in a way that makes them live, with opportunities to enter into the experience, rather than expecting a passive audience, as most of our churches do. The Passover service says that every Jew should feel for all eternity as if he or she were actually being freed from slavery in Egypt. They eat bitter herbs like raw horseradish that sting the mouth and bring tears to the eyes to remind them how horrible it was. 'Oy,' my grandfather used to lament, 'all those bricks we had to make. It was terrible.' And sitting around that table, we children believed he had really been a slave in Egypt and had more than just a passing acquaintance with Moses. At Tabernacles, to this day, people live in tents or booths for the entire eight days, so that they can actually feel how fragile life in the desert could be, and marvel that their ancestors actually survived at all. On the eve of Pentecost some sit up all night studying the Torah in penitence for falling asleep when the two tablets were handed to Moses. This is interactive story-telling, aided and abetted by food, symbol, ritual and tradition that engage all the senses and are formative in the moral and spiritual development of every human being.

That's why the most important festivals are commands, and not just an optional extra, 'when you can fit it in', or 'if you're in the mood'. That's why there are so many of them – three pilgrim festivals every year for a start, each lasting at least a week. In Jesus' day, about 100,000 devout Jews descended on Jerusalem for the duration. The mood was decidedly festive. Rabbis and others would perform party tricks such as juggling with burning torches for the vast encampment of worshippers gathered on the hills around Jerusalem. There was rich food, fire-eating, juggling and talent shows, and the new wine flowed freely. And then there were the pageants and processions as, with immense excitement and joy, the people made their way up to the Temple, accompanied by trumpets, harps, bagpipes, drums and cymbals. Faith was overwhelmingly fun. No wonder God wanted another day of it.

It all makes a bit of a mockery of the begrudging, occasional bank holidays given to hard-worked employees by the pious Christian bosses of the Victorian era, for whom work was a moral virtue, play a moral threat. It's also a huge challenge to the peremptory way our Communion services can be conducted today, as a weekly ritual rather than a great celebration of the story of God's love for his people.

The invitation is re-sent

If, historically, Christians have chosen to overlook or ignore God as the Great Party-Giver because the feasts and festivals are all set out in the Old Testament, they can't pretend the point isn't made again in the New Testament. Jesus is at pains to describe the Father's unconditional love, and the overwhelming joy he feels when a lost or wayward child rushes into his arms. At that moment, behind the scenes, Jesus says, out of the sight of mortal man, a huge party erupts spontaneously in the heavens – with clapping, cheering and loud celebration. And just in case we're still not convinced, he tells a story that has been interpreted in literature, theatre and music, because it resonates so powerfully in all of us.

Once upon a time there was a father with two sons – perhaps representing the two sides of our own nature. There's the eldest, the goody-goody, society's darling – hard-working, reliable and status-conscious. And then there is the youngest – immature and childish, who kicks his father in the teeth by asking, as I did and almost all teenagers still do, 'What have you left me in the will, Dad, and can I have it now?' Or is it only Jews who are obsessional about wills and threaten to cut their children out? What he's actually saying is, 'If you were dead, Dad, I could have your money, since it's going to be mine anyway.'

Wisely, Dad lets him go and make a mess, and even gives him the wherewithal to do it. And before long, as his father knew he would, he's squandered the lot on booze, bad company and wild parties. Here is a very accurate description of pseudo-partying – no real friendship or loyalties, no one there in the morning, no meaning, no lasting satisfaction. Destitute and down at heel, he heads for home. His father doesn't even wait for him to cross the threshold. He rushes out to gather him in a huge embrace. The selfish, exaggerated, empty, abusive exploitation of the son is met with selfless, generous, exuberant acceptance. For his lost one he throws a real kind of party – one that celebrates restoration, recreation and redemption.

Jesus' story reassures us that for all his wayward 'I did it my way' children, the Father waits with love and patience, arms wide open. When we recognize our madness and head for home, we find the party invitation already waiting on the dresser in the hall.

Later in the story the father becomes aware that his other son is sulking outside in the shadows and goes out to find him. This lad resents the celebration. He loathes flamboyance of every kind. It's waste. He represents the sensible, measured, rather sour side of ourselves that we so often project onto God. 'After what he's done! How can you take him back, let alone throw him a party?' But the Father reaches out and touches a hand or an arm, reminding him that he too is loved, urging him to let go of that gnawing negativity and rejoin the celebration.

Later in the Gospels, when Jesus is asked what heaven will be like, he tells a story about a fabulous banquet, a free dinner-dance, that isn't a mere one-off. It lasts for all eternity and everyone is invited. But despite the RSVPs that say 'Yes', when the spread is ready, the champagne on ice and the wine uncorked, the guests find excuses not to attend: 'I've just bought a new telly and have to set the channels'; 'I've just got married and we need some time at home alone.' What pathetic apologies, full of the paltry here and now. You have the rest of your life, for goodness' sake. How can such temporary pleasure take precedence over what is lasting, eternal and real?

The host is frustrated, as I am when I have stood and cooked for guests who can't be bothered to make the effort. The Jews, who have first call on his hospitality, have turned up their noses. So he turns to the marginalized and dispossessed instead, the Gentiles who've never really received such an invitation before. This is their moment. They can hardly believe their good fortune.

Some years ago I went to the Sea of Galilee with the actor and *Stars in Your Eyes* presenter Matthew Kelly to make a TV programme in a series where celebrities were taken on retreat and given a chance to find God. He was a charming, gracious companion with a wonderful sense of humour, and we had a lot of fun. God seemed to have a way of turning up in Matthew's dreams. One in particular left a lasting impression on both of us. He had been invited to a party and when he got to the door he could see that it was by far the best he had ever been to. But the house was so packed that to get in, he would have to limbo dance through a gap under the door. In his dream he thought about it for a long while, then decided he'd rather have his own party and that it would be just as good.

Knowing him, I don't doubt it would have been fabulous, but I also knew it would never match the one he had just missed. I told him his dream reminded me that heaven was described in the New Testament as a fantastic party, but entry had one condition: we had to stop being so grown up, divest ourselves of our sophistication, and become child-height. Only children really know how to play. Only children never turn a party invitation down. That's why the invitation is a party invitation in the first place. God wants his children to share his fun.

Ideas for reflection or discussion

- Describe or draw God as you see him in your imagination. Where does your representation come from? Does it reflect what you actually know about him?

- Is the Hebraic idea of never making a 'graven image' or representation of God helpful or not? Do Jesus' parables of the Father influence your perspective?

- How well do you know the roots of your own faith – the history of ancient Judaism, and the early church, and how would it make a difference to you if you did?

- How important is it to have an overview of the entire Bible, and what might you do to achieve that?

- Design your own calendar of the feasts and festivals that you might want to celebrate every year. Here is one to get you started:

Calendar of festivals and annual celebrations

1 January	New Year's Day	
5 January	Twelfth Night	The close of Christmastide. Taking down of the Christmas decorations.
6 January (day)	Epiphany	The arrival of the Magi (wise men) and the first public presentation of the baby Jesus.
25 January	Burns' Night	The birthday of Scotland's most famous poet, Robert Burns (1759–96) and a chance to eat haggis.
21 January	Holocaust Memorial Day	In memory of the liberation of Auschwitz A chance to remember victims of the Holocaust, and of all genocides since.
January	Chinese New Year	
2 February	Candlemas Day	
14 February	St Valentine's Day	Festival celebrating the patron saint of love.
February	Shrove Tuesday	The Eve of Ash Wednesday and the beginning of Lent. A time for pancakes.
February	Ash Wednesday	The beginning of the 40-day period of Lent (excluding Sundays) that leads up to Easter Day. In some churches ashes are used to mark the cross on believers' foreheads. It's a time for spiritual reflection and therefore can be marked with fasting.

1 March	St David's Day	St David is the patron saint of Wales. A time to wear a daffodil, or even a leek – national symbols of Wales.
March	Mother's Day	Mothering Sunday is a chance to give thanks for all who 'mother', in whatever way.
17 March	St Patrick's Day	St Patrick, patron saint of Ireland, along with St Brigid, was one of the first to bring Christianity to England.
1 April	April Fools' Day	Jokes and tricks have to be done before midday.
April	Palm Sunday	Festival celebrating the entry of Jesus into Jerusalem. The day begins Holy Week and can be observed with processions and the giving out of palm crosses.
April	Maundy Thursday	A commemoration of the last supper, when Jesus was betrayed and captured by the Romans. A Communion is traditional.
April	Good Friday	A day to remember the crucifixion of Jesus.
April	Easter Sunday	Resurrection day.
23 April	St George's Day	St George is the patron saint of England.
May	Ascension Day	Commemorating the ascension of Jesus to heaven after his resurrection.
May	Purim/Feast of Esther	
June	Pentecost/Whitsun	
24 June	Midsummer's Day	Was a day for parties and revels.

15 July	St Swithin's Day	St Swithin was bishop of Winchester. It was said that 40 days of bad weather would follow if it rained on this day.
September	Succot (Tabernacles)	
September	Harvest Festival	
31 October	Halloween	
1 November	All Saints' Day	A day for honouring saints, known and unknown.
5 November	Guy Fawkes Night/Bonfire Night	Anniversary of the Gunpowder Plot.
November	Remembrance Sunday	In commemoration of those who gave their lives for their country in the two World Wars.
30 November	St Andrew's Day	St Andrew is patron saint of Scotland.
December	Advent	
24 December	Christmas Eve	
25 December	Christmas Day	

Useful books that help to give an overview of the entire Bible

David & Pat Alexander, *The New Lion Handbook to the Bible*, Lion.
John Drane, *Introducing the Old Testament*, Royal.
John Drane, *Introducing the New Testament*, Royal.
Gordon D. Fee & Douglas Stuart, *How to Read the Bible for All Its Worth: A Guide to Understanding the Bible* (3rd edition), Zondervan, 2002.

Grove Booklets issued a challenge to readers to summarize the entire Bible in 750 words. The results are on their website at: http://www.grovebooks.co.uk

Jesus, Man of the Party

At the beginning of the last century, so the story goes, an elderly lady of the kirk complained to her minister that the Queen had been seen out rowing on the lake at Balmoral on the Lord's Day.

'Ah, sister,' said the minister, quickly gathering his thoughts, 'did not our Lord row on Lake Galilee on the Sabbath Day?'

'Ay, Minister,' she retorted, 'that he did. But two wrongs don't make a right.'

For centuries, people of some faith and none have tried to reduce Jesus to manageable proportions, depicting him in a way that reflects our personal, comfortable preferences. But we will never be free to be fully celebratory until we release him from the strongbox of our self-made imitations, and let him lead us by example.

It is hard to remember my early impressions of Jesus as a Jewish child, with no secular or Sunday school lessons to predetermine any mental image, but I don't think they were very flattering. He always seemed a rather pallid individual, with a mournful expression and the cares of the world reluctantly on his shoulders. Since the only representations I had ever caught sight of were crucifixes, or paintings of the crucifixion, I now see that was hardly surprising. On the lips of a teacher, 'You look as if you have the cares of the world on your shoulders' wasn't a compliment. It usually meant that audible sighing was not going to win you any sympathy or support with that impossible maths problem.

On the other hand, he did have a lot to be miserable about, since, according to my junior-school classmates, we Jews had killed him. How could I have killed someone I didn't even know? I couldn't get my head round such carelessness. But none of them ever suggested to me that he was Jewish. And apart from that Aunty Sadie-like, long-suffering expression, he certainly didn't look it. Not with that straggly blond hair, insipid complexion, and tall, spindly figure. No Jew I knew would be seen dead in a white bathrobe and sensible sandals.

But it's not only Jewish children or children of other faiths who pick up some very erroneous notions of what Jesus was actually like. My friend Richard told me that from the age of eight to eighteen he was a choirboy in a cathedral that had a large reredos depicting a gaunt, black-bearded, sombre, rather frightening Jesus. Years later, as a man, he came to realize that small children would never have wanted to go up to Jesus and sit on his knee unless he was approachable and fun. But to his immense frustration, to this very day, whenever Richard thinks of Jesus he still cannot quite rid himself of the negative mental image he acquired in his youth.

The almost universally sombre, gloomy depictions of Jesus have probably prevented many adults from creating a positive representation in their imagination, blighting their ability to feel secure in his love and acceptance. Even in Da Vinci's famous painting of the Last Supper, one of the few that put Jesus at a meal table, he hardly looks as if he is enjoying himself. Admittedly, it was his last party – on earth, at least – but he loved the Passover and had said quite clearly that he was really looking forward to it. It could hardly have been the endurance test that Da Vinci conveyed.

Today, of course, vast numbers of people are stuck with the contemporary, Hollywood Jesus of Nazareth with the never-blinking, rather disturbing stare; or the Jesus of Mel Gibson's *The Passion of the Christ*, subjected to the most appalling physical pain.

There are no paintings of Jesus having fun, no snapshots of him with his head thrown back in laughter at that wonderful wedding party at Cana, no statues of him with a wine glass in one hand, his robe raised by the other, ready for the Galilean equivalent of a jig. Jesus, man of sorrows, not Jesus, man of the party, is the traditional, subconscious image of the person my father referred to disparagingly as 'the Christian God' – a sad, suffering Messiah.

Neither Catholic solemnity nor Protestant austerity has ever done Jesus justice. The Free Church building I attended at the very beginning of my Christian journey was largely colourless and dour, a throwback to Puritan Brethrenism that aimed at simplicity but was simply dull. The Jesus who belonged there was the Jesus of the old lady of the kirk. It took me a very long time to free myself from such a lack of imagination and find a recognizably Jewish Jesus. But as I hunted my way through the Gospels, I found the buried treasure I was after.

Jesus was a big man

If there's one activity Jesus appears to enjoy more than any other, it's eating. There are at least thirty references in the Gospels to him tucking into food. He could eat for Israel. This was no lean and hungry Saviour. This was a full-blooded, life-loving gourmet of a Messiah. No wonder Martha enjoyed cooking for him and gave dinner parties in his honour. Any Jewish woman worth her weight in chicken soup would have given her *kishkas* for a man with his appetite.

More of Jesus' significant sayings and stories recorded for posterity were spoken at the meal table than at the synagogue or the Temple. After the resurrection, at Emmaus, in the upper room, or on the Galilee beach, when he shares out food and starts eating, it's then that the disciples recognize Jesus and are finally convinced that he really has risen from the dead.

John Bell, Chaplain of the Iona Community, recounts how when people arrive on the island for a retreat or conference, he sometimes shows them a variety of pictures of Jesus and asks them to choose which most reflects the impression of him they hold in their imagination. No one, he says, has ever opted for one particular picture – a big, bouncy Jesus. They all opt for the wan, slim, sylph-like versions. Yet the broad, strapping Jesus is probably much nearer the truth. There was no shortage of tasty, healthy food in the Middle East – olives, grapes, aubergines, tomatoes, figs, almonds, lamb, chickens, home-baked bread and cakes. This man must have enjoyed the whole range of tastes and delicacies the Mediterranean has to offer – yet in every portrait ever made of him he looks like a Weightwatchers success story.

Reading about Jesus for the first time was a revelation. Hidden under the bedclothes in the bedroom I shared with my little sister, I had two forbidden books – *Lady Chatterley's Lover* and the New Testament. As I read them both, more or less concurrently, by torchlight, slowly, John's Gospel won. There was nothing in *Lady Chatterley* that this precocious teenager didn't know already, whereas there was almost nothing in John's Gospel that I knew. I never realized how attractive Jesus was, how dynamic, authoritative, affectionate, outspoken and true. Why had no one ever captured that merry twinkle in his eyes, his wonderful sense of the absurd, his fun with his friends (and with the Pharisees, often at their expense), and his capacity for living life to the full? Even as the cross begins to darken his horizon, never once is he heard to say, 'Mine has been such a bum existence that dying is the best thing that can happen to me.' In fact, his ultimate pain and suffering, his death at the tragically young age of thirty-three, is all the more poignant in the face of his exuberant love of life.

This life of his in all its superabundance, the life he held out to me some two thousand years later, wasn't some miserable, 'I'll get through it somehow because it'll be wonderful when I die' existence. It was life now, richer than in my wildest dreams, encompassing the full gamut of emotion and experience - passionate, sad, funny, exuberant, sorrowful, and pleasurable.

Jesus was a funny man

If Jesus was altogether bigger than I imagined, he was also more Jewish than I ever expected. Not exactly Jewish in the way I was. Contemporary Judaism isn't quite what it was in the first century, though there were familiar elements nonetheless.

Jesus went up to Jerusalem with his parents, then later with the disciples, to party at the great pilgrim festivals, Passover, Pentecost and Tabernacles, three times a year. It was a three-day journey there by foot, and three days back. The seven- or eight-day celebration in the middle effectively meant a minimum of six weeks' holiday a year. He may well have stayed with friends or family, or camped on the hillside with many other pilgrims outside Jerusalem, sharing in that heady mix of carnival and worship, pageant and praise. With the many warnings about the dangers of excess and empty carousing in Psalms and Proverbs, there must have been a risk that some would abuse God's best gifts, but generally, there was a good-humoured interweaving of the holy and high spirits into grand celebration.

This indistinguishable blend of sacred and secular was the hallmark of Jesus' spirituality. In Hebraic thinking, which was very different from the Roman approach, human beings didn't just *have* a body - they *were* a body. It couldn't be separated from mind, soul and spirit, and, frustrating though its demands could be, it wasn't of any less value. For example, as a single man, Jesus appears to have been perfectly comfortable with his sexual feelings. He didn't balk when a woman of doubtful morality prostrated herself in front of him, unbound her long hair and began to caress his feet with it - a fairly erotic act even by today's standards. And hadn't some of the men there known her in just that other context? How embarrassing for everyone. But Jesus didn't shake her off for making them both objects of ridicule. Instead, he accepted her offering for what it was – an expression of pure, unselfish, lust-free love. The expression of emotion didn't faze him. He could reach out and touch in comfort, allow close physical contact, weep openly when he was moved.

He gave his imagination free rein, allowing it to unearth holy treasure, like nuggets of buried gold, in the mundane goings-on of ordinary people. In his stories he uses bread, wine, fish, sheep, birds, flowers, lamps, brooms and trees as symbols, infusing them with new meaning and significance. His celebratory spirit made him highly sensitive to his environment, to what he saw, heard, smelt, touched and tasted. He said, 'listen to the wind', 'look at the lilies of the field', 'open your eyes and see the harvest', 'watch the agricultural labourer', 'drink and you'll never thirst again', 'smell this perfume and think of my burial', 'touch me and see that it's really me', 'eat bread and wine and remember me'. The implication is, 'Wake up to what's around you, use all of your God-given senses to wonder, marvel, learn and grow. Let your imagination feed your spirit, and colour your world.' But much of the church, with its suspicion of all but the brain, appears to have missed his meaning altogether.

They also lost sight of Jesus' endearing and mischievous sense of humour. In his day shepherds were the fall-guys, the butt of jokes, like the Irish for the English, or the Polish for South Africans. What self-respecting businessman would risk his entire company for one unreliable employee? But a shepherd might risk virtually his entire flock for one little wandering sheep. 'Bah, typical, eh?' laughed the disciples, probably missing the point entirely – until, with a gulp, they suddenly realized that Jesus was identifying himself with the shepherd's daft behaviour. The best humour can make a powerful point. There is no gentler, cleverer way of turning our presuppositions on their heads than making us laugh, and there is nothing Jesus seemed to enjoy doing more.[4]

His world is filled with amusing and affectionate cameo portraits of the people he knew and saw every day – the housewife sweeping her entire house out in her hunt for that blooming one lost penny; a wine merchant sorting out his contrary and difficult staff; a businessman who finds a pearl and rushes to sell his entire livelihood; families who light lamps and hide them in the dark instead of putting them in their windows. His more biting humour is reserved for those pedlars of hypocrisy and cant, mostly religious leaders, and for anyone who abuses or thinks himself superior to a fellow human being. How can you tell that someone has a tiny speck in their eye when you're blinded by the dirty great log sticking out of your own? Would we ever criticize anyone else if we saw ourselves as we really are? 'You put a gauze over your drinking water to stop the flies falling into it, and whoops, a dirty great camel falls into it instead.' The idea is totally absurd. Camels don't fly, for a start. If they did fall from the sky, they would destroy the entire house, not just the jug of drinking water. This is a clever visual way of exposing the futility of trying to hedge the law around with a myriad of unnecessary rules and regulations, so much more than an ancient and original take on the 'waiter, waiter, there's a fly in my soup' joke.

There is no doubt, from the disciples' perspective, that Jesus was wonderful company. Would they have followed so readily, or survived three years of wandering around Galilee without a permanent base or decent bed, if he had been a miserable killjoy? And would children have wanted to snuggle up to him or climb all over him if he had been fierce, or a gloomy sober-sides?

Jesus was a generous man

It is hardly surprising, then, that with such an instinct for celebration and enjoyment, Jesus tends to use a perfectly ordinary commodity to turn an occasion into a party. And he does it in style.

The first major miracle, the one that launches his ministry, takes place at a wedding in Cana, not far from his home in Nazareth. It's a little, local celebration, of minimal significance in the grand scheme of things – except, no doubt, to the bride and groom and their parents. Jesus, the local lad, is invited with his mother. Maybe she was half hoping he'd find a nice Jewish girl and settle down at last. That's what weddings were for. But none were like this one.

Half way through the proceedings the conversation suddenly dies.

'Psssst, Jesus,' mouths Mary from further down the table, 'the wine has run out.'

'Mother,' he says, witheringly, only too aware of the situation, 'your powers of observation never cease to amaze me. What do you want me to do about it?'

'So you'll think of something!' she says.

What Mary thinks Jesus will do and why she thinks he'll do it is a mystery – except that she must already be aware, possibly from their trips to Jerusalem for the holidays, that her son isn't one for letting a host be embarrassed or a good party go to waste. And her instincts are more than just sound.

He converts 800 litres of water into wine – and not just any old wine at that – the best *Beaujolais nouveau*, or its Galilean equivalent, which has to be a great deal better than the current Israeli wines. It's the equivalent of around 1,000 bottles. This isn't just generosity. It's downright irresponsibility. Jesus is risking mayhem. Sadly, we have no record of how the rest of the evening panned out.

Yet another of his most famous miracles involves creating a grand day out from one little boy's packed lunch. Five loaves and two fishes – that's all it takes for 5,000-plus (the women and children haven't been counted) to sit down to one of the best picnics they have ever been to, and there's enough left over to make the kids' school dinners for a week. As they're picking up the leftovers, perhaps Peter says ruefully to James, 'When he told us to go and feed all those people with five loaves and a couple of fishes, I knew we shouldn't have laughed!'

But Jesus must have laughed – sometimes until he was bent double – at the confusion and antics of his friends, like on the occasion when a miserable failure of a night's fishing turned into a superabundant catch that broke their nets. The disciples probably had a good long grumble while they were mending the nets, made worse by the sight of Jesus watching them or even working with them, trying to control his laughter, until eventually they too began to see the funny side of it. They couldn't possibly have eaten all that fish themselves, but no doubt the whole town dined out on Jesus that night, and toasted him during the feasting.

The provision Jesus makes isn't just adequate or enough. It isn't merely generous. It's completely over the top. How responsible is it to destroy the fishing nets, for goodness' sake? No wonder the Pharisees cannot bear him. His generosity highlights their meanness of spirit. His sense of fun shows up their pomposity. His *joie de vivre* makes them look miserable. The worst insult they can hurl at him is that he is a glutton and wino. No one could suggest that Jesus ever overstuffs himself or is inebriated – but all the same, there is no smoke without fire. This man really knows how to enjoy himself. He dines out with the Pharisees, and parties with the riff-raff, not to make a point, or to use it as a preaching opportunity, but because he genuinely welcomes the hospitality and loves their company. He applauds the generosity of the Mary who lavishes an entire box of perfume all over him. If a tiny bottle of Chanel costs the earth today, what must a boxful of the best fragrance have been worth then? 'Simon, Simon,' he says to his tutting host, 'my only regret is that you didn't do it too.'

As Jesus sets off for Jerusalem one last time, faced with the enormity of his destiny, it's with a breaking heart that he still insists on one last party with his disciples. And that is a bitter-sweet, somewhat muted occasion. They eat and sing and celebrate the familiar Passover service together, with the burden of separation and bereavement hanging heavily in the air around them. Jesus uses the vivid symbolism to explain what he is about to do, and reassure them of his constant love and eternal presence, then leaves the meal table and goes out alone into the darkness.

The nearest equivalent, perhaps, is the celebration of the Passover during the last war by the Jewish community in the Warsaw Ghetto. It's hard to imagine what celebration might have looked and felt like in those circumstances.

And then, when Jesus finally appears in his resurrection body in Galilee, is there lightning, thunderbolts, illuminated lettering in the sky to let the disciples know he is there with them? No, he makes them a barbie. Another mighty catch of fish on the lake is enough to make John realize who is there on the beach, and he alerts Peter, who instantly leaps into the water, even though the shore is so close it would have only taken a few minutes to row to it. I often try to imagine what Peter was thinking as he sank to the bottom of the lake and then began his glug-glugging ascent. After all, he has betrayed his Lord, Master and Leader, done what he vowed he would never do and disowned him. But as he surfaces he sees the rings of smoke. In the Middle East a meal is a symbol of reconciliation and fellowship, so Peter knows the barbecue represents his forgiveness. Little does he know, it will also turn out to be his commissioning party.

Jesus sends out invitations to the party

Everything Jesus ever taught, he tells his followers in John's Gospel, is 'so that my joy may be in you, and that you may experience a joy that is full, total and complete.'[5] And even if it was the last meal he spent with them, I can't imagine he said that in a lugubrious voice and without a blink, à la Hollywood-style. What Jesus taught he modelled, and no one who lived such a life of pure, uninhibited joy could have spoken about it without so much as a smile of remembrance crinkling the corner of his lips. What wonderful times they had all had together in the past three years.

That's why it's so offensive when Christianity is portrayed as ascetic, austere, dour, and guilt-ridden. That's why it is so sad when its followers appear gloomy and sober and disapproving. Joy is the hallmark of any Christian who wants to reflect their leader. 'Well done,' says the boss to the productive employee in the story he tells about the constructive use of our skills, 'enter into the joy of your master.'[6] Despite the awareness of his ultimate destiny, it's for the 'joy set before him' that Jesus does what he has to do and faces the cross with determination and courage.

So it is no surprise then that when Jesus invites people into the kingdom of God, it usually comes as the invitation to a party. There are the made-up stories he tells – of the child who kicks his father in the teeth, then is welcomed home with a huge, celebratory feast; of the lord who gives a magnificent banquet and invites in all and sundry from the streets.

There are also the real personal encounters. To that wretch of a little tax collector, Zaccheus, hiding up a tree, the gospel or good news is simply, 'Come down, Zaccheus, it's your lucky day. I'm having tea at your house today.' Jesus probably turned and beckoned his disciples, 'Come on, lads, the party's at Zac's.'

Nowhere does it record that Mrs Zaccheus was pleased to see the arrival of a dozen or so hungry, local oiks on her doorstep. 'I haven't cleaned,' she probably whispered to her husband, 'I haven't cooked. There's nothing in the house. Why didn't you warn me you were bringing friends home to dinner?' Zaccheus was probably too full of joy to care. And knowing Jesus, there would have been plenty to go round.

In the Book of Revelation, to the church in Laodicea that has slammed the door in his face, Jesus says, 'I'm not going to go away. I'm still outside knocking. So why don't you open the door and let me come in, and then... I'll tell you what a pain you are.' No, he actually says, 'and I will eat with you.' In other words, 'We'll be reconciled, we'll have fellowship, we'll sit down and party together because there is nothing I enjoy more.'

Of my few truly breathtaking experiences of the presence of Christ, one remains most vivid in my memory. I was around seventeen years old at the time and a very new Christian, living at home with Jewish parents who were horrified at what they perceived as the deepest of betrayals. It was Christmas Day and my mother had sent me to dry all the bedroom windows, lest the condensation form rivulets that in turn made puddles on window ledges, that might ultimately damage carpets or curtains. Christmas Day was, after all, a day like any other. As I stood at my post, wash-leather in hand, with numb fingers and a heavy heart, every bit of me yearned for Christmas dinner, presents, decorations, a tree. Out of the window I watched the people walking to the church at the top of our street, and ached to follow them. Imperceptibly, I became aware of a presence standing right next to me, so close that I feared, if I as much as moved a fraction of an inch or reached out a hand, I might touch him. And as I stood there, enfolded in an extraordinary sense of warmth and love and comprehension, it seemed as if a voice whispered quietly in my ear, 'I am Emmanuel, God with you. I am all the party you need.'

Now I have the dinner, the tree, the presents, the decorations and more church than I know what to do with. In fact, I'm often completely Christmassed out – and love every minute of it. But I have never forgotten that Christmas all those years ago, when I had nothing – and yet I had everything, because the partying Jesus was with me, transforming my lonely circumstances into a special occasion.

For personal reflection or group discussion

- How did Jesus integrate the sacred and the secular in his life and his teaching?

- List as many of the symbols that he used as you can think of. How do they enrich your understanding of his teaching?

- Make your own list of things that have become symbols for you and think of some potential new ones. A bell could become a reminder of God's constant presence. An ambulance bell means someone needs our prayers.

- In a home group, bring some of the more accessible symbols and explain what they mean to you and why.

- Alternatively, set aside 10–15 minutes or so at some point during the proceedings. Invite each member of the group to spend some time in silence wandering around the room (or downstairs in your home), allowing God to speak to them through something they can see, hear, touch, or smell. Pray together first as a group that God will say something to each person present; then, when everyone comes back together, invite people to share what they have learned. There should be no pressure to share in this way. For some it may have been a private, personal word. Others may find it hard at first to use their imagination and senses in this way – but listening to the rest of the group will encourage them to try it out for themselves with more confidence.

I have never yet known this exercise fail – even in the dankest, dullest church halls!

Useful websites

www.rejesus.co.uk

www.jerusalemperspective.com – this is an invaluable site for anyone wanting a deeper understanding of the Jewish world and sayings of Jesus. You will need to register for full access to the site, but thirty-two free sampler articles are available and more can be emailed to you on request.

Useful books

Brad H. Young, *Jesus the Jewish Theologian*, Hendrickson Publishers, 1995.

Rob Lacey, *The Liberator*, Zondervan, 2006 – tells the story of Jesus, based on the four Gospels, in contemporary language.

A Partying People at Home

eal, Jesus-style spirituality should be like breathing, with the holy imperceptibly entwined in the ordinary, like a flowering clematis growing up a stone wall. The get-it-out-and-parade-it-around-on-Sunday model, that is wrapped up in the evening in crepe paper and put back in its box until the following week, seems unreal in the cold light of a Monday morning when the baby's been up all night, the kids can't find their homework, the cat's gone missing and the car won't start. It seems even less real after the rush-hour crush, at the office, hospital, classroom or school gate. If spirituality can't make that transition, the problem is Sunday, not the rest of the week.

Many people perceive this lack of integrity in those who claim to follow Christ, and to them it looks very much like hypocrisy. In an age where there's antipathy to 'religion', and institutions, authorities and hierarchies appear suspect, churchiness of every kind leaves people cold. They see an alien culture at odds with their day-to-day issues, and reject it before they ever have any notion of its beliefs. But the search for spiritual satisfaction is more popular than ever. The twin gods of consumerism and materialism don't fill the God-shaped hole, however much the media manipulate us into believing they can. The alternative appears to be a host of options dangled in front of a stressed-out society by pedlars who offer rituals and systems that pander to the symptoms, but don't address the issue. Coping techniques are largely done alone rather than with the family or community, and tend to be inward-looking and self-indulgent. They are not the thirst-quenching, artesian well-gushing streams of endless life that Jesus offered a woman whose whole existence had, until that moment, revolved around the succession of men in her life.[7] Drink this water, Jesus said, and you'll never be thirsty again. This free and unlimited resource alone has the power to transform the ordinary, fairly meaningless daily grind into a quality of life most people see only in their dreams. And all we have to do is demonstrate to them that it is real. But that may mean a radical change of perspective.

When Christianity first came to the British Isles, before the faithful felt any need to enclose God in a monolith, the Celtic Christians wove their faith into their home and working lives, worshipping God with what they called the 'five-stringed harp' – all five of their senses – as they sang and crooned and prayed their way through the milking, the sowing, the weaving, the breastfeeding and the baking. They blessed God for daily comings and goings, for hearth and field, for kind and inclement weather, for harvest and autumn, for good news and bad, for welcomes and farewells. Instinctively, their model of worship was Hebraic. Home was their day-to-day spiritual centre. But they also enjoyed small, synagogue-style, weekly gatherings, open to every member of the community, with whom they shared their food, purse, leisure and worship. Larger centres, such as minster churches or religious communities, based largely in the north, opened their hearts and doors to pilgrims, taking on the celebratory role of the Temple. They were led by charismatic figures such as Cuthbert, Bede and Hilda, who lived lives devoted to poverty and simplicity, and encouraged the work of skilled artisans by establishing poets, minstrels and craftsmen in residence.

Fearing the consequences of such independent religious thinking, it wasn't long before the Roman Empire sent Augustine and other emissaries to establish their kind of church. The destruction of Celtic spirituality and the earthy roots of the British church is a sad and bloody story, full of ungodly political machinations and physical force. Canterbury Cathedral, that vast, vaulted, unwelcoming stone edifice, stands to this day as a symbol of the enforced, rather soulless form of Christianity that was imposed upon the people. The formal, sophisticated model had well and truly replaced the homey, extended-family, Hebraic-style church, and the faithful have had to live with the consequences through the centuries right up to the present day. A building, not the home, became the central spiritual focus of people's lives. Gradually, it became increasingly divorced from the humdrum, everyday culture of home and working life, and integrating the sacred and the secular every waking hour became very much harder.

Recent research in the USA carried out by the Barna Group[8] discovered that people find home groups more satisfying than conventional church – whether it's older Christians seeking a deeper and more intense experience with God, or young adults interested in faith and spirituality but with little interest in the outdated structures and institutions of traditional church. It seems as if the Hebraic–Celtic model, with home as a major spiritual centre and a Temple-style venue for grand celebration, may well have a great deal of relevance in the coming age for what it means to be church.

The church at the centre

Having spent a great deal of my childhood helping prepare festivals at home, I remember thinking how odd it was that for Christians most significant religious activities took place in the church. What was more, these activities seemed to consume most of their spare time and energy, leaving little for home and family.

As a typical practising, but not ultra-orthodox family, we only went to the synagogue for special festivals. In the three- or four-hour service, there was a great deal of praying and a great deal of Scripture, but since my knowledge of Hebrew was little more than rudimentary, I only knew this from the rather stilted English translation on the opposite page of the prayer book. That was before I lost the place altogether, gave up and made eyes at the boys downstairs instead. There was definitely a sermon, because that was in English, which was a relief. In fact, Christians would recognize the basic structure of a synagogue service. It would seem familiar. But what they don't have is the most immediate, meaningful and memorable part of any Jewish occasion – the blessings, the singing, the eating, the joking, the fighting, the atmosphere – because they happen at home, around the meal table.

Historically, the church took on the role of the synagogue. But that wasn't all. It absorbed the rituals of both the Temple and the home as well, formalized and systematized them, and made itself the community's one and only spiritual centre. Today, a church's customers shop around like consumers for the one that will best 'service' their family's entire spiritual needs. It's hardly surprising that we're so picky when the spiritual well-being of those we love depends upon it. As John Atkinson comments: 'Like the patrons of "one stop" petrol stations we pull into the church to fill up our spiritual tanks in the hope that the high octane worship or sermon (preferably both) will see us through the week's journey.'[9]

For centuries this served the needs of the institutionalized church well because it created dependency. What it did for its members was far less positive. Faith became a matter of individual belief. God was made distant, inaccessible. Physical barriers were erected to keep the people out of the sanctuary, from rood screens in medieval times to steps and rails in the Victorian era. Only the special few in their funny dresses had direct access to the divine. Spirituality was carefully controlled, 'done' for and on behalf of the people.

The cleft between the sacred and secular became so deep that the importance of the home as the spiritual centre was virtually done away with altogether. The Hebraic matriarchal tradition that entrusted the vital arrangement of feasts and festivals to an all-powerful mother, responsible for the religious rituals and routines in her own home, was completely undermined. And so was the role of the father as the priest of his family.

My father never really mastered ancient Hebrew. As a lad he truanted from Hebrew classes and went out playing with his friends on the beach of his native Redcar instead. Nonetheless, he managed a passable Sabbath service every Friday night when he finally ushered the last patient out of the surgery, took off the white coat that doctors had to wear in those more germ-conscious days, donned his skull-cap and rushed to the dining-room table, where his family, salivating at the aromas that seeped out of the kitchen, had been bemoaning his absence for at least an hour. It was a role he took seriously, which never ceased to surprise us children, as he was serious about little else in Judaism, and loved irritating my mother and her mother with his scant regard for Sabbath rules – especially if Newcastle United football team was playing at home.

Duty was important to my father. So was the moral uprightness of Judaism. It was incumbent on every Jewish man to teach his children Torah, a trade and how to swim – in other words, the rudiments of faith, education, morality and survival. It was the husband or father's responsibility to resource and bless his family, to nurture his children spiritually, to teach them the meaning of the festivals, the history of God's relationship with his people, and to prepare them for faith-full adulthood. All the home-based rituals of Sabbath and festival were presided over by the father. But within a hundred years of the birth of the church, they were replaced with the Communion service, which was formalized, removed from the home into a church building only, and overseen by a spiritual professional who even took the title 'Father'.

I can't think of any equivalent responsibility for the male in the Christian home. Today there's a suggestion that women, with their new freedoms, their careers, and their opportunity for church leadership, have usurped men's role, leaving them feeling a disempowered, emasculated spare part. But historically, it's the church that has taken over the responsibility for the spiritual education of our children (and incidentally, leaves most of it to women), that has done the most to sabotage the key and vital male role in the family.

Celebration at the centre

People imagine a place of G-dliness as a place for seriousness, a solemn place, a place that fills you with trepidation. The fact is, where there is G-d, there is joy. That is why our every moment is a moment to celebrate and fill with joy. Because at every moment we are fulfilling our mission of bringing G-dliness into this world. Not just the obviously joyful matters, such as meditation, study, prayer and good deeds, but also regular, mundane activities and the ways we earn an income and go about life – all are ways by which we know Him and bring Him into our world.

Jewish sage

When the church, not the home, took over responsibility for the entire spiritual well-being of its members, we became a schizoid people, split into two halves we could never quite pull together, with all pleasure and fun relegated into the inferior category. It was as if the wheels of our wagon became stuck in the muddy, obstructive notion that churchy things are spiritual, whilst everything else is not, and it transformed the free and joyous momentum that a journey of faith should be into something resembling more of a slog. Going to church is spiritual, going to work is not. Going to a home group is, going to a party is not. Reading the Bible is, watching the TV isn't – unless it's *Songs of Praise*, of course. But when did solitary worship replace the shared, communal variety, except for the housebound?

It was at a home group one night, in one of those moments that are a professional hazard for a journalist, when we find ourselves the outside observer looking in, that it struck me how much we divide and box our lives. There we were, laughing, bantering, catching up on all the gossip as we slurped our coffee in that semi-exhausted but happy state that signals the end of another long working day, when the bright spark who happened to be leading the 'official' proceedings said uneasily, 'I suppose we'd better open with prayer.' The banter died instantly. A polite, but rather forced silence descended, and we rearranged our faces and bodies into suitably holy mode. Even the language of prayer was different. It was almost whispered, reverent, with unusual phraseology, hard to speak if you were not fluent in it. And it seemed to me that we were actually saying, 'God isn't really with us in the normal course of events, but when we adopt the proper pose and speak the proper talk, an angel in heaven kicks him on the shins to let him know we're expecting some action.'

I thought long and hard about whether there was any way of doing it differently, more naturally and seamlessly, as Jesus would have done, acknowledging that God had been with us in the chatter, the laughter and the banter as much as in the study and the conscious prayer. But when I suggested alternatives, though people greeted the idea warmly, they almost immediately slipped back into the more comfortable, cultural habits – head down, eyes closed, minimal connection with everyone else in the room, and so off-putting for visitors.

A friend said to me recently, 'In my home group it's study one week, and ten-pin bowling the next.' We're either serious or frivolous, but never any combination of the two, and frankly, I find each on its own, without the other, fairly arid. But despite the fact that Jesus instinctively integrated the sacred and the secular, that for him study was play, and play was study, and both were equally significant, we simply don't know how to do it.

Aristotle, Plato and the rest of those classical philosophers have a lot to answer for, lauding mind over matter, treating the body with contempt in favour of the finer, moral, spiritual side, despising life's ordinary, routine, daily necessities. I have to admit, my body lets me down continually, especially in the mornings when I can't go anywhere without a dozen annoyingly disruptive loo stops. And I'm certainly not too keen on the damage currently wreaked upon it by age and gravity. But I'd be a shadow of my former self without it. At the end of the day, God made it in all its wonder and weakness, and the Hebraic Jesus' view of body, mind and spirit as one entity seems to make much more sense. I cannot function at all, let alone spiritually, without sleep, food, friendship, relationship, well-functioning internal plumbing, and lots of laughter.

When we try to split ourselves into categories, we deny the lovely Hebraic concept of *shalom*, or wholeness, and disintegrate instead. Across the centuries, more than a few of the great saints have sought to address what they see as this unnatural division. The great teacher of prayer, Teresa of Avila, spoke about 'God among the pots and pans'; Brother Lawrence practised the presence of

God as he worked in the monastery kitchen. But generally, especially after the influence of the Protestant Reformation, with its suspicion of ritual, Christians became accustomed to seeing the world through Graeco-Roman, rather than Jewish Jesus, specs. We mistrusted our senses, and revered, as the ancients did, the exercise of head over heart, the brain over the senses, learning over obedience, solemnity over fun.

Celebration starts when we begin to pull the various bits of ourselves together and discover the wholeness or integration that is our second birthright, the real gift of salvation. Only then will we cease to expect the church to be the one-stop shop and start to live out our faith in a variety of creative ways – in our homes, communities and workplaces.

Many home groups are stuck in the 'Bible study and discussion' model because the members haven't ever considered another way of being or doing it, have never tried experimenting with the kind of imaginative worship that would facilitate inviting in the local community, creating an environment where the neighbours feel unthreatened, involved and at ease. But now, as people are looking for a spirituality that they can take home with them, this is a golden opportunity to clear away the host of historic, cultural-church baggage that has stifled the expression of our faith, rather than given it freedom to explore, experiment and expand. It's time for our imaginations to wake up.

The home at the centre

In Judaism almost all the significant threshold events, from birth to death, are centred around the home. The dedication of a new baby, including the circumcision of a boy on the eighth day, takes place at home, in the heart of the extended family. After a death the coffin remains at the deceased's home, with their lit Sabbath candles on top, watched over until the funeral, by members of the community who come and go in shifts, day and night. After the funeral, for the seven days of official mourning, members of the community will visit the bereaved at home for prayers, morning and night. It's known as *shivah*, the Hebrew word for 'seven', and it makes a helpful, healthy start to the bereavement process.

When my father died, many years ago now, I still remember how comforting it was to wake up to the chanting of those hauntingly sad, yet beautiful words from the Hebrew Scriptures rising softly up the stairs to my room. 'Blessed be the Lord. The Lord gives and the Lord takes away. May the great name of the Lord be blessed forever.' It is a wonderful song of praise and trust, transcending all pain and sorrow, one of the most familiar prayers of the Jewish people. It creates the right emotional atmosphere for shared tears and still has the power to bring a lump to my throat.

Throughout the day my mother, brother and sister and I sat on low stools, receiving visitors, who arrived laden with food – pots of chopped herring and liver pâté, chicken casseroles, fried fish, the inevitable smoked salmon (a lifeline in every trial), green salads, fruit salads, cheesecakes, sponge-cakes, home-made biscuits. It amused me to see my mother's non-Jewish friends arriving with bouquets of flowers, while her Jewish friends, ever practical, heaved in vast tureens of chicken soup. Not having to shop, plan meals or cook at a time when we least wanted to eat was such a relief. Resting on the loving support of others meant we had time and space to grieve without distraction.

Although *shivah* can hardly be described as a celebration, there were moments when sharing precious memories of my father with so many visitors became a kind of celebration of his life, and there were times, after evening prayers were over and most had gone, when deciding what to eat created an almost party atmosphere.

In Western Christianity those key rites of passage have been removed from the home into the church, where they are institutionalized and sanitized. Birth and death are no longer a normal part of daily life. The most important spiritual moments in most people's lives happen outside their usual orbit. Traditionally that begins very early in a person's life, when their spiritual education is devolved entirely to an institution, be it church or school. But this kind of education cannot create an emotional feel for a way of life.

For many people religious instruction at school or Sunday school has been dull and meaningless. Religious ritual in school assemblies and churches has been fairly boring and joyless. Reduce any faith down to doctrine and morals and it will be questioned, then rejected, if there are no satisfactory answers. That's why the church cannot alone be responsible for a child's spiritual development. They need so much more than head knowledge. In any case, we probably develop concepts of God long before church or school get hold of us.

Celebration in the home revolves around lived experience. Beliefs and values are implicit, not drummed into the participants. Around the table, set for an occasion, resplendent with candles and other symbols of God's presence, we are no longer merely spectators. At whatever age, we worship in the fullest sense, with our entire being, heart, soul, mind, senses and strength.

This kind of celebration must be play, it must be fun. That's why I've called it 'party'. If it becomes a burden, if it's lacklustre and can't compete with TV, the entire point is lost. That does not mean that rituals cannot be repeated from year to year, or even week by week. Children need patterns, structure and consistency, as do most adults. We all find change unsettling and like to fill our orbit with familiarity, predictability and anticipation. They give us a sense of rhythm and security. But rituals also need forethought, preparation, updating and adapting to the needs of whoever is going to be present on each occasion. My grandmother used to moan as certain festivals approached, particularly Passover. They were so much work. But a bit like childbirth, the pain and effort was forgotten in the joy of having the family gather, the children overwrought with excitement. Once we were there, my six-foot uncle, only four years my senior, would take hold of her tiny frame and dance her round and round the kitchen until her protests dissolved in laughter, she hung her pinny up on a peg and joined us in the dining room.

As people arrive, the smell of the food or flowers, the sight of a beautifully dressed table, the music in the background, what they touch, taste, hold and feel, is as much a part of creating the right atmosphere for the occasion as having the right words, stories and songs. Every family or group will establish their own favourite traditions, but traditions are only saved from meaninglessness when they exist for a purpose. And their purpose is to point to the eternal reality beyond.

None of us, adult or child, live without moments of terror. Newspapers sell by raising anxiety and panic levels. Our media perpetually blasts us with reminders of life's unexpected vicissitudes – the mass of potential tragedies, horrors and disasters. Children imagine and dream of all kinds of evil and often hide the fact as well as any adult. In this transitory and temporal world of ours, where pictures of war, pain, suffering and injustice assault us on every side, celebration at home affirms eternal truth and goodness. When we share the stories and symbols that have sustained our ancestors through good times and ill, adversity and prosperity, we are reminding our families and home groups of our safe and secure place within God's historic and perfect plan. These are vital weapons in combating fear, and nurturing faith, goodness and courage.

I remember vividly one Passover service in my grandmother's home when

I wondered for the first time why – if God had conquered that tyrant, Pharaoh, and freed his people – he was so remote and so silent during the Holocaust. As I said the familiar words, 'Pharaoh has not been the only tyrant who tried to annihilate us. There have been others in every generation, but the Holy One, blessed be he, delivered us out of their hands,' I realized that my very existence was testimony to the truth of it. I did not live through the Holocaust. And because I was not there, our story as a people, mine as a child of promise, continues.

Stories and symbols reach beyond our intelligence to the parts of us that all the sermons, education and talks in the world, important as they are, cannot touch. They enable us to experience God and not just explain him. They allow him to whisper something different into the hearts of everyone present. Like art and music, they feed our awe and wonder as they give us a glimpse into a world that will be ours one day, but not quite yet. I have never yet invited guests, whatever their background, however atheistic or cynical, to a simple Sabbath meal, who did not want us to pray for them and their families, and were not deeply moved and touched both by the fact that we did so, and by the entire experience.

This kind of celebration is particularly appropriate for children because it doesn't require any level of understanding before they can participate fully. Any simple meaning they take will grow with their ability to understand. They are very comfortable with mystery. It is we adults who so easily disrupt it with our need to explain, rather than live it with them.

In an age where television, computer games and the internet risk turning our children and young people into passive observers and consumers, here is a vibrant, meaningful way of engaging their attention, and encouraging full participation in family and community. Not only that, it also provides them with the tools for survival that they will need in a world of constant change, reminding them that there is an unchanging, eternal purpose for their lives. This kind of celebration creates a safe harbour, so that many years later, when our children find themselves adrift in what can be a very lonely, hostile sea, the symbols and memories become the lighthouse that will guide them back to their true home.

Some basic principles for celebration in the home

- The Hebraic concept of 'the family' did not mean today's nuclear variety – mum, dad and two kids. It meant extended family – parents, grandparents, surrogate parents, aunts, uncles, cousins, out-of-town visitors, and whoever else may be alone on special occasions. If your own children are grown up, there's plenty of opportunity to bless everyone else's, and their parents in the process. Children of single-parent families thrive in home groups that really care for them.

- Hospitality is not an optional extra. It is as near a command as it's possible to be (Romans 12:13; 1 Peter 4:9). In the Old Testament hospitality was much more than entertaining friends. It also meant receiving strangers as honoured guests, providing them with food, shelter and protection, because the Israelites themselves were once strangers in the land of Egypt. Jesus received hospitality from people he knew well and from those he didn't. All of those meals seem to have been significant. When I was a student and cut off from my family because of my new faith, I was shocked at how little practical support there was from the local church. In Judaism it would have been unthinkable for a young, single person to eat alone on the Sabbath, let alone Easter Day. How many opportunities for party have been missed because we are just too busy or too self-conscious about our cooking to invite strangers back to lunch on Sundays?

- If you are on your own there is no point sitting at home alone and lonely, lamenting the fact that 'no one ever invites me'. Be a bit more Hebraic and invite them instead. In Hebraic thought, it's the doing that counts – faith in action. This is why the Apostle James says, 'If you believe, let's see that you do' (James 2:14). The question Peter was asked at Pentecost was, 'What must I do to be saved?', not 'What must I know to be saved?' Besides, single people are often the most creative home-celebration makers.

- Any meal can become an occasion if the atmosphere is right. It does not depend on the cooking! Music, candles, flowers, table decorations, coloured serviettes, can all make a feast of a takeaway.

- Any spiritual component should be as normal and natural and integrated as possible. No one needs to shut their eyes just because they are praying. It can embarrass guests if they think there are special rules to follow – and they don't know them. In my childhood home the ceremony went on despite dozens of interruptions – children fighting, mother rushing to and fro to the kitchen, friends chattering, grandparents snoring, uncles telling silly jokes.

- Create your own traditions and rituals. In this context, familiarity does not breed contempt, if they are freshly planned and prepared. In fact, they just get better, treasures that become part of the fabric of our spiritual inheritance over a long period of time, full of warm and happy memories that carry us through happy times and sad. It's when they become empty gestures or a burden that they lose their meaning. To stay meaningful, they must be enjoyable, not a chore, or a boring alternative to watching TV or a night out. Celebration soon loses its party feel when it's mandatory and dull.

Some reflections and ideas to get you started

- Read Psalms 148 and 150, exchanging the word 'praise' with 'celebrate'. The Hebrew word *Hallal* means both 'praise' and 'celebrate'. Even creation continually celebrates its Maker.

- Read Psalm 98 and try to decide how you can recapture some of the suggestions the psalmist outlines here in your own worship in a family gathering or a home group.

- In what way has the Hellenistic (Greek–Roman) influence impacted your spiritual life? Does it matter? And if it does, what might you want to change?

- Begin to create new 'symbols' that have meaning for you. Set aside fifteen minutes, once a week at least, and take a 'prayer walk'. Ask God to speak to you as you walk. Use all of your senses – touch, taste, smell, sight and sound – and you will probably get a very pleasant surprise.

- In a survey in the *Independent* newspaper, 70 per cent of those who were questioned thought children should be taught to pray at school. It was far too embarrassing and too private to do in the context of home. How many different ways can we help children learn to pray?

- The contemporary Jewish sage, Rabbi Abraham Heschel, said, 'Wonder, not doubt, is the beginning of knowledge.' How can we give the children in our family or home group a sense of wonder?

- Make home a 'spiritual space'. Homes have great significance in biblical history. God created the first spiritual space in creation – a place where man walked with God in a glorious garden. Make your home and garden a 'sanctuary' for you and God. Create 'spiritual spaces' – corners or places for quiet, for art, for music, for sharing stories, for prayer. You could create an altar out of a small table, with a candle or candles, and some of your most meaningful symbols laid out on it. It should be a place of retreat, of calm and quiet in your busy world.

A useful model

'Godly Play', developed by Jerome W. Berryman, based on Montessori methods of learning, is a fun way of encouraging and developing the spirituality of children, but it can be adapted for people of any age and would work particularly well in a home group.

It involves welcoming children into a specially prepared environment, with the 'telling' or 'enacting' of a Bible story, using figures or symbols that they can touch and hold, that allow them to enter into or live the story. The children are not told what the story means, but are invited to reflect on what they felt as they were listening. They then recreate what the story seems to be saying to them – in writing, dressing up, crafts or artwork. You will need to have lots of card, paint, glue, glitter, ribbon, felt etc. to hand. By engaging all of their senses, the children are far more likely to absorb the messages of the stories, and learn to study and apply them for themselves.

In a home group this may involve:

- Setting up the room in a way that is conducive to worship, that is more than rearranging the armchairs. Lighting, candles, scents, symbols, music all have their place.
- The dramatized telling of a Bible story, without explaining what it means. After all, a text can have many different interpretations, and different meanings or applications at various times in our lives.
- A chance for everyone present to share what the story meant to them – or what especially struck them.
- An opportunity to recreate those feelings in some form of artwork.

End with a 'feast' of some kind, and a personal blessing for all those present.

Useful websites

www.centeringprayer.com
www.godlyplay.org.uk

Useful books

John Leach, *How to Use Symbol and Action in Worship*, Grove Booklets, Worship 184.
Martha Zimmerman, *Celebrate the Feasts*, Bethany House Publishers, 1981.
Sara Wenger Shenk, *Why Not Celebrate?*, Good Books, 1987.
Olive M. Fleming Drane, *Spirituality To Go*, Darton Longman & Todd, 2006.
Bob Hartman, *The Lion Storyteller Bible*, Lion, 1995.

A Partying Community

The seventeenth-century diarist Samuel Pepys once visited a synagogue in London during *Simchat Torah*, that special day at the end of the Feast of Tabernacles when the entire congregation abandons any attempt at sedate behaviour, and gets up and dances, or even prances, behind the sacred scrolls. The men kiss their prayer shawls, then reach out and touch the silver casings with the spot their lips have touched. Better not use naked flesh. Remember Uzzah, who steadied the Ark with his bare hands and dropped dead for his pains? No lessons are ever wasted.

Pepys was deeply shocked by what he referred to as the 'laughing' and 'sporting' and general cavorting, and described the worshippers as 'more like brutes than people knowing the true God'. Admittedly, Pepys had never had the pleasure of attending a present-day football match, though there was no shortage of other secular roistering around him, and he appears to have had no problem with that. It was the partnership between religion and fun that caused his outrage – the apparent lack of the reverence that God could and should expect. It's an attitude buried deep in the British psyche, though Islam, with a very different cultural background, is just as solemn and earnest. Religion, sadly, tends to make people take themselves too seriously, and faith without humour so easily becomes fanaticism, bearing no resemblance whatsoever to any Judaeo-Christian festive legacy.

Party is more than just a knees-up

So is celebration simply an excuse for a good romp? There's nothing wrong with letting one's hair down every now and then, but true celebration is so much more profound. It begins with our inner life. It's an attitude to life. It's a way of life. It can be quiet and dignified. But often, in company, it will burst out into party. Not everyone welcomes that idea. When I once described my vision for a partying church to a group of counsellors, one of them asked, 'Where does that leave introverts like me?' Hmmmm, I thought, Jesus turned so many occasions into parties – dinner parties, tea parties, even breakfast parties. Was he an introvert or an extrovert, and did it have any bearing on his lifestyle? All those occasions were an opportunity to form relationships, share fellowship, and eat with his friends, which is what God has always planned and loved to do from the beginning of time.

But when I told my husband that I was writing about partying, he said, 'That sounds a bit frivolous to me.' Another introvert, parties fill him with dread rather than anticipation. But it's what the word conveys that's the prob-lem. Just as 'celebration' has been devalued, so 'party' tends to convey images of groups of strangers, standing stiffly, wine glass in hand, making stilted conver-sation, or a drink-induced, raucous disco, where everyone invades each other's space as they yell above the thudding drumbeat and spray each other with bits of potato crisps. That kind of party is enough to make even the extrovert quake and it certainly isn't the biblical variety.

I love the spiritual writer Henri Nouwen's definition of celebration as 'the acceptance of life in a constantly increasing awareness of its preciousness. And life is precious not only because it can be seen, touched and tasted, but also because it will be gone one day.'[10] The Hebrew sages of old agreed that ingrati-tude was our greatest sin. We so quickly take for granted the grace, mercy and protection that sustain us from day to day. Celebration is the discipline that forces us to look at life from God's perspective, to recognize its daily blessings, whatever the difficulties we face, and give grateful thanks. It is worship at its very best, pouring like a waterfall from a heart overwhelmed with love and gratitude. It is the alabaster box of oil that a woman broke over Jesus, then, unashamedly and very publicly, massaged into his feet with her hair. It means lavishing all we are on him, body, soul and spirit – often in a communal, public act. To those looking on, like Samuel Pepys, it can seem frivolous, wasteful or downright uncomfortable. But then, in the context of our busy lives, if worship isn't a holy, glad and willing waste of time and energy, what is it?

Several times, people in churches we have been in have told me they did-n't come to a particular celebration because life was tough and they weren't in the mood. Perhaps that's the best time to party. In pain, bereavement, or depres-sion, it can be very hard to do – a real sacrifice. But in the Book of Leviticus,

God commands his people to be joyful at a festival: 'You shall rejoice before me.' There is no 'if' or 'except', no 'whether you feel like it or not', no special dispensations. But nor does any sacrificial offering ever go unnoticed. The word 'sacrifice' comes from the Latin *sacrum facere*, 'to make holy'. There is something sacred and special about celebration that is an act of the will, a determined response to the superabundant goodness of God, even when that goodness may seem a distant, inaccessible reality. It is a mark of exceptional spiritual character to be able to hang onto the truth like the psalmist and say, 'I'm going to thank you for all the amazing and wonderful moments life holds, even if I'm too bruised and befuddled to enjoy them fully at the moment. I believe that the well of tears will dry up, and a new dawn will come.' Interestingly, Jewish law excuses people from dancing at parties for the first year of any bereavement. It doesn't suggest they shouldn't attend. That's the time when they most need their community, when they most need to fasten onto God's good gifts and remember that joy has not gone forever.

Party creates community

It's almost impossible to party alone. Celebration creates community – that deep sense of connectedness with others that drives away the loneliness that hounds our society. In a recent national survey carried out by the Department of Health, asking people what they most needed from Social Services, second on the list was company. There has to be something very sad about a society that expects professional carers to fill the emotional holes in our lives.

I am only beginning to appreciate the full potential of party. A couple of years ago I invited a work colleague to a performance at our church of the Riding Lights touring company's Christmas play. Meriel, one of the congregation, had the foresight to lay on mince pies and mulled wine afterwards, and it created a real sense of occasion. My colleague turned to me and whispered, 'I'd love to belong to a community like this.' Several weeks later she appeared in my office and asked, 'Do you do the Alpha course at your church? Can I come?' And she's been coming ever since.

'Community' has become another of those devalued words. According to council newspapers, I am a member of my local community simply by dint of living in the same council area as a large number of people I have never met. It requires no acquaintance, no commitment on my part. Belonging has been reduced simply to sharing a postcode rather than sharing the ups and downs of life.

If it means anything, community is about having and being a neighbour. One of Boots' free magazines recently carried a feature called '9 easy ways to unleash your inner optimism'. Reaching out to others was one suggestion – not for any altruistic purpose, but because it does us good. Research at the University of Toronto has apparently discovered that spending more time at home alone rather than socializing can cut our life expectancy: 'One US study demonstrated that the most important characteristics shared by the 10% of the people with the highest levels of happiness and the fewest signs of depression were their strong ties to friends and their commitment to spending time with them.'

Whatever our motives, getting together and eating together is an antidote for the individualism that besets our society, and the current notion that religion or spirituality can be personal and private. It is polyfiller in the relational cracks experienced by countless people who have been abandoned or abused by family or wounded by the alienation around them. It could and should be deeply healing.

At one of our annual Passovers, after the meal, when the church was heaving with horas and congas, as people wove their way around the tables, Peter noticed Barry drop the hands of the people on either side of him and pull out of the circle. He stood for a while, mopping his brow, with an untypical, huge grin on his face as he watched the manic progress of young and old and all in between, in and out of doors, up and down steps, all around the building. Barry had sustained the cruellest physical and mental abuse throughout his childhood, which had robbed him of joy in relationships and threatened to blight his adult life.

'I just love occasions like this,' he said, as Peter went up and joined him. 'It suddenly struck me, this is my family now. This is my community. I've found somewhere where I know I can love and be loved, where I am accepted exactly as I am. This is where I belong.'

Party is a chance to play

If church isn't fun, people are simply not going to come. Why give up a morning or evening to be bored? Play is instinctive, yet so many people feel they ought to leave it behind when they become grown up. It seems to happen at around the age of eighteen, possibly when we first leave home. During our Harvest Tabernacles service the children and adults have a wonderful time and move freely around the building waving palm branches and ribbons, disappearing into the large makeshift tabernacle for quiet prayer and reflection, lighting night-lights during the intercessions, having water poured over their hands, or even heads, as a sign of receiving the Holy Spirit. Students who come – many of them for the first time, since it's the first Sunday of the new academic year – watch wide-eyed. The more the rest of the congregation gets into festive mood, the more some of them stand on their dignity. They find it very hard to let go and engage in the service in any way other than sitting still and listening. It could be our beloved education system that has reduced them to passive observers. It could be that they feel they have come to university to be adults, not to play like children. It certainly is peer pressure and not wanting to make fools of themselves.

Play is essential for the health and well-being of all living creatures. That's why God gave it to us as a gift, enshrined in the command to Sabbath. The pinnacle of God's creative imagination was not in designing humans on day six, but in giving them rest on day seven. Sam Wells says the beauty of play is that it is not 'purposeful, productive, efficient, economical, measured, effective or strategic' – all the useful, grown-up things we have to be in the workplace every day. Instead it's 'exuberant, passionate, joyful, reckless, wholehearted and unselfconscious' – all the childlike things we really need to be from time to time.[11] If the church community isn't providing an alternative to the relentless pressure of work, if it is not offering an element of fun and play, it cannot send its members back into the world refreshed, reinvigorated, recreated and ready for the week's battles.

'Unless you become like a little child,' Jesus said, 'you'll never really appreciate the most wonderful, magical things in life. You'll never allow your imagination to run riot, giving you a glimpse into the glories of the kingdom of God.' Children are an excellent barometer of a church's temperature. If they find it dull, difficult and a chore, there's a chance that so will the adults. Of course, worship has to be age-appropriate, but many adults welcome the chance to get away from the cerebral and intellectual model from time to time. I have never seen a child bored by our Passover, Tabernacles or Pentecost services. There's far too much to engage the senses and the imagination, far too much fun to be had. Play, writes Sam Wells, 'is a corrective to any solemn Gospel that seeks to make disciples more earnest than God.'

Play is also education. It teaches children to share, and sharing doesn't always come naturally these days. I have been staggered on occasions, when we have a 'bring and share' communal lunch at church, that by the time my poor husband has dispensed with his pastoral duties and made it to the buffet table, there is often nothing left except a few shrivelled, crusty sandwiches or gloopy, empty pastry cases, although they did make up for it recently with a wonderful party to celebrate the 25th acciversary of his ordination. On the other hand, a monthly shared lunch at the little church we attend in France from time to time is a gourmet's and a gourmand's paradise. Everyone brings their best, their favourite dinner-party treat, and there is always more than enough for everyone – including the half dozen or so unexpected visitors who always turn up and don't, of course, know that they needed to bring food. One of the English members of the congregation thought it a waste and stopped attending. But I have to admit that from our first experience, when we arrived for a service one Sunday, knowing no one, with nothing, and were welcomed and fed like royalty, this feels more like the generosity of God. It is an enormous privilege to share our purses, our food, and our homes, to welcome strangers and lavish on them a token of the superabundance we have received.

Yes, it can be costly. We open our warm, comfortable church centre to the homeless every week and provide a meal. At Christmas it is theirs for the whole festival. There has never been such damage to the church, and on Christmas Eve, when they joined us for the candle-lit service, handbags disappeared into the ether and church members found themselves at the police station reporting theft, rather than at home with their families. Is it worth the distress, the inconvenience, the extra work? We have to believe it is. Sharing what we have with those who have nothing is a recurring biblical theme, an essential part of any celebration.

The Governor's great party

Celebration doesn't have to come packaged as party, but when it's communal, it often looks like one. My favourite biblical party story is in the Book of Nehemiah. Liberated from long exile and captivity in Babylon, the people return to their beloved Jerusalem. After several years of intense opposition, they have finally managed to build the Second Temple, where they assemble for the first time to celebrate the Feast of Trumpets, or New Year. Ezra the Priest and Nehemiah the Governor bring out the Book of the Law, and begin to read it out loud, and as they hear God's loving expectations of his relationship with his people, so long forgotten or ignored, they begin to weep with shame and regret. Ezra welcomes their penitence, but Nehemiah reminds him that this is neither the time nor the place. The Feast of Trumpets is a major festival, and the law commands rejoicing, not wretchedness, on a festival. So Nehemiah tells them to dry their eyes and sends them home to party. 'Go and enjoy choice food and sweet drink, and send some to those who have nothing prepared. This day is sacred to the Lord. Do not grieve...and then, the joy of the Lord will be your strength.'

Throughout my life, in times of trouble and adversity, some bright spark has slapped me on the back and reminded me in a doom-filled voice full of resignation, that the joy of the Lord is my strength. Not out of context, it isn't – at least, not in this story. The joy that gives us strength here is a direct consequence of the partying.

In his commentary on Nehemiah, Derek Kidner says, 'Three times in this short paragraph (Nehemiah 8:9–12) it is pointed out that holiness and gloom go ill together. What makes Nehemiah's words striking, to our ears, is the calm assumption that it should go without saying.'[12] No one was holier than Jesus, and he was the least gloomy person who ever lived. Writing about this verse, Matthew Henry, the great commentator, said, 'Holy joy', not misery or the martyr-spirit, 'will be oil to the wheels of our obedience.'[13]

It's the little luxuries that turn a meal into a feast. Nehemiah spells them out. 'Drink sweet wine.' He manifestly knows *kosher* wine. It's as sweet as diluted treacle. In the Book of Leviticus, anyone who hasn't enough money for wine at Passover may withhold their tithe and use it for that purpose. And then he tells them to 'share your food with those who haven't prepared any.' The very nature of hospitality is to provide, unstintingly, for others, in the certainty that there will always be enough to go round. Then, there will be no more room for tears. 'The joy of the Lord will be your strength.'

In Hebrew thinking there are traditionally four stages or levels of rejoicing – that ultimately lead to the fullness of joy that is our intended birthright. The first is *chedvah*, the word used here. *Chedvah* is a tiny ray, pinprick, or laser beam that pierces the numbness of our despair. The first step is taken, the darkness has been penetrated, even if it hasn't yet been dispersed. The second stage is *gilah* – that moment when a faint stirring of joy can actually be felt, like a butterfly in the pit of the stomach. The word doesn't appear in Nehemiah, but it is used in the Book of Habakkuk, where the prophet says, 'If all else fails, yet will I still joy in you.' The third stage or level of joy is *simchah*, which in Hebrew is synonymous with partying, and refers to a communal outpouring of thanksgiving and joy. In chapter 12 of Nehemiah, the people return to Jerusalem some two weeks after the Governor has sent them home, this time for the Feast of Tabernacles, and now, joyful partying or *simchah* breaks out spontaneously across the whole of the town and impacts everyone in its orbit. The ultimate and final stage of joy is *sason* – total elation, an experience of the glory of God that is so overwhelming that it leaves us flat on our face. It may not happen to us very often and doesn't appear to happen in Nehemiah, but it was certainly the experience of the psalmist, who seemed to swing between all four emotional levels on a regular basis.

In Auschwitz some of the inmates danced on *Simchat Torah*, just as they would have done in the synagogue on such a day. Speaking of it, the writer and Holocaust survivor, Elie Wiesel, wrote, 'For them the commandment to rejoice on your festival was an impossible commandment to observe – but observe it they did.' If celebration is an obedience rather than simply a bonus ball for the favoured, perhaps it isn't strange that the poorest church, the church that suffers the most – the African church – has the most to show us about celebration.

Party as a rehearsal

In Luke's Gospel, the shepherd who finds the lost sheep, the woman who finds the lost coin, and the father whose lost son comes home, call in their friends and neighbours for a grand celebratory party. Jesus says this is a picture of what goes on in heaven every time one of God's children discovers their true inheritance. Celebration down here is a reflection of what the Father loves to do up there.

That means that celebration is not only instinctive, it's prophetic. It points to a future reality. It is a demonstration of our hope. We live in a world where people are so desperate to celebrate that they imitate it most weekends, using a variety of artificial stimulants to deliver amnesia and give the necessary high – drugs, binge drinking, free sex. Only oblivion can blot out an unhappy past and an even more unpalatable, empty future.

Authentic celebration recognizes forgiveness for the past, freedom for the present and a future without fear. A few years ago, some very special Roman Catholic nuns who worked on the staff of our local hospice told us that Christians, particularly the evangelical variety, tended to find it much harder to cope with terminal cancer and come to terms with their death than those who had little or no faith. I hope that's because we so love and appreciate the life we have been given, but I also wonder whether it might have something to do with the unreality of eternal life. Henri Nouwen explained that when we have been able to celebrate life in all its most decisive moments, in its gains and losses, its joys and pains, 'we should even be able to celebrate our own dying because we have learned from life that he who loses it can find it.'[14]

My Great Aunt Rae's only child was the impersonator, Eddie Arnold, who appeared regularly at the London Palladium and on ITV on Sunday evenings. But he died, tragically, of a brain tumour, while he was still in his thirties. At every family event, on the happiest occasions, Aunty Rae would whisper a quiet but stark reminder: 'Nothing lasts forever.' As I get older I find that notion increasingly sad. The writer to the Hebrew Christians said something very similar: 'Here we have no lasting city.' But he at least added that that was because 'we are looking forward to the city that's to come.'[15] Further on,[16] he paints a rather alluring picture of what that eternal home will be like. I hadn't noticed it, until my husband, who was reading the New Testament in French, pointed it out. The writer says we will join thousands upon thousands of angels who are already *en fête* – in other words, in party mode. The Greek word he resorts to, translated as 'joyful assembly' in English, is *panegyria*, which isn't used anywhere else in the New Testament. In ancient Greece a *panegyria* was a great religious festival that included processions, prayers to the gods, amusements, games, and gymnastic and musical competitions. It was the Gentile equivalent of a Hebrew festival.

Celebration is a taste now of the eternal party that is to come. The Hebrew word for feast days is *moedim*, which also means 'holidays' and 'a rehearsal'. One or two of the most important Hebrew holidays are more than a rehearsal – they have already had their opening night and a full run to a grand finale. Passover, as a rehearsal of our ultimate deliverance and freedom, was fulfilled in the crucifixion and the resurrection. *Shavuoth*, or the Feast of the Firstfruits, as a rehearsal of a grand, spiritual harvest, was fulfilled at Pentecost. But others, like the Feast of Trumpets and the Feast of Tabernacles, are still in rehearsal for the wrapping-up of time as we know it, the final harvest and resurrection of all the dead. That's why authentic party can be the antidote to the meaninglessness of daily living, to being bombarded by bad news from all over the world, and the hopelessness it engenders. It calls people to live as they were meant to live, in a relationship and a companionship with God that will last for all eternity. If we're offering people an invitation to the final and eternal party in heaven, we may as well start by inviting them to one down here.

Celebration recognizes that no matter how things may seem, no matter how we feel, God is on his throne and all's well with the world. Such is God's love that injustice and suffering never have the final say. One day there will be no more tears. Sorrow may last for a night, but joy will come in the morning – even if it is not until the very last morning. So as we party, we effectively say with Mother Julian, 'All is well and all will be well and all manner of things will be well.'

My friend Laura has cerebral palsy. She's confined to a wheelchair, has little use of her arms, and cannot speak, except with the help of a plastic alphabet sheet. She has a degree in Social Sciences and is highly intelligent, but it takes a long time to communicate and she has to be incredibly patient with our stumbling attempts to understand the slight head movements that cost her immense effort, and tell us whether we're on track or not. But Laura refuses to be caged by her wayward body. Sometimes, when she's in a really celebratory mood, one leg begins to swing backwards and forwards, slowly at first, then gathering momentum, until eventually one shoe will spin over her head across the congregation, and woe betide anyone in its path. Then she starts on the other leg, but by that time we're all ready to duck.

Laura knows that one day her body will be as free as her spirit, and when we all eventually get to the greatest party of all – the one that will last forever – I have no doubt that it will be Laura who will lead us in the dance.

For group discussion

The three pilgrim festivals in Jerusalem were party time for the entire community of every age. So were *panegyria*, the equivalent for the Gentile community. They involved feasting, camping, playing games, cabaret acts, drama, procession, pageant, music, worship, symbolism.

- How can that atmosphere, that mix of spiritual and secular, be reflected in our festivals today, both at home and in the wider community?

- Which of the above can you incorporate, when and how?

To do

1. Form a 'make a festival' group

At a seminar that Peter and I led at New Wine, participants suggested setting up a 'make a festival' group, consisting of several families and friends, of all ages, who would work together to come up with ideas for celebrating the festivals in small groups or in the wider community, including:

- Designs for decorations for home, the church, school or church hall. Visuals always work best if they are planned and there is an overall scheme, design or theme. Some can be made by members of the group. Think big – large objects work best! One group at our church transformed the building into a *favella*, or village, for a South American evening, creating walls and houses by painting cardboard boxes. Recreating Bethlehem, or a huge tomb, or a tabernacle isn't difficult with a bit of imagination. People with experience of stage or museum design can be very helpful.

- Choosing appropriate music – that can be performed, or simply listened to. Contemporary or classical music played over loudspeakers can be as powerful as singing, if the pieces are carefully chosen.

- Choosing readings – scriptures, poems, monologues, stories. A wide range is available in bookshops and on the internet. The group may want to write their own dramas or stories.

- Writing simple liturgies. Some are included in this book, but they are just a basis and can be adapted to each and every circumstance.

- Writing background study or explanation notes, with suggested alternative ways of celebrating the festival.

- Compiling recipes or suggested menus – with cost and the accessibility of the food in mind.

- Choosing symbols – they are inexhaustible: stones, shells, greenery, candles, colours, string, balloons. They look their best if they are grouped together in bigger displays. Try to think of new and original symbols.

- Choosing visuals – pictures, photographs, cuttings, displays, overheads, DVDs.

2. Create a spiritual space at work

Every Friday at my workplace the Muslims all went to the mosque together to pray. I was impressed by their commitment, and they were impressed when the half dozen or so Christians in our office decided to meet together weekly too. They asked if they could join us to see what we got up to. Sadly, it never actually happened, but that, and being invited to pray for healing for various colleagues, made me realize how effective it could be to set up a 'spiritual space' in the workplace. The two websites below offer some very creative but simple ideas for how this might be done.

www.thesoulgym.org
www.rejesus/spirituality/sacred_space

Useful websites

www.biblicalholidays.com

www.woodlands-junior.kent.sch.uk/customs/questions/festivals – this is a
   lovely website created by a small junior school. A mine of information
   on festivals.

www.crivoice.org

www.cpas.org – it is worth subscribing to *Church Leadership*, CPAS' magazine
   for church leaders. It's full of useful resources, such as liturgies, clip-art
   and creative ideas.

www.rootsontheweb.com

www.somethingjewish.co.uk

www.yashanet.com – provides some excellent theological background to the
   Jewish festivals.

Useful books

Mark Fraser, *Christian Festivals, Retaining a Biblical Theology*, Grove Booklet
   Renewal Series 23.

Margot Hodson, *A Feast of Seasons*, Monarch Books/Olive Press, 2000.

Ron Cantrell, *The Feasts of the Lord, Rehearsals for the End*, Bridges for Peace,
   1999.

Lucy Moore, *Messy Church*, BRF, 2006

Part 3

The Main Course

Celebrating in the Daily and Ordinary

elebration starts in me. Only when I give my imagination free rein and operate beyond the bounds of
my rational intelligence, only when I discover things
to enthuse, entrance, inspire and transfix me, not just in a glorious view or
at a fabulous concert, but also at the kitchen sink and the office desk, can I
create a celebratory environment at home, at work, and in my community.
That way of living then has the power, not just to transform my daily grind
into a place where God speaks, but to attract everyone in my orbit who, up to
now, has lived very happily without any sense of 'transcendence', or awareness
of that otherness who is God.

Living with attention

Rejecting the institutional church has left people with a spiritual hole, and
an increasing interest in finding meaningful rituals. The traditional Anglo-
Catholic spiritual discipline of 'living with intention' – capturing each
moment by investing everything with spiritual significance – has been appropriated by the secular lifestyle coaches and the time-management gurus. 'Life
by Choice, Intent, Design' is what they offer – in other words, since this life
is all there is, you need to take control of it, and not let it control you, if you
want to achieve your dreams.

In an attempt to help women create more time in their busy lives,
Deanna Joseph, 'inspiration editor' for *Bella*, an American magazine for
women, lists her 'intentions' on the *Bella* website:

> *I want to remember that it's never too late and that nothing ends until it is over...to make some space for the new to enter...to bring kindness to others...to leave a creative legacy, something I've sewed, or painted, or written that will be here after I'm gone...to ensure my outside reflects my inside, to take care of my health, find time each day for creative and spiritual moments, and appreciate the riches that I already have.*

It's all very noble and loosely Christian, but still too self-obsessed and finite to reflect the kind of vibrant, eternal life that Jesus had in mind.

The Hebrew sages never spoke about living 'with intention'. They spoke instead about 'living with attention'. Intention is about remembering to give spiritual meaning to the ordinary. But that intention has a tendency to go out of the window the moment we do anything that requires using our brain elsewhere, whether we're good at multitasking or not. Intention has another problem. It is self-focused. It asks, 'How can I get in touch with God?' or ' What will make me feel better, more spiritual?'

Attention has a different motive. It wants to know what God has to say to me in the ordinary things of life, and how I can do what he wants me to do. One of the best examples of Jesus 'living with attention' is in Matthew 23 – one of his most forceful sermons against hypocrisy. Anyone standing in the ruins of the Second Temple in Jerusalem, where he was standing as he spoke, could actually see or imagine every illustration he used – the altar, the gold, the dishes and cups, whitewashed tombs, and bones. He probably pointed at or towards them as he preached. Surroundings that were so familiar to most of his listeners that they normally took them for granted, were suddenly invested with new meaning as he pressed home his point. Each in turn became a kind of visual aid, a symbol of the blindness and hardness of the Pharisees that broke his heart. Would anyone hearing that sermon ever look out from the Second Temple again without his words ringing in their heads?

I spend my life thinking what a wonderful, spiritual being I would be if I didn't have a house to keep clean on top of a busy career. If I didn't have to wash the pots and pans, stock the pantry, wash the loo and empty the bins, imagine what time there would be for reflection and meditation. The rabbis at the time of Jesus said, 'This is exactly why you were created – to clean the toilet, do the mending, repair the car, change the baby's nappy, sit in the motorway queue.' This is what puts you in touch with Reality – God himself. It's in the discipline of giving attention to what you're doing, as you keep your ears and eyes open, that you may hear God's gentle, quiet voice or even catch a fleeting glimpse of his eternal glory. There are so many lessons to learn in the ordinary – humility, patience, application, courage, love, service, gratitude and grace. As you do the chores well, with all of your heart, for the sake of others, God can guide, challenge and encourage you, and move you into a deeper awareness of his ways. This is why Jesus was alert to every moment, to who and what was around him, to direction from above that would reveal its wider, spiritual significance.

One summer evening, when I was trying to learn how to do this better, I took a walk alone up to the top of the town, trying to be more sensitive to my surroundings, listening to what God might say to me through them. Gradually, as I walked, I became aware of the myriad, tiny patches of garden fronting the endless rows of terraced housing. Small as they were, they were all different: some a dump for unwanted furniture, some concreted over, some neglected and full of weeds, some fussy and overfilled with tubs and baskets, but some thoughtfully and lovingly cultivated with just the right variety of shrubs and colours.

And it seemed to me that an inner voice whispered, 'That's what the world is like – full of lives that are messy, bland, boring or overbusy. Have a look at your own. You think, by living at the hectic pace you do, full of thoughtless, frenetic activity, that you are creating the kind of garden I want, but what I really need is a tranquil garden that I can simply enjoy, a garden that's a delight to look at, where you can be rather than do, where I can set up my deckchair and share your company.'

I can't say this revelation transformed my life, but it contributed to my decision to give up my more-than-full-time job in senior management in the NHS.

Gradually, anything and everything around us can become a symbol, a vehicle that God can use to converse with his friends. 'I haven't called you servants because a servant doesn't know what his master is doing; but I have called you friends, for all that I have heard from my Father I have made known to you.'[17] But we need to give him the chance. And that requires concentration, imagination and attention.

Christians have tended to be a bit limited with their symbols – there's the cross, the candle, and the elements of bread and wine. The Catholic tradition venerates them and makes them inaccessible. Evangelicals have feared exactly that, so throw them out of the window. Neither way encourages us to give the quality of attention that listening to God really requires.

In the Hebraic tradition symbol has always been very important, as long as it is just that – an inanimate, meaningless object in itself, but with the power to bring a deeper reality to mind. Take, for example, a simple stone. Jacob used a stone as a pillow on the night he dreamed he saw a ladder into heaven. The Children of Israel used them at various times as monuments and reminders of the reliability of God. One was called *Ed*, or 'witness'. Jesus called one 'Peter': 'On this stone I will build my church.' He also said that if we didn't worship him, the stones would. Stones are cast into the sea at the Day of Atonement as the symbol of sins that are covered and gone forever. Stones, not flowers, are placed on graves. A stone doesn't die. It outlasts and outlives us.

In the pre-*nouvelle cuisine* days, when restaurants decorated a customer's plate with a piece of parsley, I would almost always, subconsciously, pick it up and wave it around between my thumb and index finger, because in the Passover service it's the symbol of the hyssop used to daub blood on the doorposts of the Children of Israel so that the Angel of Death would bypass their houses. Instantly, the whole salvation story has popped into my mind, and a tiny sprig of parsley has made me grateful again, not just for dinner, but for the amazing inheritance that is mine.

Walking the walk

A poor man, lost in the woods, found himself at nightfall without his prayer book. So he said to the Almighty, 'Dear God, I have done a very stupid thing. I have such a poor memory that I can't recite the prayers by heart, but I have left my prayer book at home. But you know all the prayers, Lord – so I'll just recite the letters of the alphabet, and you put them together in the right way.'

And the Almighty took note of that prayer because of its sincerity, and thought it more worthy than any of the others he had heard that day.

Traditional Chasidic story

Living with attention doesn't happen overnight. It is an art to be acquired little by little. In Hebrew, becoming more adept at the art is known as *halachah*, which means 'progression' or 'purposeful walking'. Help on the way is provided by countless *berachot* or 'blessings' that are said every day, even several times a day, for every imaginable aspect of life – getting up in the morning, washing your face, brushing your teeth, eating bread, eating fruit that grows on a tree and fruit that grows from the ground (and you have to know which is which), seeing a rainbow, even smelling a nasty smell. In fact, there are blessings for everything from the moment people wake up to the moment they lie down to sleep. Every action, great or small, becomes an opportunity to bless God. It's a great idea, but I think the ideal is often lost in the ritual.

I well remember as a child, the one occasion I tried to get out of Hebrew Translation practice, to which I was subjected for an hour four times a week, by asking if I could be excused. When I arrived back in the classroom some ten minutes later and slid, smugly, onto my chair, the rabbi held up the class and asked, 'And the blessing, Malchah?' Malchah was my Hebrew name. It means 'a queen', but that was the last thing I felt when I was made to stand before the whole class and read what felt like the longest blessing in the prayer book. Now I realize that it's something we all have to do so often, it might as well be a spiritual experience. The actual blessing, which speaks of flesh returning to the earth, is a reminder of our mortality. I find it less morbid to attach my prayerboard, covered in photos of those I love, to the toilet wall. That way I have to pray for them all several times a day. I did once find the board face down on the floor outside the door. I asked my son what it was doing there and he said, 'I don't like all those people looking at me while I'm in there.'

Rediscovering a spirituality for the home takes a little effort and practice. Once we have developed a listening, attentive spirit ourselves, once we have learned to hear God's voice in the daily chores, it is no step at all to sharing those symbols with family, friends and neighbours. The Mennonites say we need 'bridges into transcendence' – ordinary, everyday happenings that will remind us of God's existence and fill us with a sense of his presence. Here are some small bridges that I hope may help.

Daily prayer

The vast expanse of the sea; Wedgewood skies decorated with fluffy, cotton-wool clouds; the seemingly infinite galaxies of stars that twinkle in the night sky; lush, rolling, verdant hillsides; dignified trees and shadowy forest glades; a single, resilient flower forcing its way through hard earth or a brick wall; musical birdsong at dawn... Our world is designed to stagger our imaginations – if we let it. For some people a tree is an object of wonder. For others, it's simply a nuisance in the way as they try to park the car. Any one day provides countless triggers to worship, as we catch a peek into the inestimable beauty and glory of God.

But access to natural beauty is not essential for a celebratory spirit, as

Robert Siegel's lovely hymn of praise shows. When we really let our imagination guide us, a toothbrush, a dressing-gown and a shower – the ordinary things of life – become a celebration of its Maker:

A Song of Praises

for the gray nudge of dawn at the window
for the chill that hangs around the bed and slips
        its cold tongue under the covers
for the cat who walks over my face purring murderously
for the warmth of the hip next to mine and sweet lethargy
for the cranking up of the will until it turns me out of bed
for the robe's warm caress along arm and shank
for the welcome of hot water, the dissolving of
        the night's stiff mask in the soft washcloth
for the light along the white porcelain sink
for the toothbrush's savory invasion of the tomb of the mouth
        and the resurrection of the breath
for the warm lather and the clean scrape of the razor
        and the skin smooth and pink that emerges
for the steam of the shower, the apprehensive shiver and then
        its warm enfolding of the shoulders
        its falling on the head like grace
        its anointing of the whole body
        and the soap's smooth absolution
for the rough nap of the towel and its message to each skin cell
for the hairbrush's pulling and pulling, waking the root of each hair
for the reassuring snap of elastic
for the hug of the belt that pulls all together
for the smell of coffee rising up the stairs announcing paradise
for the glass of golden juice in which light is condensed
        and the grapefruit's sweet flesh
for the incense of butter on toast
for the eggs, like twin peaks over which the sun rises
        and the jam for which the strawberries of summer have saved themselves
for the light whose long shaft lifts the kitchen into the realms of day
for Mozart elegantly measuring out the gazebos of heaven on the radio
and for her face, for whom the kettle sings, the coffee percs,
and all the yellow birds in the wallpaper spread their wings. Robert Siegel[18]

Ideas for daily prayer

- If you enjoyed Robert Siegel's poem, note down all your daily routines – the ones you love, if you were to stop to think about them – and write your own song of wonder and praise.

- Create a 'prayer space' – a room, a garden shed, a nook or corner which is a 'quiet' or no-noise zone, where you can retreat. Keep a notebook and jot down your conversations with God.

- Parents could have a moment of quiet reflection and prayer at the breakfast table each day, so that as each child comes down, they could have a moment's prayer with them individually for their day. This can also be done as a family with a hot drink in one shared bed! My children still remember what fun it was, when they stayed with grandparents, climbing into their double bed to share in an early morning drink and story. Their parents appreciated the extra peace too!

- Instead of putting photographs in the loo, you can pin up prayer needs on post-it notes, or attach them to a noticeboard in the kitchen.

- There is a very useful old Anglo-Catholic tradition of recollection. At the end of the day, share the highs and lows around the table before the evening meal. This teaches children and adults to look out for them, and to encourage each other to find the good things amongst the more difficult, and appreciate them.

- Let each person take it in turns to say grace, and make their own individual prayer request when their turn comes.

- Set up a 'thank you board'. Every time someone feels grateful for something someone else has done, they simply jot it down on a piece of paper and stick it to the board. We often forget to say thank you at the time, so this gives us a chance to express verbal appreciation as it pops into our minds.

- Create a mealtime prayer box. File prayer requests in a small box, and each time grace is said, take out a card and include that particular prayer request. Put the card at the back of the file. If the prayer is answered, note that down and use it as a chance to give thanks.

Daily blessings

Living life in a daily rhythm of blessings really can focus the mind. But these blessings need to be a great deal more than the 'God bless Mummy, God bless Daddy' variety, that we have so often taught our children. Like asking the minister for a blessing, they simply request vague benefits for our loved ones and can almost become a kind of talisman.

In Jewish thought blessing is thanksgiving. Each of the dozens of blessings that can be said from morning to night is directed at God and expresses gratitude for the wonder of all that he has made and done. *Berakhot* are easy to recognize: they all start with the word *barukh* ('blessed' or 'praised'): 'Blessed are you, O Lord our God, King of the Universe...' The words *barukh* and *berakhah* are both derived from the Hebrew root word meaning 'knee', and reflect the practice of bending the knee and bowing as a sign of respect. According to Jewish tradition, a person should recite 100 *berakhot* every day. Get into the habit of blessing God at all times, preferably silently for the sake of everyone else; this isn't as difficult as it sounds. It should enable us to achieve a continuous state of thankfulness.

Here is a lovely Jewish night-time blessing:[19]

Blessed are you, O Lord our God,
King of the Universe.
At your word night falls.
In your wisdom
you open heaven's gates,
you control the elements and rotate the seasons.
You set the stars in the vault of heaven.
You created night and day.
You cause the light to fade when darkness comes
and the darkness to melt away
in the light of the new day.
O ever living and eternal God,
you will always watch over us
your creatures.
Blessed are you, O Lord,
at whose word night falls.

With their Hebraic way of living out their faith, the Celtic Christians of the fourth and fifth centuries had many favourite blessings, most inviting God to protect their family, home and loved ones. Here is a Celtic version of the night-time blessing:

The Sacred Three
My fortress be
Encircling me,
Come and be round
My hearth, my home.

Fend Thou my kin
And every sleeping thing within
From scathe, from sin.
Thy care our peace
Through mid of night
To light's release.

Daily graces

The Jewish grace after a meal is much longer than the blessings said before it. Presumably, by then, we know whether we have something to be thankful for or not! Grace after a meal consists of four parts. Traditionally, the first two parts, which thank God for giving food to the world, and for delivering his people from slavery, were written by Moses. The third part, thanking him for the land of Israel, was added by Joshua. And then the prayers for the rebuilding of Jerusalem and the coming of the Messiah were an afterthought by King David. In other words, there's a little bit more to it than, 'For what we are about to receive, may the Lord make us truly thankful', and inevitably, it lasts a lot longer. It can be very entertaining to hear it sung communally at *bar mitzvahs* and weddings, when no two people know the same tune, and most guests tend to dip in and out in between conversations with long-lost relatives.

Nonetheless, there is no doubt that Jesus said this prayer regularly, as there are strong echoes of it in the Lord's Prayer – in the blessing of God's holy name, in thanking him for daily sustenance, in calling for the coming of his kingdom, in remembering the forgiving of all sins and the freeing of all slaves.

In fact, the only major difference is Jesus referring to God as 'our Father' rather than 'Sovereign of the Universe'.

Grace doesn't have to be so long-winded. But since, in many homes, it may be the only clue to a family's faith, the only daily nod and wink in God's direction, it might as well be as imaginative as possible. Here are a few graces that you may wish to use:

A simple grace
For food in a world where many walk in hunger;
For faith in a world where many walk in fear;
For friends in a world where many walk alone;
We give you thanks, O Lord. Amen.

Wesley's grace[20]
Be present at our table, Lord!
Be here and everywhere adored.
Your mercies bless, and grant that we
May feast in Paradise with Thee! Amen.

Grandparents' grace
Father, thank you for...
We are so blessed to have such special grandchildren.

Light a candle for each one and as you do so, make some specific requests for that individual.

May they come to know you more as they grow,
and find your world an exciting and loving place in which to live.
Thank you for our whole family and for (pray for their parents).
Bless this meal that we're about to share.
May it leave us with special memories to share in the future.
Thank you for all the good things you give us every day.

A Hebraic-style grace after meals
Blessed is the Lord our God,
King of the Universe
Who sustains the entire world
with goodness, tender love and compassion
for his mercy endures forever.
We thank you for everything you have given us,

for you stretch out your hand,
and satisfy the desires of every living creature.
Blessed is the Lord our God
who provides for all he has made.

We thank you, Lord our God,
for giving us a lovely and spacious inheritance,
for liberating us from the land of Egypt,
and freeing us from the bonds of slavery;
for the covenant that means we belong to you,
for your word that helps us obey you,
for life and breath to worship you.
For all these blessing we thank you,
and remember that you said,
'When you have eaten your fill,
give thanks to the Lord your God
for the good land he has given you.'
Blessed be the land and its produce.

May the Lord have mercy on his people,
on his city, Jerusalem,
on Zion, where his glory dwells,
and may he bless the reign of his Anointed One.
Grant us respite from all the world's troubles,
And may God make us dependent,
not on the alms and loans of others,
but on his generous abundance,
that we may never be humiliated or put to shame.

Blessed be the Lord, Sovereign of the Universe
who is our God, Father, Sovereign, Creator, Redeemer,
the Holy One of Jacob, the Shepherd of Israel,
who continually showers us with his kindness.
May he continue to bless us with his grace,
love, compassion, deliverance, prosperity,
redemption, comfort, and peace.

The blessings and graces here are just an example of what they might be like. Try to write some of your own, as an extended family or home group.

We meet with a group of seven friends in a cell group twice a year and always end by singing the old Anglican prayer, 'Lighten our darkness, Lord we pray, and by thy mercies, defend us from all dangers and perils of this night.' Some of us have already faced cancer or heart problems, and that one prayer, placing each other firmly in God's loving care, repeated year in, year out, has become more and more meaningful as we get older and creakier.

Rites of passage

Anniversaries are important, and we are so often consumed in busyness, that we don't stop to reflect, or give them the time and significance they deserve. Here are one or two suggestions for personal celebrations that might just start you thinking about many others.

Anniversary of the baptism or dedication of a child

Try to get the godparents together for that once-a-year celebration. It's probably best to warn them that's what you plan to do when you ask them to become godparents in the first place.

Parent says: On this day...years ago, we took you for baptism/dedicated you to God. On that day, we committed ourselves to raising you in the faith of Christ to the best of our ability. We asked God to make you a disciple of Christ and prayed that you would follow him as you grew older. Your godparents also promised to pray for you and help you grow up as a follower of Jesus.

Relight the candle the child was given on that occasion, or replace it with a new one – a heavy white candle, personalized by adding the child's name in coloured wax. Surround the base with flowers that can be replaced every year at the anniversary of the occasion.

Godparent says: Gracious God, we thank you that _____ has been dedicated to you from such an early age and is a special part of your family. We pray that he/she will grow up knowing and loving Jesus.

We pray that those of us with a special responsibility for his/her spiritual growth will not only be an encouragement, but also a worthy model of what that means.

If the child is old enough, he/she says: Father God, thank you for that day all those years ago when I was given back to you. Thank you for the care and support I have had from my parents and godparents to be the person you want me to be.

I now own the vows they made as my own. I want to say for myself that

I repent of my sins,
I turn to Christ,
I turn away from evil.

Help me to be faithful to the commitment I make to you this day and follow you wherever you lead me.

Parents and godparents offer their own prayers, and add: Dear God, we go on giving _____ into your loving hands. During the coming year may he/she learn more about your love and care, and really know Jesus as a special friend at home, at school, at university and in every part of his/her life.

Ideas for birthdays

- Before the birthday person gets out of bed, everyone in the house carries a lit candle to their bedside and serenades them into their new year.
- Have a cake for breakfast as a special treat.
- For the party, allow the birthday girl/boy to choose the menu, or better still, find out in advance from any special guests what their favourite food is, and make it for them.
- At the party, everyone present offers a word of affirmation – what they most value about the birthday person.
- The candles on the cake can be used as symbols of each thing the birthday person is thankful for.
- Every family or home-group member can sign one big card with a special greeting.
- Within families (this can be done by parents or godparents or other significant adults), make a birthday box of special moments – photos, tokens, stones, newspaper cuttings, letters, cards etc., and share them as each year comes round.

- Have a big birthday candle that comes out and is lit every year.
- Simon and Laura Walton, missionaries in Tanzania, say: 'We do have an interesting cake-feeding ceremony for weddings and birthdays and any other celebration which involves a cake, which does however depend on the financial situation of the party-givers, but is good fun. A small cake can then go a long way! The birthday person or bride actually feeds his or her guests. It's a nice way of sharing and serving!'

A short service for a birthday

Begin with the leader asking the birthday person, 'What have been the most significant events of the past year? What are your hopes for the coming year?'

Leader: Father, thank you for _____, for making him/her exactly as he/she is. We are so glad that he/she is part of our family. Thank you for giving him/her the gift of life and for making him/her so special.

Reading: Psalm 139:13–16.

Leader: Let's all think of some things we want to thank God for in his/her life. (*Everyone contributes with one or two words.*)

Birthday person: (*lighting the candles*) Father, thank you for all the love you have shown me over the years. Thank you for your faithfulness, especially in this past year. I want to thank you especially for _____.

Leader: Lord, continue to show your faithfulness to _____. We want to ask you to make this coming year a special one, full of life's most meaningful gifts.

The leader invites everyone to name some 'special presents' or spiritual treasures that they would like the birthday person to receive.

Leader: Father, help us all to be more loving and understanding to one another and those we meet. Bless especially those who can't be with us today, and thank you for this feast, a token of all the good things you give us day by day.

Coming of age

A Jewish boy becomes a man at thirteen, when, as Jesus did, he has his *Bar Mitzvah* ('the Blessing of a Son'). Unlike Jesus, young Jewish men used to be the ungrateful recipients of five suitcases, six sports hold-alls, ten alarm clocks, and twenty fountain pens, all laid out on display, so that the guests could see who had been the most generous. But a '*Bar Mitzvah* list', like a wedding list, now eradicates the problem of multiple, unwanted gifts. After all, it's stressful enough having to stand up in the synagogue on the Sabbath before your entire family and the local community and sing several portions of the Scriptures solo, your parents willing you to get it right, without having to be grateful afterwards for a set of disappointing presents.

There are now equivalent ceremonies for daughters, known as *Bat Mitzvah*, though in orthodox circles they seem to be a bit of a nod in the direction of political correctness, rather than a real commitment to supporting a young woman through adolescence into adulthood. Nonetheless, nothing can detract from the importance of this ritual transition. For one day that child is the centre of everyone's attention. When they finish singing the Scripture portion, sweets and chocolates rain down on them from every quarter of the synagogue. They're lucky to survive into adulthood. Now they are deemed old enough to know the difference between right and wrong, to exercise self-control, and to account for their behaviour. They are full members of the community, and can be called upon to read the Torah in the synagogue, lead prayers, or be elected to the synagogue council. The *Talmud* (the oral Law) says, 'Until he is thirteen, I talk to my son about God; after age thirteen, I talk to God about my son.'

The church has no real equivalent. Some denominations have confirmation. Some have adult baptism. Neither is a 'coming-of-age' in its truest sense, for they do not necessarily confer eligibility for what are regarded as strictly adult roles – reading a lesson, taking a lead in services or becoming a member of the church council. Fewer children than ever walk through the church's doors these days. If we treat them as second-class citizens and expect them to be passive observers or patronize them, if we do things to and for them, rather than receive, in humility, whatever spiritual gifts they bring to us, we can hardly be surprised when they leave us before they reach eighteen.

Perhaps it's time to create some meaningful Christian rites of passage. For example, I know several men who have taken their daughters out to dinner when their menstrual cycles started, to celebrate the arrival of womanhood.

An eighteenth birthday celebration

This idea was suggested by a friend, Dr Rhoda Knight, who only has sons, and she believes it is a truly memorable occasion. I am sure that it's possible to come up with a female equivalent for daughters. She says:

> Give your son an adventurous, manly present – hang-gliding, a spin in a motor-boat or a Porsche – something that celebrates their maleness. Then, throw a dinner party for him. Invite all the key Christian men in the church to eat with him, as a way of handing him over to their company, and have them pray and prophesy over him. In a time where manhood is often compromised, it is a lovely way to celebrate being a Christian man and all it entails.

Marriage

The festivities and symbolism of a traditional Jewish wedding are famous for being some of the most colourful in the world. The couple are married beneath a canopy – the only covering or home anyone ever had in the forty years in the wilderness. The *chuppah* represents the temporary, fragile nature of our journey on earth. The bride and groom drink from the same cup to remind them that they will share the cup of life, whatever it brings. As ever, there is much drinking of wine, the symbol of joy, and many blessings, including the famous seven recited by the rabbi:

- Blessed are you, Lord our God, Sovereign of the world, who created everything for his glory.
- Blessed are you, Lord our God, Sovereign of the world, the creator of human beings.
- Blessed are you, Lord our God, Sovereign of the world, who created human beings in his own image, in the pattern of his own likeness, and provided such a wonderful way of perpetuating the human race.

- Let the barren city be jubilantly happy and joyful at her joyous reunion with her children. Blessed are you, Lord our God, who makes Zion rejoice with her children.

- Let the loving couple be very happy, just as you made your creation happy in the garden of Eden, so long ago. Blessed are you, Lord our God, who gives great joy to the bridegroom and the bride.

- Blessed are you, Lord our God, Sovereign of the world, who created celebration, bridegroom and bride, rejoicing, jubilation, pleasure and delight, love and harmony, peace and friendship. Lord our God, may there be heard in the streets and in the town the voices of joy and gladness, the voices of bride and groom, the jubilant voices of those joined in marriage under the bridal canopy, the voices of young people feasting and singing. Blessed are you, O Lord, who causes the groom to rejoice with his bride.

- Blessed are you, Lord our God, Sovereign of the world, creator of the fruit of the vine.

After the blessings, the groom stamps on a glass. Its very fragility symbolizes our vulnerability, and the lengths we must all go to, to ensure that our most significant relationship remains intact. Once the glass has been broken, everyone shouts '*Mazeltov!*' – 'Congratulations!'

An old Celtic wedding blessing

May God be with you and bless you.
May you see your children's children.
May you be poor in misfortune, rich in blessings.
May you know nothing but happiness
From this day forward.

May you have –
Walls for the wind
And a roof for the rain,
And drinks beside the fire,
Laughter to cheer you
And those you love near you,
And all that your heart may desire.

Wedding anniversary

In biblical times, when religion and family life were interwoven, children were encouraged to ask their parents questions about their own history.[21] Significant places were often marked with large stones to prompt such questions.[22]

- As soon as they are old enough, encourage your children to celebrate their parents' relationship by organizing a special celebration and cooking a special anniversary dinner. After all, it is an achievement, and marriage is so rarely celebrated.

- On this occasion, or in their home group, the couple could lay out a series of stones or other symbols that represent the struggles, pain and joys of the previous year, and explain what each represents.

- A big anniversary can be shared with the home group or entire church by having a bring-and-share Sunday lunch or a post-evening-service meal. During the service marriage vows can be renewed, or an opportunity given for sharing the highs and lows of the past years.

A short service for a wedding anniversary

Leader: God of love, thank you for _____ and for their marriage,
which has allowed them to share their lives with each other for _____ years.
Thank you for all your faithfulness during this past year,
for the blessings and the difficulties,
for the joyful and the stretching times,
for their loyalty and their commitment to one another.

Husband and wife (to each other in turn):
I love you and again pledge myself to you in marriage.
Thank you for your patience, faithfulness and service over this past year.
Thank you for putting up with my foibles.
Forgive me for the times when I have let you down.
May God help us to go on growing together in love.

Any children present:
Thank you for Mum and Dad and for all they have done for us.
Thank you for your faithfulness to them down through the years.
Bless us as a family in all we do and say during this coming year.

The leader invites others present to pray specific prayers for the couple.

Leader: Father, we ask that your presence will go with _____ over the coming
year,
that you will lovingly guard and guide them,
that you will strengthen their commitment to each other,
that you will enrich their love and bless their home.

A Celtic blessing for a new home

A blessing upon your new home,
A blessing upon your new hearth,
A blessing upon your new dwelling,
Upon your newly-kindled fire.

A blessing upon your tallest grass,
A blessing upon your fruitful partner,
A blessing upon your growing son(s),
Upon your growing daughter(s).

A blessing upon the household's helpers,
A blessing upon the children yet unborn,
A blessing upon the wise parents,
Upon your occupation.
A blessing upon your goods and income,
A blessing upon your kith and kin.
A blessing upon you in light or darkness,
Each day and night of your lives.

Death

Kaddish, the most famous of all Jewish prayers, is recited morning and evening
for seven days after the death of a loved one, and on the anniversary of the death
every year, when a memorial candle is lit.

Lighting a candle for twenty-four hours on the anniversary of the death of a loved one (known as *Jahrzeit* or 'Time of Year') can be very healing. (Make sure it's a candle that can be left when you are out of the room – it must be in a specially designed glass.) It becomes a focal point, enabling us to reminisce, either alone or with others, to recall the funny and lovely things that a grandparent, parent or friend did and said, to express how much they meant to us and what a difference they made to our lives. For a short period of time they live again for us, as we laugh at their foibles, give thanks for the lessons they taught us and enjoy some wonderful memories. I hope someone will want to remember me in that way.

In many Catholic countries the bereaved put photographs of a loved one on their grave, and return there with their whole family at least once a year – on All Saints' Day. Mounds of colourful chrysanthemums are left behind, turning the cemetery into a magnificent garden that's a riot of colour. I rather like that tradition and have spent many happy hours in French cemeteries, enjoying the flowers and looking at the photographs, trying to imagine what the people were really like and whether they lived up to the eulogies on their graves.

Kaddish

Leader: May the great name of the Lord be magnified and hallowed throughout the world which he made according to his will, the world which he will one day make anew, where the dead will be revived and raised to eternal life. May he establish his kingdom soon and reign in glory, even during our lifetime, and the lifetime of the House of Israel.

Response: Amen. May his great name be praised for ever, and to all eternity.

Leader: Glorified, praised, exalted, honoured and magnified be the Name of the Holy One, blessed be he, though he is far above all the hymns and praises human beings can offer.

Response: Amen. May the name of the Lord be blessed from this time forth and for ever more.

Leader: May he grant us heavenly peace and abundant life.

Response: Amen. My help is from the Lord who made heaven and earth.

Leader: May the great Name of the Lord be magnified and hallowed throughout the world which he made according to his will.
May he establish his kingdom soon, and reign in glory, even during our lifetime.

Response: Amen. May the name of the Lord be blessed for ever and ever.

Leader: May comfort, healing, sustenance and deliverance be granted to all of us, and to Israel.

Response: Amen. May he who ordains peace in heaven, grant us his peace.

Other ideas for occasional celebration at home or in a home group

- Encourage home groups to welcome children from time to time, adjusting the time and content of the evening to suit the wider age range – for example, by having a meal together, by lighting candles, telling and sharing stories and testimonies.
- Have a film night – each member takes it in turn to recommend a film. The group watches it together, then afterwards (over supper) they discuss the values of the story.
- Have a monthly family activity night – chosen by each child in turn.
- Fund-raise together for a charity – chosen by the children.
- Try an informal jam session – make music, worship together.
- Have a family craft club, and invite other families. Make cards and decorations, or candles for special occasions and festivals, or stained-glass windows from tissue paper, or fabric collages with prayer requests, wishes, dreams, thanks and blessings.
- Encourage 'spiritual walks' – for example, watching a sunrise or sunset together – or 'prayer walks', stopping at various points where people want to offer prayers of thanksgiving or requests.
- Throw a Summer Ball or a Valentine's Day Ball – with a live band, and lanterns.

- Have a grand picnic, or a communal fish-and-chips meal, ending with Communion.

Useful books

Olive M. Fleming Drane, *Spirituality To Go*, Darton Longman & Todd, 2006.

Useful websites

www.godlyplay.org.uk
www.rejesus.co.uk
www.childrenmatter.net
www.cpas.org.uk /home/resources

Celebrating a Sabbath

One of the greatest challenges facing me today is preserving Sunday lunch. Our congregation likes to malinger after services and Peter often doesn't get back until he manages to eject the remnants onto the street, when his belly is greeting his backbone, at around 1.30 p.m.

At 1.50 p.m. one particular Sunday we finally sat down to our roast, just as the telephone rang. 'Yes, thank you, we did get our Yellow Pages,' I heard my long-suffering husband say, with the slight edge of forced politeness. He returned to the table just in time to see one of our gentlemen of the road walking up the front path.

'Alan, for sandwiches, again.'

'Put the carving knife down, dear,' I suggested, as he headed for the front door.

With Alan duly fed and watered shortly after 2 p.m., the joint was attacked once again and barely carved into slices when the phone rang once more – the band leader wondering whether Peter had any song and hymn choices for the evening service.

'At this precise moment?' I asked. 'No, I think you could probably have "Three Blind Mice". All he wants is his dinner. He'll ring you back.'

The fork had just reached his mouth as a complete stranger ambled up to our door. It was a Jehovah's Witness who claimed not to have seen the vicarage sign, but said he was up for a long discussion nonetheless.

'Not at this moment,' my husband said quietly, the politeness wearing thinner by the minute, 'I am having my dinner.'

'Has anyone in this country ever heard of Sunday lunch?' I said to Peter, as he sat back down, 'or are we just a pair of dinosaurs?'

No one in France, not even the most needy of callers, would dare to telephone or visit between midday and 7 p.m. on a Sunday. That weekly extended-family gathering is sacrosanct, an institution. There might just as well be a 'Do Not Disturb' notice on the door of every house. Children return home from college for it. Elderly parents and grandparents are fetched from their homes for it. Singles join together and share it. It's probably the only day of the week there is a dessert other than fresh fruit or yogurt.

But so many people in English-speaking countries have allowed this vital cement of family life to crumble away. Peter still remembers how, when he was a lad, 4 p.m. on Sundays was tea-time, when his mother would roll in a trolley laden with home-made baking. She once told me that her lasting memory of Evensong in Ashton Under Lyme in the northwest of England was the pervading odour of fish paste everyone brought with them from their Sunday tea sandwiches. But it seems that only the Women's Institute has any attachment to afternoon tea any more.

Why have we allowed so many of the old rituals and traditions to be eroded so easily? Why have we not valued the best in old English culture? Or is it only me, as the child of immigrant Jewish grandparents, with a strong sense of Sabbath, who saw something worth preserving in the tranquil Sunday, and still tries to hang onto it with cracking fingernails?

A Sabbath rest isn't just for families. It's for the single and the married, for young and old, for those in paid work and those in voluntary employment. It's such an important principle that God himself set us the example and made it one of the Ten Commandments. The Israelites on Sinai were told to keep, not make, the Sabbath holy. In other words, God made it special and gave it to them as a gift. All they had to do was unwrap the package, and treat it with the reverence and respect that it deserved. Rejecting the gift was not an option. It was far too important – a key to survival that we neglect at our peril. The Jewish writer Achad Ha-am said that instead of the Jews keeping the Sabbath, the Sabbath has kept the Jews.

Despite their civilized lifestyle, the ancient Greeks and Romans didn't understand why the Jews needed one day off in seven, and thought it was because they were lazy. But anyone who had Jewish servants, slaves or employees soon discovered that they worked much harder and better on the other six days.

I don't think I fully appreciated just how important a Sabbath rest was until Peter took a three-month sabbatical in France. Every day was a kind of Sabbath, but we were setting up a new home and I quickly got it into my head that unless we used every moment to paint, decorate and DIY, we would never get everything done in twelve weeks. Peter had a different approach. 'Tomorrow's Sunday,' he said, 'so the rebuilding of the kitchen, the decorating, and all the other chores will have to wait.' Like the ancient Greeks, I saw this as an attempt to cop out of work. But that first Sunday was a glorious day, and as we biked through little French villages in peaceful countryside, I began to see what a gift Sabbath was. No gift is as precious as the gift of time. Later, as we got to know folk and shared one of those long French Sunday lunches with them, then spent the evenings by a real log fire with a glass of Pineau de Charente, a good book and no pressure, I wished every day was Sunday because it was a little taste of heaven. That's exactly what the Jewish sages said it should be – a tiny glimpse of what it will be like when work is done away with once and for all, and we return to our original, natural, Eden habitat.

To be fair, it is much easier to keep a Sabbath in France, where shops are shut on Sundays, once the early morning bread has gone, and life grinds to a very pleasant standstill from around midday. It is indicative of a much healthier approach, and one of the reasons why 60,000 English a month are decamping across the Channel. Changing the Sunday trading laws has had a seriously detrimental effect on the British way of life. 'A society without a Sabbath is one in which we can be too busy making a living to have time to live', said the Chief Rabbi of the UK, Jonathan Sacks[23]. In this area especially, Christians may have to swim against the tide and model a better way to live.

In Israel, an even greater hush falls on the country on the Saturday Sabbath, as much of the traffic comes to a standstill. No revving car or motorbike, no engine noise or blaring stereo radio drowns the song of a bird, the buzz of the bee. There are no pollutant fumes. In the pure, fresh air, it's possible to catch the wonderful, spicy aromas of Jewish or Arab cooking, or even the scent of a rose. When we're forced to walk, we look and see, become aware of our world in a new way, reflect more. We pass other human beings, make eye contact with them, stop to say hello and pass the time of day. In the Jewish quarter in Jerusalem on a Friday night, from the open windows comes the sound of singing, murmured chatting, sporadic laughter, the clinking of glasses and of cutlery against a plate, and the tap-tapping of board-games being played.

'The Sabbath is one of those phenomena – incomprehensible from the outside – that you have to live in order to understand,' says Jonathan Sacks. It is, he claims, a 'still point in the turning world' – time out from the urgent, stressful, driving demands of earning a living, to be focused instead on the important, so easily neglected essentials that are our real treasures – family, company, community, celebration, prayer, study, and reflection.

The Sabbath isn't just a chance to be truly recreated. It has so many other implications. Having one day a week when we neither work nor employ others to work for us, when we neither buy nor sell, temporarily creates a new world order where all the hierarchies of power or wealth, all the injustices and inequalities of the workplace and the so-called free market are put on hold. It is a reminder that we do not have total control of our universe, that we cannot endlessly exploit it and those who live in it, and expect to survive intact. We too are creations, not just creators. Our employer does not own us, and we do not own our employees. Christians have a great tool against workaholism. They can say, 'I can't work on Sunday. It's against my religion.' Unless, of course, that work involves the welfare of human beings and animals. And if we cannot let go of our urge for power, control, success and achievement one day in seven, then we are seriously and dangerously out of emotional and mental kilter. 'Human freedom is expressed as much in the ability to stop as in the ability to work,' says Sacks. It demonstrates that we can be the masters, not the slaves of our busyness.

Sadly, the beautiful gift of Sabbath can so easily be turned into sabbatarianism – a restrictive, dull and rather deadly day with enforced rules and regulations, full of 'can'ts' and 'don'ts' and 'ought nots', like the old woman of the kirk. By the time of Jesus, its real meaning had already been drowned in a sea of petty law-keeping. The Pharisaic rabbis spent hours discussing such momentous perplexities as, is carrying a handkerchief breaking the commandment not to bear a burden on the Sabbath? They decided it was if it was carried in the pocket, but it wasn't if it was tied around the neck, because it counted as clothing.

My family still argue that Jesus couldn't possibly be the Messiah, as he failed to keep the Sabbath, and the Messiah would never break one of the Ten Commandments. Jesus didn't break or even dismantle the Sabbath. Healing on the Sabbath, making people well, was never proscribed in Pharisaic law. That was the restrictive, controlling human interpretation of it. When he reminded the Pharisees that the Sabbath was made for man, not man for the Sabbath, he was quoting their own teachings back at them, reminding them of the joy it was meant to be.

A Sabbath rest, whichever day we take it – and Sunday has been the norm for Christians since it was instituted by Constantine in AD 321[24] – is a wonderful God-given opportunity to do the things we never normally have time to do, like spending hours over a meal, playing silly games, reading a good book, having a lunchtime nap, taking a long walk, talking to a spouse, a child, a friend without the pressure of the phone, email or the next event. Fortuitously, none of these lovely things costs money. Sabbath does not involve great expense. In my husband Peter's childhood vicarage home there wasn't much spare cash around, yet his mother always managed to turn Sunday into a special day. Instead of a roast joint, she made a tasty meatloaf. The tea-trolley, replete with best china, was laden with dainty sandwiches, home-made cake and her mouth-watering Canadian cookies. (There are recipes for meatloaf, Guinness Cake and her scrumptious and easy date-cookie traybake at the end of the book.) In Peter's memory, Sunday was a day to look forward to. I had to learn to make Canadian cookies.

I once heard a Jewish woman describe what Friday night, the start of the Sabbath, felt like for her. 'Friday evening comes, the table is laid, the food is ready, everyone dresses and something magical descends upon the house. The atmosphere is completely different. It is a day when I am transported out of the mundane misery of everyday – it's just washed away. As I light candles I unwind.'

I decided I wanted to recreate that atmosphere somehow, so when the children were small we decided to institute a Sabbath eve family event – not just for us, but for our extended family, inviting single friends and surrogate aunts, uncles and grandparents. It became much more difficult to maintain once the children were teenagers and wanted to go out on Friday or Saturday evenings. Rather than insist they stay in, we simply had the meal first, or moved it to another night. It was wonderful, years later, to discover that Joel was keeping the tradition with his friends in his little room at university.

I always tried to make mealtimes special, and will never forget one particular night, when I had gone out of my way to cook his favourite food. It had been a difficult day for all of us, for very different reasons. None of those issues had been resolved when we sat down to eat together and we were all tetchy and at cross-purposes. As Joel put down his knife and fork he said, 'I didn't enjoy that meal at all.' At first, I thought something was wrong with the food and felt affronted – until I realized it was the atmosphere, not the cuisine that was the problem. A meal can be so much more than simply satisfying an appetite. It can be an act of fellowship, which is why I like the idea given to me by Shirley Lacey in South Africa of clearing the air at least once a week, and looking for reasons to be thankful for the day at every meal.

Ideas for a weekly special family meal

'Family' does not necessarily mean the nuclear family – it can mean extended family, home-group family, or a group of single adults.

- Encourage everyone to share something that has happened that week, for which they are particularly thankful.

- Give an opportunity for everyone to share something that has struck them during the week – from a book, a newspaper, a TV programme, a conversation, a lesson.

- Allow everyone the time to write down the things they wished they hadn't done that week, whatever might have caused hurt or pain. Or they can describe their feelings about any argument or conflict there has been during the week. Then scrunch them up and burn them. This is a chance to let go of last week and move forward with a clean slate.

- Invite surrogate grandparents, aunts and uncles, and after the meal, play some good old traditional games – Scrabble, Cribbage, Rummykub, card and board games.

Ideas for Sundays

- Have a special or different family breakfast – scrambled egg on crumpets, or fresh fruit salad – and intersperse it with Bible stories.

- Have an old-fashioned teatime, with small sandwiches and special treats – perhaps on people's knees around the fire.

A liturgy for a Sabbath meal

This service is drawn very loosely from the Jewish prayer book, but adapted to give it a Messianic feel with the help of the Anglican prayer book and Mennonite rituals. You can adapt it even further to suit whatever family or home-group occasion you have in mind. It is important to give a little time to setting the table and creating an atmosphere of rest and joy that will enfold your family and friends from the moment they arrive. That's why Friday night is such a good time to do it – even if it is a little divorced from Sunday. It is the start of the weekend, after all. You should be able to pick up several audible sighs of relief and watch people stretch and almost physically unwind as they let go of the week and its pressures.

You will need:

- **Candles:** It is traditional for the mother of the house to light two Sabbath candles at the beginning of the service and pray for everyone present. But if you prefer to have one candle or a dozen night-lights, that is entirely up to you. You may prefer to invite the eldest or youngest person in the room to light the candles.
- **Bread:** Bread is the symbol of the work of man's hands. Jews traditionally have a sweet, plaited loaf, tasting a bit like a French brioche, but a machine-baked wholemeal or a supermarket baguette will do just as well.
- **Wine:** Wine is the symbol of joy, of relaxation, but if you have guests who are teetotal or have had a problem with alcohol, grape juice is fine. In the Middle East at the time of Jesus, grape juice would have fermented in the heat anyway. Today we have fridges. What it represents is what matters.

1. Candle lighting

The mother or a child lights the candles.

Mother: God said:

All: Let there be light.

Mother: Blessed are you, O Lord our God, who has given us your living word and told us to call Sabbath rest a delight. We light these candles as we honour this time of rest that you have given to us. Your word is a light to our paths and a lamp to our feet. May the light of your presence guard, lead and guide everyone who sits at this table tonight. May we, your family, walk in all your ways, obey your word and do good to everyone we meet. Keep us free from shame, harm, grief and care, and grant that peace, joy and light may ever fill these hearts and this home. For with you is the fountain of life and in your light do we see light.

2. Welcoming the Sabbath

Leader: And there was morning and there was evening – the sixth day. The heavens and the earth were completed in all their vast array.

By the seventh day God had finished the work he had been doing; so on the seventh day he rested from all his work. And God blessed the seventh day and he made it holy, because on it, he rested from all the creative work he had been doing.

And God said, 'Six days shall you labour and do all your work, but the seventh day is the Sabbath, set aside for the Lord, your God.'

All: We rest.

Leader: We rest from our work, putting aside all the stress and pressure of it, all thought of it, remembering instead all God's good gifts of life and joy, friendship and fellowship.

All: We remember.

Leader: We remember that God made the entire universe and that he loves everything about it. We remember that he made us, and how he has cared for us this week. We also recall that just before he died, Jesus said, 'When you break bread, drink wine and eat together, remember me.' And so we prepare to remember Jesus, our saviour, healer and redeemer, the promised liberator of God's amazing universe.

All: We welcome him.

Leader: We welcome the Lord as a bride welcomes her bridegroom.

3. The symbols of bread and wine

The leader fills his/her glass and holds it up.

Leader: Wine is a symbol of rest and rejoicing, and so we say:

All: Blessed are you, O Lord our God, who gives us the fruit of the vine.

The cup is passed around.

Leader: Bread is the symbol of the work that we have to do, whether it's paid work or not.

All: Blessed are you, O Lord our God, who gives us bread from the earth.

The bread is broken and passed around. During this time, people are invited to pray for those who have no work, or no food.

4. *The blessing*

The leader or the father blesses each child present by moving around the table and laying hands on the child's head as the blessing is given. You can also pray for specific needs or requests, if the child has indicated that he/she would like it. It's best not to presume.

Leader: We bless you for _____. Keep him/her safe in your love. May he/she follow Jesus more closely week by week. Keep him/her for the life partner with whom he/she will one day be united. And the Lord fill you with his light, and his peace.

A Celtic blessing for the children:
All: O Thou, to whom to love and be are one,
hear my faith-cry for them who are more thine than mine.
Give each of them what is best for each.
I cannot tell what it is.
But Thou knowest.
I only ask Thou love them and keep them
with the loving and keeping Thou didst show
to Mary's Son and Thine.

It is traditional in Jewish homes for the father present to express his appreciation of his wife by reading Proverbs 31 and telling her that she is a woman beyond compare. A small token of that appreciation – flowers or chocolates – that all can share, isn't a bad idea. To ring the changes, some nights there may be small presents for the children, or even for dad. Try to pick some that all can share.

All: Lighten our darkness, Lord we pray, and in your mercy, defend us from all dangers and perils of this night. For the sake of your only Son, our Saviour Jesus Christ. Amen.

Celebrating the Festivals

A short summary of every Jewish holiday:
They tried to kill us, we won, let's eat.
Anon

The annual festive cycle seems to have all but vanished from the agenda of many churches, defeated by disinterest and terminal indifference, or pillaged by mass-market consumerism and drowned in kitsch. Non-denominational churches might just about manage to give Christmas and Easter a nod and a wink. Some even close for Christmas. Big conventions like Spring Harvest in the UK, which must be about the nearest Christians ever get to the great pilgrim holiday festivals in Jerusalem, don't really make a great deal of Easter. In those denominations that do extend a restrained and courteous welcome to various saints' days and major occasions – the Catholics and the Anglicans – the punters tend to wait for their ministers to do, or rather say, whatever might be necessary in the church service, rather than look for ways to celebrate in homes or small groups.

As a preamble to many of the seasonal celebrations I include here, I have described a Hebraic one – not because I expect people to observe them, certainly not in their entirety, but because we need to go back to the beginning, and digging up our roots seems a very good place to start. First of all, many are prescribed and described in the Old Testament. Secondly, they were the fabric of Jesus' life. Thirdly, they have a rich spiritual symbolism that can provide Christians with an almost limitless fund of inspiration and ideas to adapt and update. And finally, this has to be better than resorting to our pagan heritage, though I'm not averse to reclaiming paganized celebrations, since they too are a part of our cultural inheritance.

It has always amazed me how little Christians know what is, after all, their own background. How can we follow the thoughts and teachings of a Jewish Messiah without seeing him in his context? How can we grasp some of the more complex sayings of Rabbi Paul without understanding his point of reference? When he wrote his letters to the churches, Paul didn't suck the end of his pen, wondering how he could pluck poetically pleasing imagery out of the stratosphere. Every word was rich in spiritual significance, rooted and grounded in Hebraic tradition, making immediate sense to his readers. For example, resurrection day was the barley harvest, which always began the day after the Sabbath that followed the Passover. So when Paul told the Corinthians that Christ 'has indeed been raised from the dead, the firstfruits of those who have fallen asleep',[25] it wasn't simply a neat little turn of phrase. As a Jew he had made the obvious connection. The resurrection took place on just the right day to show that it wasn't simply a one-off, but the start or first sign of a brand-new process – an eternal harvest of all who believe. Without access to that background information, much of the Scriptures remain a closed book. The great 'Feasts of the Lord' are a key that opens the door to the living, breathing world of the New Testament.

All Jewish festivals have three basic facets: remembering the past faithfulness of God, giving thanks for his present care and provision, and looking forward to the future with hope. There can be no better foundation or structure for any celebration than that. These *Moedim* (Hebrew for 'holy days' (holidays) or 'rehearsals') are all tied to key future events. Passover, the great freedom festival, anticipates Easter. *Shavuot*, the festival of first fruits, heralds the extraordinary happenings at Pentecost. But the autumn festivals, Trumpets and Tabernacles, are yet to be fulfilled. They are rehearsals for the one great eternal festival to come when the Messiah will return and rule as king.

Autumn

The Jewish New Year begins in the seventh month of the Jewish calendar. This is typically Jewish – they're late for everything, but it may not be as daft as it sounds. Although the Jewish year officially starts in April with the Passover, the birth of the nation, its deliverance from captivity, its receiving of the Law and the beginning of its special relationship with God, *Rosh Hashanah* is supposed to mark the anniversary of creation, which happened in the month of...? No one appears to have been there to record the event.

On the other hand, eminently sensible Christians know that a new year begins where it should – in the first month. The only problem with that is that very little begins in January. That's because it has already started – in September. Let's face it, there is something very natural about acknowledging the new academic year – that time of fresh starts after the natural hiatus of the long summer holidays.

When I led a seminar on celebration in the home at the New Wine Conference everyone agreed that they wanted to acknowledge that new beginning – the new classrooms, new teachers, new courses, new clothes, and new adventures, but no one was very sure how to do it. The only Christian festival marking the season is Harvest, and that has little relevance for townies who have never ploughed or scattered. So since September appears to be a very good month for a new year, perhaps our Hebraic past can provide a mine of possibilities in making new year special.

There are three major autumn festivals described in detail in the Book of Leviticus, all within the space of a month, all interlinked. You can have too much fun. I had so much time off school at the beginning of the new school year that my schoolfriends began to ask what they had to do to convert to Judaism. I resented starting the year by getting behind with my work, but there were compensations – a new outfit, or 'rig-out' as my mother called it, because of the matching bag and shoes every Jewish girl has to have at the synagogue. They were also unique. There was nothing to compare with them in the Christian tradition.

Strictly speaking, the first two, *Rosh Hashanah*, the New Year, and *Yom Kippur*, the Day of Atonement, are more about self-reflection than party. An outbreak of unreserved celebration is withheld until Tabernacles. Perhaps this is because we need time and space to divest ourselves of our rubbish, a kind of spiritual spring-clean, before we can proceed, unencumbered, into a new era of our lives. In material terms, purging our homes of what we no longer need is a very salutary, liberating experience – once we pass the pain barrier. Letting go is never comfortable. I still grieve the loss of an extra-large dining-room table that I had to part with many years ago when it wouldn't fit into my diningroom.

In the great Christian tradition, uninhibited worship is always preceded by confession and repentance, a laying down of the clutter of our inadequacies, failures, grievances and regrets in the certainty of God's forgiveness in Christ. A new year strikes me as a good time for a more prolonged period of reflection, though Christians have tended to move it to Lent in time for the resurrection. Perhaps it isn't a matter of having one or the other, but both. Letting go in order to move on is a good discipline at any time in our lives.

There is also immense significance in the contrast of feasting after fasting, lack of restraint after abstinence, joy after sorrow. It reflects the very essence of our existence as a kingdom people, full of hope, who rejoice in our inheritance now, but not yet – because now we only have glimpses of what is to come, while then, we will enter fully into the Messianic age that Tabernacles points to so powerfully.

New Year

Rosh Hashanah (Head of the Year)

> On the first day of the seventh month you are to have a day of rest, a sacred assembly commemorated with trumpet blasts. Do no regular work, but present an offering made to the Lord by fire. Leviticus 23:24–25

> On the first day of the seventh month, hold a sacred assembly and do no regular work. It is a day for you to sound the trumpets. Numbers 29:1

Rosh Hashanah has little to do with binge drinking and singing Auld Lang Syne. In fact, it wasn't called New Year in the Old Testament. It was actually known as *Yom Teruah*, 'The Day of the Blowing of the *Shofar*', or *Yom Ha Zikkaron*, 'A Day of Remembering'.

Getting a note or two out of the *shofar* (ram's horn) is a skill only given to those with good lungs, grim determination and neighbours who don't mind them practising. Otherwise, all that's achieved is a duck-like squawk and a puddle of saliva, as we discover every year when we hold a *shofar*-blowing competition during our Tabernacles Harvest Festival. But a real blast on the *shofar* can make the hairs on the back of your neck stand to attention.

The *shofar* first appears in that extraordinary story of Abraham's testing. Would he, could he, sacrifice his beloved only son in whom he had invested every lovely dream and hope, his future and the future of his people? All of history, our history as children of Abraham, hangs in the balance. But Abraham has made no idol of his Isaac. He trusts God implicitly, and yields what he loved most in the world – not reluctantly but in humble obedience. This is a turning-point in the eternal story of God's dealings with humankind. A ram is substituted in Isaac's place, symbolized forever after by the *shofar*.

Originally, it was used as a kind of bush telegraph or early email, sending messages across the miles, such as 'Wakey, wakey, danger on the horizon', or the happier, 'Down tools, lads, the Sabbath's almost here'. Then it took on a greater significance – as a kind of a spiritual wake-up call. Just as God's arrival on Sinai was heralded by a terrifying trumpet blast, so today the *shofar* rouses a congregation from complacency, and reminds them that they stand in the presence of the living God.

The ear-splitting noise is also a reminder that one day the creation that we have so badly messed up will be gloriously restored – a theme seized on by the Apostle Paul in his letters to the churches at Corinth and Thessalonica. An archangel, he writes, with unrestrained excitement, will deliver one final, spine-tingling blast on the *shofar*, Christ will appear in triumph and the dead will rise. In the Book of Revelation, the Apostle John, condemned to hard labour on the island of Patmos, with chains gouging the very flesh out of his limbs, also hangs onto that vision of the trumpet announcing final judgement and the eternal reign of the Messiah.

The festival only became a New Year celebration after the destruction of the Temple in AD 70. But by then the tradition of having a special celebration of God as Creator and King of the universe was already well established. The arrival of a king is always heralded by trumpets. But on this occasion, they not only announce his arrival, they also proclaim the opening of the Book of Life which contains a record of the deeds of everyone living. Ultimately, each human will pass in front of him to receive their end-of-term spiritual report.

All four key themes of *Rosh Hashanah* – the kingship of God, his sovereignty over his creation, his judgment of all our doings, and his promise to make all things new – are significant Old and New Testament themes. And even if *Rosh Hashanah* doesn't look much like Hogmanay or any other typical secular New Year celebration, it's still a time to lay to rest mistakes of the past year and make resolutions for the one to come.

A liturgy for a New Year celebration

Begin the evening with a short review of the past year – what things are there to be thankful for, what has been difficult, what things would people like to do differently in the coming year? If a journal has been kept – individually or communally – look at it together.

Leader: Blessed are you, our God and Father, who gave us life and breath, who has watched over us since our birth and brought us to this new year.

All: Read Psalm 47.

Confession
Leader: If we say we have no sin, we deceive ourselves and the truth is not in us; but if we confess our sins, he is faithful and just to forgive us our sins and to cleanse us from all unrighteousness (1 John 1:8–9).

All: For the sin we have committed in our lack of love for you,
for putting other loves first,
for our fear and lack of absolute trust in you,
for our pride, arrogance and self-reliance,
for turning away from our responsibilities and commitments,
for falsehood and lying,
for wrong thoughts,
for resentment and hatred,
for being insincere in relationships,
for breaking promises,
for speaking ill of others and being quick to spread rumours about them,

for being rude to colleagues, teachers, bosses or parents,
for scoffing at or ridiculing others,
for being aggressive, hurtful, rude and unloving,
for our lack of justice and concern for the poor,
for our love of money and things,
for indulging our own selfish wants too much,
for not putting the needs of others before our own,
Father, forgive us.

Quiet reflection

Leader: As you said the confession, what specific things came to mind?
What items that you borrowed might you want to return?
What debts might you need to pay off?
What promises might you want to keep?
What memories might you want to lay to rest?
What words do you regret?

These things can be written down and burnt, or written on stones and thrown away communally. ('Taschlich' is described at the end of the liturgy.)

Leader: For all of these, God and Father of forgiveness, forgive and pardon us and grant us your peace.

There is one God and one mediator between God and human beings, the Messiah, Jesus Christ, who gave himself as a ransom for us and makes all things new.

And you shall love the Lord your God with all your heart, and with all your soul, and with all your strength.

Thanksgiving

One or two in turn thank God for the blessings of the past year.

Intercession

Leader: God has graciously hidden the future from us. We have no idea what it will hold, but he does.

Reflect briefly, either quietly or together, on:

- *What relationships might need some extra work?*
- *Who might you want to visit?*

Share out some apple slices and dip them in honey. Each in turn shares his/her hopes and fears for the coming year, and one or two at the table pray specifically for them.

Now break the loaf and share it.

All: Lord, we commit ourselves and this new year to you. Thank you for all your provision in the past, represented by this bread we share. You told us that whenever we eat together in this way we should remember you, and so we thank you too that your body sustains us day by day.

Now share the cup of wine.

All: Lord, our life on this earth is a mixture of many joys and sorrows. We pray that whatever may befall us this year, we will go on trusting in your abundant grace, in the hope of the eternal joy that you have promised to those who love and follow you.

Discuss: Set out some goals for the coming year. Write them down.

Blow the Shofar.

The blessing
All: Lord, the year ahead is an unknown, but we face it with you. Help us to take hold of your hand and to walk into it with trust, confidence and strength, and whatever it may hold, let there be moments of sweetness for each and every one of us.

Leader: The Lord bless you and keep you;
the Lord make his face shine upon you and be gracious to you;
the Lord turn his face towards you and give you his peace.

Taschlich

On the first day of *Rosh Hashanah*, some Jews go down to the sea, a river or a stream and symbolically cast off (*tashlich*) their sins by throwing pebbles into the water. The ceremony is based on verses from the prophet Micah: 'You will cast all their sins into the depths of the sea' (Micah 7:19). It can be a fun and meaningful experience.

Gather a bagful of stones, and let everyone take as many as they want, and write on them with a felt tip whatever wrong thoughts or deeds they have committed in the past year, or whatever memories or difficult situations they want to forget.

Then, go down to the sea or a fast-flowing river and throw them in, one at a time, as far as you can, while reading this verse from Psalm 103: 'As far as the east is from the west, that's how far he has removed our transgressions from us.'

See if you can find the stones again. Hopefully you can't. And then there may be some child who wants to hold onto one because it looks or feels pretty – and that also makes a powerful point.

A time of repentance

This is to be a lasting ordinance for you: on the tenth day of the seventh month you must deny yourselves and not do any work...because on this day atonement will be made for you, to cleanse you. Then you will be clean from all your sins. It is a Sabbath of rest, a lasting ordinance.   Leviticus 16:29–31

It seems strange to put ideas for a time of repentance into a book about party and celebration, but actually, they go hand in hand.

On *Yom Kippur*, the Day of Atonement, the holiest day of the year, a Sabbath of Sabbaths, life in Israel comes to a virtual standstill. A holy hush descends and envelops every city. There is no radio or TV, no meals to prepare, no shopping or traffic, no email or phone. It feels as if the world is holding its breath.

On *Rosh Hashanah* God has judged mankind and has recorded his judgment in the Book of Life, but there is a ten-day reprieve. On *Yom Kippur* the Book of Life is finally closed and sealed. Those who have repented of their sins during that time are ready to move forward into the new year, with freedom and joy.

In Temple times, when animal sacrifice was made, the rituals were hugely complex. Two goats were involved. One, the *azazel* or scapegoat, carrying the sins of the people, was taken out into the desert and pushed backwards over a cliff. The other was killed in the Temple. The High Priest then sprinkled its blood before the Ark in the Holy of Holies, as he made intercession for the people. *Kippur* means 'covering'. All wrongdoing was now officially covered.

After the destruction of the Second Temple in AD 70, when animal sacrifice ceased, the rabbis faced the difficult challenge of keeping some of the rituals of *Yom Kippur* intact. They maintained a part of the liturgy from Temple times, and reconstructed the day by shifting the emphasis to prayerful penitence and the giving of charity. Sacrifice was replaced by twenty-six hours of self-affliction – no food and drink, no washing or shaving, no anointing in an attempt to cover any body odours, no wearing leather, and no marital relations.

Now that Christ has dealt with sin on the cross once and for all, there is no necessity for Christians to observe a Day of Atonement. But an occasional time set aside for repentance and prayer on behalf of our nation, at any time of the year, can be very significant. Years ago I was part of an organization called 'Intercessors for Britain' which encouraged members to give an hour a week to pray for the country. I don't know why an hour became such a chore at times (my snoring husband was a sleeping partner), but the results were incredible. Watching the news became fun as I began to see specific answers to the prayers I had prayed.

Try fasting from food occasionally if you can, unless it's against medical advice. It isn't necessary to abstain from drinking water. The Jews believe that as the body is purged of its poisons, the spirit is symbolically cleansed of its waste matter. Christians have tended to see fasting as a more forceful way of getting answers to prayer. But far better to see it as an act of love. With no planning, shopping, cooking or washing up, God, who is often pushed into second place by the clamouring of eyes, mouth and stomach, now receives our full attention. There is so much more time to give to him when we don't have to worry about what to eat. And during that time set apart from the normal humdrum, he can prepare us to be the answer to our prayers.

Twenty-four hours – from one evening meal to the next – will normally do. In Judaism children fast completely from the age of thirteen, but it may be better instead to encourage them to give up something for the occasion – biscuits or chocolate.

This is a good time to share the extraordinary story of Jonah, with its themes of obedience, repentance, forgiveness and second chance – for both Jonah and the Assyrians. It's no small wonder Jonah was afraid and resisted God's will at first. Nineveh was the capital of Assyria, and the Assyrians were world-renowned for their cruelty. They would drag their captives home behind their horses by ropes attached to rings through their lips or jaws. Once they got them there, they would cut off their thumbs or big toes or tongues, then sell them into slavery. From Jonah's perspective, no one who did such things deserved forgiveness. But with his lack of compassion and understanding of God's mercy, does he?

If God can forgive a nation like Assyria, and bring about its transformation (the Assyrians enjoyed 200 years of relative peace after their national repentance at this time), if he can take an unwilling, argumentative and disobedient servant like Jonah and use him to such effect, then clearly no thing and no heart is too hard for God. If very small children are present, leave out the gruesome bits of the story and construct a whale instead.

Here a communal confession may be helpful. It was written after the Blitz, when Coventry Cathedral was destroyed. The huge nails that fell out of the roof timbers and survived the fire were formed into crosses and sent to communities all over the world that were prepared to work for reconciliation and peace. It can also be used on Remembrance Sunday.

The Coventry Cathedral Litany of Reconciliation

Leader: All have sinned and fallen short of the glory of God. The hatred which divides nation from nation, race from race, class from class,

All: Father, forgive.

Leader: The covetous desires of people and nations to possess what is not their own,

All: Father, forgive.

Leader: The greed which exploits the work of human hands and lays waste the earth,

All: Father, forgive.

Leader: Our envy of the welfare and happiness of others,

All: Father, forgive.

Leader: Our indifference to the plight of the imprisoned, the homeless, the refugee,

All: Father, forgive.

Leader: The lust which dishonours the bodies of men, women and children,

All: Father, forgive.

Leader: The pride which leads us to trust in ourselves and not in God,

All: Father, forgive.

Leader: Be kind to one another, tender-hearted, forgiving one another, as God in Christ forgave you.

A ten-day meditation before a beginning or a new start

Alternatively, you may prefer to use this ten-day meditation, based on the Ten Commandments. It is a Hebraic tradition to set aside the ten days leading up to the Day of Atonement as a time for self-reflection, clearing out the spiritual rubbish, making restitution, putting wrong right. They are known as the Days of Awe, or the Days of Repentance, or even, the Days of Turning.

You can in fact use this meditation any time that suits you – leading up to Easter, to a new academic year, to the start of a new job, to New Year – in fact, to any new beginning or turning-point. It can be done alone, or with your family, or with a small community. It only need take five to ten minutes or so each night and can be done as an add-on to saying grace. Keep a record of your thoughts or discussions and review them at regular intervals.

The Ten Commandments are not an onerous, dry set of rules, but God's hopes for the human race – his blueprint for the best possible world. That's why they make such a good spiritual thermometer.

If you have a *shofar* (ram's horn) to hand, or any other noisy instrument for that matter, give yourself a good wakey-wakey call with it at the end of your reflection.

Day 1
All: I am the Lord your God, who brought you out of the land of slavery. You shall have no other gods before me.

Leader: God is King of the entire universe and all that is in it. He created it and made human beings because he wanted our friendship. It breaks his heart when we turn away, and seek satisfaction for our needs elsewhere. Yet his love still pursues us, and sets us free from the snares and the selfishness that enslave us.

Discuss:

- Does God really have first place in our lives? What other 'gods' might be taking up more space in our hearts than they should?
- What might be our 'Egypt' today – holding us in slavery, instead of letting us live in the freedom that has been won for us?
- What things have filled us with awe and wonder, and a totally fulfilling sense of God's glory in this past year?

All: Jesus said, 'Hear, O Israel, the Lord our God, the Lord is one. Love the Lord your God with all your heart and with all your soul and with all your mind and with all your strength. And love your neighbour as yourself. There is no commandment greater than these' (Matthew 22:37–40).

Blow the shofar, then say:

All: We blow the *shofar* because trumpets remind us of God's kingship. Let's bow before our King. Then, in freedom, let's lift up our heads and go forward into the future as children of royalty.

Day 2
All: You shall not make for yourself an idol in the form of anything in heaven above or on the earth beneath or in the waters below. You shall not bow down to them or worship them.

Leader: An idol is not a statue. It isn't even a hobby like golf or football, that we really love. An idol is anything we rely on for security, rather than placing our trust in God. It can often be our money.

Discuss:

- Look back over the past year. Which things have made us afraid?
- In what ways do we not trust God for all our needs?
- Where is our real security, and how may we learn to handle our fear constructively?

All: Don't be anxious about anything, but in everything, by prayer and petition, with thanksgiving, make your requests known to God, and the peace of God, which transcends all understanding, will guard your hearts and minds in Christ Jesus (Philippians 4:6–7).

Blow the shofar, then say:

All: We blow the *shofar* because trumpets remind us of God's kingship. Let's bow before our King. Then, in freedom, let's lift up our heads and go forward into the future as children of royalty.

Day 3

All: You shall not misuse the name of the Lord your God, for the Lord will not hold anyone guiltless who misuses his name.

Leader: God's name is his character. And his entire character is love, justice, kindness and faithfulness.

Discuss:

- Being called a Christian brings responsibility. How might we have diminished God's character, and therefore misused his name, in the eyes of others in the way we have behaved towards them?
- How might we reflect his character in the days to come?

All: Be kind and compassionate to one another, forgiving each other, just as in Christ, God forgave you (Ephesians 4:32).

Blow the shofar, then say:

All: We blow the *shofar* because trumpets remind us of God's kingship. Let's bow before our King. Then, in freedom, let's lift up our heads and go forward into the future as children of royalty.

Day 4

All: Remember the Sabbath day by keeping it holy. Six days you shall labour and do all your work, but the seventh day is a Sabbath to the Lord your God.

Leader: The Sabbath was the crown of creation. God gave us a day for play, rest and recreation, then set us an example by enjoying the Sabbath himself.

Discuss:

- Have we really taken time to rest and play, to set aside one day of the week as holy or special, a day for God, for family and friends?

- Have we honoured God's creation by having one day when we don't exploit the earth's resources?
- How might we do so in the future?

All: The Sabbath was made for human beings, not human beings for the Sabbath.

Blow the shofar, then say:

All: We blow the *shofar* because trumpets remind us of God's kingship. Let's bow before our King. Then, in freedom, let's lift up our heads and go forward into the future as children of royalty.

Day 5

All: Honour your father and your mother, so that you may live long in the land the Lord your God is giving you.

Leader: We live in a society where there is not much respect for older people, and little sense of responsibility for those who can no longer care for themselves – whether they are our parents or not.

Discuss:

- How have we cared for the older generation, whether they are our responsibility by blood, or by adoption into the Christian family?
- What more might we want to do for those who are lonely, and have no one near them to honour them?

All: If a widow has children or grandchildren, these should learn to put their religion into practice by caring for their own family and so repaying their parents and grandparents, for this is pleasing to God (1 Timothy 5:4).

Blow the shofar, then say:

All: We blow the *shofar* because trumpets remind us of God's kingship. Let's bow before our King. Then, in freedom, let's lift up our heads and go forward into the future as children of royalty.

Day 6

All: You shall not murder.

Leader: God breathes life into every human being and each is known and precious to him. When Cain killed his brother, Abel, it horrified the Giver of Life. Today there are so many ways of 'killing' people without actually taking their physical life.

Discuss:

- What cruel words, gossip or murderous thoughts of ours have killed off someone's hopes and dreams, or diminished them in the eyes of others?
- How can we be someone who speaks and gives life to others instead?

All: Love is patient, love is kind. It does not envy, it does not boast, it is not proud. It is not rude, it is not self-seeking, it is not easily angered, it keeps no record of wrongs. Love does not delight in evil, but rejoices with the truth. It always protects, always trusts, always hopes, always perseveres (1 Corinthians 13:4–7).

Blow the shofar, then say:

All: We blow the *shofar* because trumpets remind us of God's kingship. Let's bow before our King. Then, in freedom, let's lift up our heads and go forward into the future as children of royalty.

Day 7

All: You shall not commit adultery.

Leader: God is utterly devoted, utterly committed, utterly faithful to his people. His relationship with us is a picture of marriage at its very best. But in our world relationships have become very cheap, and their importance for our security and well-being is undervalued.

Discuss:

- How committed am I to the most important relationship in my life? Do I rejoice in it, invest in it, and nurture it – or do I seek my emotional fulfilment elsewhere?
- What might I do in future to ensure that this relationship remains healthy and strong, as God wants it to be?
- Am I supporting or undermining my friends' marriages?

All: The Apostle Paul says, 'Marriage should be honoured by all, and the marriage bed kept pure.'

Blow the shofar, then say:

All: We blow the *shofar* because trumpets remind us of God's kingship. Let's bow before our King. Then, in freedom, let's lift up our heads and go forward into the future as children of royalty.

Day 8

All: You shall not steal.

Leader: The love of money is the root of all evil – and advertising panders to materialism, our inexhaustible yearning for more. It leads to burglary, shoplifting, handbag snatching, muggings, human trafficking, mistrust and misery, but also to tax evasion, taking stationery home from work for private use, wasting other people's time, taking their gifts for granted.

Discuss:

- How does materialism affect and infect us?
- Where might we have been not altogether honest?
- What debts do we need to pay off?
- What items we have been loaned do we need to return? (Have a look at the bookcase!)

All: Jesus saw the rich putting their gifts into the Temple treasury. He also saw a poor widow put in two very small copper coins. 'I tell you the truth,' he said, 'this poor widow has put in more than all the others. They gave their gifts out of their wealth; but she, out of her poverty, has put in all she had to live on' (Luke 21:1-4).

Blow the shofar, then say:

All: We blow the *shofar* because trumpets remind us of God's kingship. Let's bow before our King. Then, in freedom, let's lift up our heads and go forward into the future as children of royalty.

Day 9

All: You shall not give false testimony against your neighbour.

Leader: We live in a world where lying and cheating are accepted as a way of life. But lying always involves deceit and deceit spins a web around people that is hurtful and demeaning and destructive.

Discuss:

- When have we told an untruth that puts us in a better light than someone else, and diminishes or demolishes them?
- When have we 'told a fib' that gets us out of a tight corner?
- How might we now put that right?

All: The psalmist says, 'Surely you desire truth in the inner parts, you teach me wisdom in the inmost place.'

Blow the shofar, then say:

All: We blow the *shofar* because trumpets remind us of God's kingship. Let's bow before our King. Then, in freedom, let's lift up our heads and go forward into the future as children of royalty.

Day 10

All: You shall not covet your neighbour's house. You shall not covet your neighbour's wife, or his manservant or maidservant, his ox or donkey, or anything that belongs to your neighbour.

Leader: We are constantly tempted to want what others have – their lovely homes, possessions, gifts, jobs – and before long, even their relationships.

Discuss:

- How many times have I wished I were someone else, or had the opportunities, the privileges, the skills they have?
- What impact does this have on my own spiritual progress?
- What opportunities might I have missed thinking I was just not good enough?

All: Keep your lives free from the love of money and be content with what you have, because God has said, 'Never will I leave you, never will I forsake you.'

Blow the shofar, then say:

All: We blow the *shofar* because trumpets remind us of God's kingship. Let's bow before our King. Then, in freedom, let's lift up our heads and go forward into the future as children of royalty.

A Tabernacles Harvest Festival

Succot or Tabernacles is the third and most important of the three major Old Testament annual festivals. It is so unique that it is often simply referred to as *Ha Hag* – 'the Feast' or 'the season of our rejoicing'. It is the culmination of the three autumn festivals which are designed, progressively, to take us on a journey deeper into the grace and mercy of God. It represents an opportunity for us to revel in his creating us, caring for us, forgiving, protecting and providing for us – now and forever.

The church loosely observes two of the pilgrim festivals, those that have been fulfilled in the coming of Jesus and the gift of the Holy Spirit – Passover and Pentecost – but ignores Tabernacles altogether, in favour of a Harvest Festival that has more pagan overtones and little relevance for an increasingly urbanized society that nips down to the supermarket for its daily bread.

Yet no festival is richer in symbolism or Messianic significance than Tabernacles. None gives such a panoramic overview of the history of God's involvement with his people, and none is as much fun, especially for children. It readily lends itself to an all-age service or school assembly, and for those reasons alone I have included a service outline that can be used in church and home groups or adapted and shortened for smaller family networks. Within the text is an explanation of the meaning of Tabernacles, and of each of the key symbols. It lasts around ninety minutes. If this is too long, the symbols can all be explained the previous week, or on the back of an order of service.

Tabernacles is so much more than a Harvest Festival. It provides us with an opportunity to share communally in a great treasure – celebrations that Jesus knew and loved, and used as a major teaching tool, that will be fulfilled in the fullness of time.

What's more, in recognition of the fact that the children of Israel were told to do it forever, it formed the basis for the American celebration of Thanksgiving.

On the fifteenth day of the seventh month, when you have gathered in the produce of the land, you shall celebrate the feast of the Lord for seven days. On the first day shall be a solemn rest, and on the eighth day shall be a solemn rest. And you shall take on the first day of the fruit of splendid trees, branches of palm trees and boughs of leafy trees and willows of the brook, and you shall rejoice before the Lord your God seven days. You shall celebrate it as a feast to the Lord for seven days in the year. It is a statute forever throughout your generations... You shall dwell in booths for seven days...that your generations may know that I made the people of Israel dwell in booths when I brought them out of the land of Egypt.Leviticus 23:39-43

A service for a Tabernacles Harvest Festival

The Sunday or week before the service, explain to the congregation that they will need to bring a citrus fruit to hold, and a selection of branches to wave. If they don't want to cut branches from the trees, make them out of paper, or bring ribbons to wave instead.

Build a *sukkah* or tabernacle somewhere central in the church where all can see it. It needs to be large enough for people to sit in. A large tent frame is ideal. Cover it with netting and then push pine or other scented branches through the holes until it is entirely covered in greenery. If you are really ambitious you can use flowers or grapes as well, but be warned, with children around they don't last long. Put some bowls of dried fruit inside, along with prayers and Scripture texts on cards. You will need:

- jugs of water
- bowls
- a *shofar* (ram's horn)
- spare branches and citrus fruits for those who forget or are visitors
- a tray of sand filled with night-lights or a large church candle
- a selection of texts and meditations to go on A4-sized cards in the *sukkah*, or beside the candles

The Welcome
Leader: We are celebrating Harvest today as the biblical Feast of Tabernacles. This is a festival that Jesus himself celebrated each year in Jerusalem for eight days.

It focuses on the God who in faithfulness has sheltered and protected his people in the past, who tabernacles or dwells with us and cares for us today, and will in the future take us to tabernacle or live with him forever.

Please participate from the very beginning. Wave your branches. Get up and move around. Celebration the biblical way is experiential. It should engage your senses as well as your mind. I will explain the symbols we use as we go along.

The Confession

SYMBOL 1: The Tabernacle/tent/shelter

Leader: Our first symbol is the Tabernacle or *sukkah*. Over the years the Israelites constructed a variety of flimsy, tent-like structures where they could eat and pray and worship for the eight days of the feast. The *sukkah* was a reminder of the forty years in the wilderness that followed the exodus from Egypt. The people had no permanent dwellings – they learned to depend on God entirely.

- He sheltered them with his presence – a pillar of cloud by day, a pillar of fire by night.
- He fed them with manna.
- He provided water out of the rock.
- He gave them his instruction (the law).

The Bible repeatedly picks up the idea of God being our shelter or Tabernacle. 'He who dwells in the shelter of the Most High will rest in the shadow of the Almighty', yet we so often fail to recognize his protection and care, and either rely instead on our own financial resources, or worry and fret about the lack of them.

Lord, we repent of our materialism.
All: We are sorry for the way it ensnares us, almost without our realizing it.
We are sorry that we often fail to recognize your provision and protection.
We are sorry that we so often want more than we need.
We are sorry that it unwittingly makes us exploit others.
We are sorry that we make possessions our idols, because we trust in them and
    turn to them, rather than to you.

John's Gospel says, 'The word became flesh and tabernacled among us'. Thank you, Lord, for breaking into our world, for dying for us so that we might be free, and for your ongoing presence and care.

Come at *any time* to pray on your own or with someone, or with your child or children. Ponder the texts you'll find on the floor.

Let's now say together Psalm 47:

All: Clap your hands, all you peoples;
shout to God with loud songs of joy.
For the Lord, the Most High, is awesome,
a great king over all the earth.
God has gone up with a shout,
the Lord with the sound of a trumpet.
Sing praises to God, sing praises;
sing praises to our King, sing praises.
For God is the king of all the earth;
sing praises with a psalm.

Simultaneously with the word 'trumpet', sound the shofar.

Go immediately into a hymn or a selection of songs, the instant the words 'with a psalm' are said.

Reading: Deuteronomy 16:13–15:

> *You shall keep the feast of tabernacles or booths seven days, when you make your ingathering from your threshing floor and your wine press; you shall rejoice in your feast, you and your son and your daughter, your manservant and your maidservant, the Levite, the foreigner, the orphan, and the widow who are within your towns. For seven days you shall keep the feast to the Lord your God at the place which the Lord will choose; because the Lord your God will bless you in all your produce and in all the work of your hands, so that you will be altogether joyful.*

Leader: On this festival it is a command to be joyful! Verse 14 says, 'You shall rejoice' – whether you feel like it or not. For some of you who are going through a difficult time, this may be a sacrifice, but you have branches in your hands that are to be used for that purpose. Use them as an act of will, a sign of your desire to worship. There is a tradition to point them north, south, east and west, up and down, signifying God's sovereignty over the entire universe.

A hymn or more songs, as branches are waved.

Leader: Please sit down. (The quieter section of the service now follows.)

SYMBOL 2: The Fruit and Branches

Leader: The Book of Leviticus specifies three kinds of branches that are to be waved: palm, myrtle and willow. No one is very sure why, but it's thought they might represent the wide variety of people there are in the world, whom God has created and loves.

The citrus represents the fruit of the trees and God's provision. Look at it and:

- Give thanks for God's provision of the fruit of the earth – for food, clothing, shelter, warmth, trade and business, work and livelihood.

- Think about the seeds inside it – the promise of future harvest, future fruitfulness, God's ongoing care for creation and our task in cherishing it.

- Reflect on the seeds of hope for your future. Commit your dreams and aspirations to God, for him to fulfil as he sees best.

Pause in silence.

The Intercessions

SYMBOL 3: The Light

Leader: Light is a key element in the celebration. In Jesus' day the entire Temple was floodlit. Four huge braziers outside drew pilgrims from far and wide. The Court of the Women in the Temple precincts, which is where most people milled around together, was lit by 400 lamps. For seven nights the people would wait for the High Priest to return with a golden pitcher full of water from the pool of Siloam, and as he arrived they would celebrate and worship and dance for joy. The men went on dancing all night in the streets of Jerusalem with flaming torches.

Please stand.

Reading: Exodus 13:21:

> *And the Lord went in front of them by day in a pillar of cloud to lead them along the way, and by night in a pillar of fire to give them light...the pillar of cloud by day and the pillar of fire by night did not depart from before the people.*

Leader: In silence let us stand to worship the God of glory from our hearts. (*Don't worry about noisy children – in Jesus' day all the children would be present, even* *in the quiet moments.)* It was at the Feast of Tabernacles that Jesus said he was the light of the world.

You may here refer to items in the news that need prayer. Either light the candle, or invite people to come forward and light a night-light. They can do so as a token of their desire for God to shine his light into whatever circumstances or people they are praying for today. As they do so:

Readings: John 1:3–5, 9; 8:12:

> *Through Jesus all things were made. And without him nothing was made that has been made. In him was life and that life was the light of men. The light shines in the darkness but the darkness has not overcome it. The true light that gives light to everyone was coming into the world.*
>
> *Jesus said, I am the light of the world. Whoever follows me will never walk in darkness, but will have the light of life.*

Hymns or songs on the theme of light. Still standing:

The Dedication

SYMBOL 4: Water

Leader: During the worship, the water that the High Priest would carry in a golden pitcher from the pool of Siloam up into the Temple would be poured on the altar. After a long dry summer when water was at a premium before the coming of the early rain, this was a costly sacrifice and a proclamation of trust that God would indeed send the rain. It was also a prophetic act. The water would then run out of the Temple area into the Kidron valley, which leads eventually to the Dead Sea, in anticipation of the words of the prophet Ezekiel.

Reading: Ezekiel 47:

> *Then he brought me to the door of the temple; and there, water was flowing from below the threshold of the temple towards the east, flowing south... Then outside the temple I saw that water was flowing out of the temple area. One thousand steps further on and he led me through the water and it was ankle deep. One thousand paces further on and he led me through and it was knee deep. Further on it was waist deep, and a thousand paces further it was a river that I could not cross – it was deep enough to swim in, a river that could not be crossed.*

Start to pour the water from one of the jugs into a bowl beneath and continue:

Leader: At the Feast of Tabernacles, John 7:37–39 records:

> *On the last day of the festival, the great day, while Jesus was standing there he cried out, 'If any one thirst, let him come to me and drink. He who believes in me, as the scripture has said, out of his heart shall flow rivers of living water.' Now this he said about the Spirit whom those who believed in him were to receive.*

Lord, thank you for giving us the water of life. Thank you for sending the rain of your Holy Spirit to refresh us and flow through us.

Come, therefore, as we sing and allow this water to flow over you, and let God speak to you about its significance for you – washing, refreshing, filling with the Spirit, renewal, commitment...

Come to the *Sukkah*, the Tabernacle, and know and receive his protection. Come and stand by the candle, as an act of dedication.

Several adults or responsible children come and pour water from the jugs over the hands of all who come forward into the bowls beneath. As the jugs empty, pour the water from the bowls back into them and keep going...

Leader: Don't be distracted from your act of dedication or commitment, or from receiving a fresh anointing of God's Holy Spirit, even as we move into celebra-tion, with dances like the people did at the festivals in Jerusalem.

Begin with quiet hymns and songs, then change gear into several more Hebraic 'dance' songs, all unannounced.

SYMBOL 5: The Ram's Horn

Leader: This final symbol has many meanings, but the most important is that it announces the approaching presence of God. It is a warning to prepare for his coming. It's a call to obedience. Jesus said, 'Repent, for the reign of God is here.' This is not just a kingdom reign for the future, but one that has started already and is here now. So as we hear it, let's be aware – for in its call is both judgment and salvation. Paul writes in 1 Thessalonians 4:16–17:

> *For the Lord himself will descend from heaven with a cry of command, with the archangel's call, and with the sound of the trumpet of God. And the dead in Christ will rise first; then we who are alive, who are left, shall be caught up together with them in the clouds to meet the Lord...*

Blow the shofar.

Slight pause (10 seconds) before reading together Revelation 21:1–4:

All: Then I saw a new heaven
and a new earth;
for the first heaven
and the first earth
had passed away...

And I saw the holy city
new Jerusalem,
coming down out of heaven from God,
prepared as a bride adorned for her husband.

And I heard a great voice from the throne saying,
'Behold, the dwelling of God is with people.
He will *tabernacle* with them,
and they shall be his people,
and God himself will be with them.

He will wipe away every tear from their eyes,
and death will be no more,
neither shall there be mourning nor crying nor pain any more,
for the former things have passed away.'

Immediately into a hymn or song.

The Blessing
Leader: Zechariah tells us that when the time comes for God to bring history to its climax, then the nations of the world will go up to Jerusalem every year to celebrate the Feast of Tabernacles.

The traditional Hebrew festival prayer:

All: To you alone we give thanks.
If our mouths were filled
with song as the sea,
and our tongues with
jubilation as the multitude of its waves,
and our lips with praise
as wide as the heavens,

and our eyes shining
like the sun and the moon,
and our hands spread out
as the eagles of heaven,
and our feet swift as the wild deer,

we would still be unable to thank you sufficiently
and to bless your name, O Lord our God,
for even one of the millions of benefits
which you have performed for us
and for those who believed before us.

Leader: May the Lord bless and keep you.
May the Lord make his face shine upon you,
and may he be gracious to you.
May the Lord turn his face to you
and give you his peace.

As the final song is played, please pick up your citrus fruit and quickly follow us
and the water out into the church entrance.

Final hymn or song.

*As it's played the bowls of water are carried by several members of the congregation,
including children, behind the leader, followed by the entire congregation, into the church
steps or porch.*

Leader: Lord, send the rain of your Holy Spirit onto our neighbourhood like
streams of water onto the thirsty ground, and bless the people who live here
abundantly.

*Pour the water down the path or street, or over the ground as a symbol of rivers of living
water flowing through the area. The citrus fruits are then collected and are turned into
fruit punch so that everyone can drink. It may help to have several juice extractors ready
for that purpose.*

Ideas for celebrating a Tabernacles/Harvest at home

- Create a bower inside the porch, or at the entrance of your home with
  trellis or a tent frame. Cover with fruit and greenery, and give every visitor a piece of fruit or a few flowers to take home.

- You can build a *sukkah* for children out of a makeshift tent virtually anywhere – in a conservatory, under a table, in a corner. Have some refreshments there at some point. Allow the children to spend at least one night in it. This is great fun if it's the night before the last night before going back to school. They may want to spend it literally under the stars, but they tend to creep into their own beds in the middle of the night when it gets cold.

- Use a very shortened version of the service above, focusing on the five symbols.

- Build a human tabernacle, as a symbol of our vulnerability and need for God to hold our lives together. Some people simply lie on the floor, forming a square; some stand at the four corners and along the sides, forming the walls; they should hold up children or slightly built adults lying horizontally to form the roof beams. Other children can now help to decorate them if they choose – it depends how sturdy and lasting the design is! Read Psalm 127 if they can stay up that long, then let the edifice collapse to make the point.

- Make an edible tabernacle out of gingerbread.[26]

For the gingerbread:
- 340g/12oz pl flour
- 85g/3oz soft brown sugar
- 85g/3oz margarine
- 2 tablespoons golden/corn syrup
- 1 tablespoon black treacle
- 3 teaspoons ginger
- 2 teaspoons cinnamon
- 1 teaspoon baking powder
- 1 beaten egg
- 1–2 tablespoons milk

Melt the margarine, sugar and syrup in a pan over a gentle heat until just melted. Add the dry ingredients and bind together with a wooden spoon, adding the egg and enough milk to make a dough firm enough to roll out.

Divide the mixture in half, and roll out one half of the dough into a rectangle – 25cm by 13cm (5in by 10in) and place on a greased baking tray. Divide the other piece in half again and roll out two squares 13cm by 13cm (5in by 5in). Place the two squares on another greased baking tray (or two) and bake all three pieces on gas mark 4/180°C for 15 mins, or until golden brown. Cool on a wire rack.

For the icing:

- 1 egg white
- 227g/8oz icing sugar
- 1 teaspoon lemon juice

Once the cake slices are cool, whisk the egg white until it forms peaks, then slowly beat in the icing and lemon juice.

To assemble:
Bear in mind that if the mixture has spread unevenly you may need to cut the cake pieces (your tabernacle walls) into one 15cm by 25cm (6in by 10in) piece and two 15cm by 15cm (6in by 6in) squares, so that they fit together.

Arrange your gingerbread pieces to make the three walls of the tabernacle, with the longest at the back, on a cake-board or bread-board. Cement your walls in place by piping icing along the bottom edges of the pieces to attach them to the board, and along the sides that touch each other to fix them together.

Decorate the walls with tiny sweets (preferably ones that look like fruit), attached with icing sugar.

To make the roof: you can either use lengths of uncooked spaghetti, cementing them with icing sugar across the side walls and covering them with pieces of greenery, made either out of green crepe paper or sprigs of herbs like rosemary; or, if you plan to eat your cake (and that's the best idea), cement a piece of edible rice paper to the top of the walls, and cover it either with green crepe paper greenery that can be removed before eating, or colour the remainder of your icing sugar green with food colouring and make some leaves to rest on top. Attach some too, to your outer walls.

You could also make a carpet out of rice paper or icing sugar and place some doll's-house furniture and characters inside.

An alternative Halloween

This idea came from Christine Jensen of Heaton Baptist Church in Newcastle upon Tyne. She and a few of her friends have been looking at original ways to celebrate for some years. She says, 'How about using Halloween as an opportunity to get together with our wonderful children, flatmates, families or friends to impact our community in the name of Jesus?'

This is the plan

Several families get together in the last week of October. We all dress up in things that could be described as bringing light and life and joy. Monks, clowns, angels, rubber chickens, if you can get them! Then we go out into our streets with large baskets full of flapjacks or cookies, some New Testaments, and along the way we say the following blessing:

> The Lord bless you and keep you.
> The Lord make his face shine on you
> and give you his peace.

Then we start knocking on doors. They answer and we politely refuse their gifts, but we give instead. They expect to be told of evil and trickery, but we bless them with words of Scripture. When we leave them, they are holding something nice to eat, the words of God to read, the blessing of God in their ears, and a little note saying who we are and why we've been. Halloween has been turned upside down and the evening is now a hallowed one in the name of Jesus.

Practicalities

Here are a few top tips from last year's pilot study!

- You can't have too many lanterns and lights! It really should look like a door-to-door light-seller has arrived! The more distinctive we look, the more effective our message is at getting through. If we look dark and dreary, yet say we're bringing light, we're not going to be that convincing.

- It's cold out there so layer up, unless you want to freeze, or completely ruin the effect of the fabulous costumes and sparkling brightness with a bulky dark winter coat!

- Explain before you go out, until *everyone* understands, that you're 'blessing and treating', and *not* accepting anything that's offered, however scrummy it looks.

- Pray, pray, pray before you go out, for safety, practically and spiritually. Pray God's light and life into the homes that you visit.

- Have some special goodies for any kids when they get back, as a 'thank you' for being self-controlled and blessing their community. Maybe even have a meal together, or some yummy hot chocolate and treats, and thank God for what he will do.

- A big bright sign on a stick might be a good idea, unless you want to explain to each household that you're an *alternative* to Halloween.

- Remember as you do this, that you are standing at the doors of people God has made, loved and died for. It is a huge privilege to bring God's light into their lives.

All Saints' Day

Alternatively, replace Halloween altogether with an 'All Saints' fancy dress party. Each person comes dressed up as a saint of old, from any of the previous centuries, ready to share that saint's story and what it means for them. It may be fun to withhold the saint's name initially and see how quickly people can guess their identity.

Or, if you don't want to involve fancy dress, invite people simply to come together, each with the story of a chosen saint – historic or contemporary – who has had a profound influence on their lives. They should be ready to tell that story and explain why they are grateful to God for that person. Sit in a circle, around a table or on the floor, with a tray covered in night-lights in the middle. When each person finishes their story, they light a night-light in thanks for that particular saint, who was, for them, a true light shining in the darkness.

Winter

I hate having a November birthday. Dismal and drizzly, with a chill that seems to penetrate bone marrow, this first winter month brings enough gloom without heralding the passage of yet another year. All I want to do is hibernate until spring. But wishing the season away is dumping the precious gift of time in the rubbish bin.

The years seem to pass faster the older we get because, with every successive birthday, a year represents a tinier fraction of our lives. At ten a year is a tenth of our lives. At fifty, it's a fiftieth. That's a good enough reason for appreciating the moment. And winter does have its compensations – hoarfrosts, crisp, clear walks through ice and snow, cosy evenings around the fire, piping hot soups, and of course, Christmas.

Ideas for Thanksgiving

In the USA Thanksgiving is as important as Christmas. Celebrated on the fourth Thursday of November (the second Monday in October for Canadians), the annual one-day holiday is a kind of Harvest Festival. Stories abound about how it actually came into being.

They all start with 11 December 1620, when the first pilgrims, a group of Puritans fleeing religious persecution in Europe, landed at Plymouth Rock in Massachusetts on the *Mayflower*. That first winter was devastatingly hard. By the following fall, they had lost 46 of the original 102 who had set sail. But the harvest was bountiful, so they shared a thanksgiving with the native Indians who had helped them survive. There was no turkey, no pumpkin pie, not for devout Puritans, who in true Calvinist style would have observed the day with prayer and fasting, not feasting. In fact, the native

American people had celebrated the harvest, in one form or another, for several thousands of years prior to European colonization.

Two years later, during a severe drought, the pilgrims gathered to pray once again. When their prayers were answered the following day with a long, steady rain, Governor William Bradford proclaimed a day of Thanksgiving. But there wasn't another until June 1676, when the governing council of Charlestown, Massachusetts, decided it was time to express thanks that their community was now well and truly established. It was 1789 before George Washington proclaimed a national Day of Thanksgiving, not without criticism from some quarters that the struggles of a few settlers hardly merited such a celebration.

Some of us, however, welcome any opportunity for thanksgiving, so perhaps the time has come at last for the Brits to join our cross-Atlantic cousins in celebrating God's faithfulness to their nation, because:

- There's little to celebrate in November and it has to beat having a Bonfire Night to celebrate a terrorist like Guy Fawkes. Besides, the Puritans were the founding fathers of the Presbyterian, Baptist and Congregationalist churches. Immense freedom was given to women for the first time and, against much opposition, they often held the equivalent of Alpha courses in their homes.

- Instead of a traditional grace, pass a candle from person to person. As they receive it, each offers a prayer of thanksgiving, or a short testimony about something they have learned or for which they are thankful in the past year.

- Have a fireworks display in the garden.

- Reflect on this moving quotation from the *Diary of Anne Frank*, who died in 1945 in a concentration camp, when she was only fifteen years old:

  > I do not think of all the misery, but of the glory that remains. Go outside into the fields, nature and the sun, go out and seek happiness in yourself and in God. Think of the beauty that again and again discharges itself within and without you and be happy.

Ideas for a Festival of Lights

For with you is the fountain of life,
in your light we see light.   Psalm 36:9

Many nations and faiths celebrate the victory of light over darkness, good over evil at this time of year. Light is a symbol that reaches into all of our hearts, especially during the long, dark days of winter, but no light compares with Jesus, Light of the World, whose life illuminated history and whose radiance drives away the shadows of doubt and despair.

- The Hindus celebrate Diwali in November. Diwali, which means 'array of lights', symbolizes the triumph of good over evil, and is enjoyed now by people of every religion. Indian hospitality is legendary, and when we lived in Coventry, we were always invited into local homes at Diwali to share their samosas, bajis, curries and sweetmeats. Advent or Christmas can provide a lovely opportunity to return the compliment with traditional European delicacies.

- The Dutch remember St Martin for his kindness to strangers on 11 November. One winter night, as he was returning home in a snowstorm, a homeless man appeared in the darkness and Martin gave him half his cloak. Children go from house to house, carrying lanterns, singing for sweets and other treats.

- In Sweden, 13 December, the shortest day of the year, is dedicated to the gentle and gracious Lucia, patron saint of light. Girls dress up as Santa Lucia wearing a white dress with a red sash and a crown of candles. These days, for safety, the candles are battery operated. The girls hand out a cake called Lussekatter and spicy gingerbread biscuits. The boys carry a candle and wear a kind of white pyjama suit and pointed hats with golden stars on them.

- During the Christmas season in the Philippines people decorate their homes with star lanterns of every shape and size. They're often very elaborate and families pass down their expertise in lantern making from one generation to the next.

- For the nine days before Christmas, Mexican families march from house to house with candles looking for a room at the inn. In South

America Christians, including the children, eat their Christmas dinner at midnight on Christmas Eve.

- Christians in China celebrate Christmas by lighting their houses with paper lanterns.
- The Germans, who gave us the Christmas tree, began decorating them with wax tapers in the 1700s. They also have a tradition of putting candles in windows to light the holy family's way to Bethlehem.

The Jewish festival of light is called *Hannukah*, which means 'dedication'. There is no mention of it in the Old Testament, which is hardly surprising, as the event it recalls didn't happen until the inter-testamental period. But it is referred to in the New Testament:

> *Then came the Feast of Dedication at Jerusalem. It was winter and Jesus was in the temple area, walking in Solomon's Colonnade. The Jews gathered around him saying, 'How long will you keep us in suspense? If you are the Messiah, tell us plainly.'*   John 10:22–24

The coming of the Messiah would have been very much on people's minds at the Feast of the Dedication, as it commemorates not only the dedication of the First Temple of Solomon, and the Second Temple of Nehemiah, where Jesus was walking, but also the events of 165 BC.

Antiochus, the Greek King of Syria, tried to force the Jews in Judaea to worship his gods. He seized the Second Temple and dedicated it to Zeus, defiling the holy altar by killing a pig on it. The Jews, under the remarkable guerrilla leadership of Judas the Maccabean, managed to drive the Syrians out. Since both previous dedications had taken place at Tabernacles, they lasted a whole eight days. But when the Jews came to purify and rededicate their beloved Temple, they discovered there was only enough sacred oil to light the huge menorah for one day. Miraculously, the oil lasted eight days until a messenger could return with more.

There are actually nine candles in the special *Hannukah* menorah. One, known as the *shammas* or 'servant candle', usually smaller than the others, is the only one to be lit with a match, and is then used to light each of the other candles, one the first night, two the second, three the third and so on, until all eight are alight on the final night. In other words, forty-four candles are needed in all.

It was at *Hannukah*, more than at any other time, that the Jews prayed for another Judas Maccabeus to free them from Roman rule. 'Is that who you are?'

they asked Jesus. 'If you are, say so clearly.' And Jesus speaks to them about sheep who listen to his voice and receive eternal life. In other words, 'Sorry chaps, you've got it wrong. There's no military solution this time', and in their bitter disappointment they seek to stone him.

In contemporary Judaism the *shammas* is the synagogue verger – the lowliest of community servants. Just as the *shammas* or servant candle gives light to all the others, so Jesus gives light to his people and his church. 'You are the light of the world,' said Jesus in the sermon on the mount. And he follows it with one of those wonderfully funny, absurd pictures of people lighting a lamp and then putting a cover over it. 'Put it on a stand, for goodness' sake,' he says, 'so that everyone can see it, just as your good deeds will reflect the glory of your Father in heaven.'

A Messianic Service of Light[27]

This is a lovely service that can be used:

- By a family, either over the eight nights leading up to Christmas Day, or on one evening before Christmas, possibly on Christmas Eve itself. Just as people put their Christmas trees in the window for everyone to see, the candles can be placed on a window-sill to shine out into the neighbourhood – but watch the curtains!

- By a home group, on one night, as a special informal Christmas service in a home, to which they can invite relatives, neighbours and friends. Have a buffet of special Christmas food from all over the world – a French *buche de Noel* (chocolate log), a German *stollen* cake, and Swedish spicy ginger biscuits. The small French church we attend from time to time does this every year in the local Tourist Office to accompany their carol service. Last year, as a result, two new families were added to the church.

You will need a candelabra with at least nine lights, or a taper and a tray of eight night-lights or candles. You will also need to explain that one candle represents Christ, the Servant, who gives light to his people.

Open the service in darkness.

Leader: Blessed are You, O Lord our God, King of the universe, the source of all light, whose light brightens the deepest darkness.

Light the first candle or taper, and sing 'O Come, O Come Emmanuel'. Tell a relevant story – either the story of Esther saving her people (see below), or the story of the Maccabees, or of some victory of the oppressed over the oppressor.

Leader: As we gather to light these candles, we remember with gratitude and joy the many miracles which God has performed for his people down the genera-tions. In particular, we remember the miraculous way in which he gave victory to _____ against all the political and military odds.
We bless you, Lord, for preserving the light at that time.

All: We bless you, Lord, for preserving the light in every generation.

Leader: We bless you, Lord, for sending Jesus, the Light of the World.

All: Come to us, Lord Emmanuel, and be the light of our lives.

Leader: Give us light to inspire us to do what is right.

All: Give us light to encourage us to make a stand for what is just.

Leader: Give us light to help us know and speak the truth.

All: Give us light to see that neither political power nor military might can help us, but only your Spirit, Lord.

Leader: The Lord is my light and my salvation – whom shall I fear?

The one candle or taper is now passed round, and each person who receives it lights another candle until all eight are lit. The people say the numbered responses below. (If you are planning to use this liturgy over eight nights, simply say (1) on the first night, (2) on the second, and so on.)

(1)   The people walking in darkness have seen a great light.

(2)   The people walking in darkness have seen a great light.
       Arise, shine, for your light has come,
       and the glory of the Lord rises upon you.

(3)   The people walking in darkness have seen a great light.
       Arise, shine, for your light has come,
       and the glory of the Lord rises upon you.

Your word is a lamp to my feet and a light for my path.

(4) The people walking in darkness have seen a great light.
Arise, shine, for your light has come,
and the glory of the Lord rises upon you.
Your word is a lamp to my feet and a light for my path.
Though I have fallen, I will rise.
Though I sit in darkness, the Lord will be my light.

(5) The people walking in darkness have seen a great light.
Arise, shine, for your light has come,
and the glory of the Lord rises upon you.
Your word is a lamp to my feet and a light for my path.
Though I have fallen, I will rise.
Though I sit in darkness, the Lord will be my light.
So let us put aside the deeds of darkness
and put on the armour of light.

(6) The people walking in darkness have seen a great light.
Arise, shine, for your light has come,
and the glory of the Lord rises upon you.
Your word is a lamp to my feet and a light for my path.
Though I have fallen, I will rise.
Though I sit in darkness, the Lord will be my light.
So let us put aside the deeds of darkness
and put on the armour of light.
For God, who said, 'Let light shine out of darkness',
made his light shine in our hearts
to give us the light of the knowledge of the glory of God
in the face of Jesus Christ.

(7) The people walking in darkness have seen a great light.
Arise, shine, for your light has come,
and the glory of the Lord rises upon you.
Your word is a lamp to my feet and a light for my path.
Though I have fallen, I will rise.
Though I sit in darkness, the Lord will be my light.
So let us put aside the deeds of darkness

and put on the armour of light.
For God, who said, 'Let light shine out of darkness',
made his light shine in our hearts
to give us the light of the knowledge of the glory of God
in the face of the Messiah.
For you were once darkness,
but now you are light in the Lord.
Live as children of light.

(8)   The people walking in darkness have seen a great light.
Arise, shine, for your light has come,
and the glory of the Lord rises upon you.
Your word is a lamp to my feet and a light for my path.
Though I have fallen, I will rise.
Though I sit in darkness, the Lord will be my light.
So let us put aside the deeds of darkness
and put on the armour of light.
For God, who said, 'Let light shine out of darkness',
made his light shine in our hearts
to give us the light of the knowledge of the glory of God
in the face of the Messiah.
For you were once darkness,
but now you are light in the Lord.
Live as children of light.
If we walk in the light, as he is in the light,
we have fellowship with one another,
and the blood of Jesus purifies us from all sin.

Refrain: 'O Come, O Come Emmanuel', or sing 'Light of the World, You Stepped Down into Darkness'.

Leader: In the beginning was the Word, and the Word was with God, and the Word was God. He was with God in the beginning. Through him all things were made; without him nothing was made that has been made. In him was life, and that life was the light of men. The light shines in the darkness, but the darkness has not understood it. There came a man who was sent from God; his name was John. He came as a witness to testify concerning that light, so that through him all men might believe. He himself was not the light; he came only as a witness to the light. The true light that gives light to every man was coming into the world. When Jesus spoke again to the people, he said, 'I am the light of the world. Whoever follows me will never walk in darkness, but will have the light of life.'

All: Blessed are you, O Lord our God, King of the universe, who has sent us Jesus, the true Light, who gives light to all.

Children can play a game here with a spinning top. I collected several miniature plastic versions from crackers at the office party. Last Christmas we challenged each other to see who could make them spin the longest. The tradition of playing with a top, or dreidl, originated at the time when the Syrians wouldn't allow the Jews to read the Scriptures, so they kept a top handy in case they were caught in the act and needed to pretend they were playing games.

Leader: Blessed are you, God and Father, for the freedom you give us. And yet, Lord, we so often take this precious gift for granted.

All: We have not thanked you enough.

Leader: We have not been as concerned as you are about our brothers and sisters in parts of the world where they have no such freedom.

All: We have not mourned as you have over the imprisonment, torture and murder of those who have chosen martyrdom rather than deny their faith.

Leader: We confess the weakness of our own witness.

All: We confess that we have not been the lights in the darkness that we were called to be.

Leader: Lord, forgive us, and inspire us to be lights in the dark world around us.

Take the candles to a window facing a street, and put them where they can be seen by any passers-by. If possible, people should move to stand beside them.

Leader: Just as we cannot light the candles except by the light from the servant candle,

All: So we confess that we have no light of our own; we need Jesus' light in our lives.

Leader: Therefore, Lord, as we place these candles in the window to be seen by all around,

All: So we pray that the light of Jesus will shine through our lives and be seen by the whole world.

Leader: Blessed are you, O Lord, the source of all light, whose light brightens the deepest darkness.

All: The Lord is my light and my salvation – whom shall I fear?

Leader: Bless us now, Lord, as we seek to live for you.

All: The Lord is my light and my salvation – whom shall I fear?

Ideas for Advent

Advent boxes

This ingenious idea came from Kate Porteous in Lancaster. I will let her describe how it developed over the years, as her children got older:

Twenty-four small boxes are filled and then individually wrapped and numbered. They can then be strung together to make a decoration and hung against a wall.

Filling the boxes is great fun! I started quite simply and used the figures from a cardboard nativity set, when the children were little. Each day a new figure would be added to the scene, finishing with the baby Jesus on the 24th. (Extra angels and plastic sheep from the farm were added to make 24!) Then I came across 24 mini books that told the Christmas story and these went in the boxes with the appropriate figure. After a couple of years the cardboard figures were getting a bit tatty, so I made up kits out of household junk and craft materials to make each of the figures, and these went in the boxes.

That was the year we started 'no telly during Advent' and instead of switching on the TV after school, we opened the box and made a figure for our nativity. It was such a success that I had to find a way of doing it again the following year, but by then the children were attached to the figures they had made, the pipe-cleaner camels and beautiful doily angels.

Instead of the figure kits I included 'something to do' with a little instruction card. It became a way of getting all the jobs done before Christmas! So there would be:

- glitter and card with the instruction to make cards for relatives and friends,
- sticky paper with the instruction to make paper chains and decorate a room,
- wrapping paper and ribbon with the instruction to wrap their presents,
- Christmas biscuit cutters with the instruction to make biscuits for the school Christmas fair, and so on.

Alongside this we kept the little books and figures so that the Christmas story unfolded during Advent. When Playmobil brought out their nativity figures, they replaced the home-made ones. They even did a little Father Christmas to go in the box on 6 December, St Nicholas' Day!

Now I have to put aside a few hours the weekend before Advent to plan the Advent boxes. Larger 'Christmas tasks' go to weekend days and on busy school nights there might be a Christmas jigsaw, a CD of Christmas music, a pair of Christmas socks or a badge to wear. On one of the first Saturdays in December there is a £20 note in the box with the instruction to go and buy a Christmas tree. If I know the dates in advance, I plan for the various Christmas events; for example, the day before the school Christmas parties, the task in the box will be to make the party hats.

Over the years the contents of the boxes have changed as the children have grown. I have never replaced the little books (Advent boxes wouldn't be the same without them) but I have added the proper Bible readings to read out. Last year only the Bible reference was given in the box and the children had to look it up and then read it out. It gave me the opportunity to put in some of the Old Testament prophecies about the coming of the Messiah. One of my friends is now experimenting with tiny Advent boxes that can be put in the post to university students.

Advent has become a very special time for us as a family. There is great excitement on the evening of 30 November, knowing that in the morning the Advent boxes will be up. Each day we spend some time as a family getting ready for Christmas, and working on the projects draws us together. Each day we hear a little more of the story of the first Christmas, and the older children try and remember which figure will come out that day. (They spend quite a time trying to work out which of them will be opening the present from the first king, as the gold is always accompanied by a gold chocolate coin.) I have had to keep a record of whose turn it is to open number 24; opening the box containing the baby Jesus is very special, even though they know what's inside.

And isn't this what Christmas should be like – full of anticipation? We know the story, but eagerly await the day when we remember how our God took the form of a child and broke into human history.

The Jesse Tree

Isaiah 11:1 says, 'A shoot will spring forth from the stump of Jesse, and a branch out of his roots.' The prophet Zechariah also refers to the Messiah as 'my servant, the branch'. The Jesse Tree is an alternative Advent calendar cum Christmas Tree that vividly communicates the story of God's eternal plan.

To make a Jesse Tree, bring in a large branch from the garden. It must have lots of smaller branches on which to hang decorations. Paint or spray it white or silver, trim it with tiny Christmas lights and fix it in Oasis in a vase or pot, filled with pebbles or scented pot-pourri. Each day throughout Advent encourage children or visitors to make and hang a decoration. Each one, made out of card and decorated with pieces of fabric, buttons or glitter, should represent the Old Testament names for the coming Messiah. There is 'Prince of Peace', 'King of Kings', 'light', 'star' – and so many more.

An Advent wreath

This is the more traditional approach. Buy a circular piece of florist's Oasis with a hole in the middle. Place four purple or red, long, fairly thin (so that they can be pushed into the Oasis) candles evenly around the wreath. Fill in the gaps with holly, ivy or any other greenery. I use some very good silk alternatives – with a few plastic apples and imitation birds. In the middle of the wreath place a large, fat, white candle – the special Christmas candle.

Each Sunday before Advent, at the main meal of the day, one more candle is lit. Here is a simple liturgy, adapted from one created by the Mothers' Union in Australia, which may help:

An Advent wreath service[28]

First Sunday of Advent: the candle of hope

Child: What will we find at the stable in Bethlehem?

Parent: We will find HOPE. We will not be able to see it, but we know that Jesus is the hope of the world – the hope of new beginnings, and we look forward in hope to the time when he will come again and there will be a new heaven and a new earth.

We light this candle of hope as a sign that we trust in the hope that will be there in the manger. Jesus is the light who shines in the darkness, and the darkness cannot extinguish that light.

Second Sunday of Advent: the candle of light

Child: What will we find at the stable in Bethlehem?

Parent: We will find hope (light the first candle) and we will also find LIGHT. We may not be able to see it, but Jesus is the light of the world – He will show us the right way to live our lives, until he comes back in glory.

We light this candle of light as a sign that the light of God has come into the world, praying that we may follow that light and see clearly the way we should live. Jesus is the light who shines in the darkness, and the darkness cannot extinguish that light.

Third Sunday of Advent: the candle of love

Child: What will we find at the stable in Bethlehem?

Parent: We will find hope (light the first candle), and we will find light (light the second candle), and we will find LOVE. We will not be able to see it, but we know that God so loved the world that he sent his only Son to rescue us. Jesus is love, and can show us how to love one another.

We light this candle of love, trusting that the love of Jesus will fill the whole world and asking that we may share it with everyone we meet. Jesus is the light who shines in the darkness and the darkness cannot extinguish that light.

Fourth Sunday of Advent: the candle of joy

Child: What will we find at the stable in Bethlehem?

Parent: We will find hope (light the first candle), and we will find light (light the second candle), and we will find love (light the third candle), and we will find JOY. We will not be able to see it, but we know that in God's presence there is nothing but joy. Jesus radiates that special joy to us, and one day there will be perfect joy when he comes again.

We light this candle of joy, trusting that the joy of Jesus will spread from us to everyone we know. Jesus is the light who shines in the darkness and the darkness cannot extinguish that light.

Christmas Day: the fifth candle
Child: What special thing will we find at the stable in Bethlehem today?

Parent: Today we will find Jesus lying in the manger. We can now see the hope (light the first candle), we can now see the light (light the second candle), we can now see the love (light the third candle), and we can now see the joy (light the fourth candle) in this baby, because Jesus is our hope, our light, our love and our joy.

God has come to earth as one of us, a human being, and we must help to build his kingdom, and bring hope, light, love, joy and peace to the world.

Together: Jesus is the light who shines in the darkness and the darkness cannot extinguish that light.
We light this Christmas candle.
May the hope of Jesus encourage us.
May the light of Jesus shine on us.
May the love of Jesus touch us.
May the joy of Jesus fill us.
And may we help to bring peace to this world.

An Advent Candle Service[29]

First Week of Advent
Scripture reading: Isaiah 9:7.

As the first candle is lit say: I light this candle in memory of God's promise to send a leader who will deliver all people from oppression and injustice.

Sing: First verse of 'O come, O come Emmanuel'.

Second Week of Advent
Scripture reading: Isaiah 40:1–5; 43:13.

Light the first candle, repeating what was said the previous week.

As the second candle is lit say: I light this candle in memory of God's promise to send a Comforter and a Saviour.

Sing: First two verses of 'O come, O come Emmanuel'.

Third Week of Advent
Scripture reading: John 1:1–5; 8:12.

Light the first two candles, repeating the text said for each.

As the third candle is lit say: I light this candle for Jesus Christ, who is the light of the world.

Sing: First three verses of 'O come, O come Emmanuel'.

Fourth Week of Advent
Scripture: Luke 1:26–33.

Light the first three candles, repeating the text said on previous weeks for each.

As the fourth candle is lit say: I light this candle for Jesus Christ, whose kingdom will have no end.

Sing: First four verses of 'O come, O come Emmanuel'.

Christmas Day
Scripture: Luke 2:1–20.

Light the first four candles, repeating the text said on previous weeks for each.

As the Christmas candle is lit say: I light this candle for Jesus Christ, who was born in a lowly stable.

Sing: First verse of 'O come all ye faithful'.

Other ideas for Advent and Christmas

- Decorate the house little by little, possibly more each Advent Sunday. Build the nativity scene gradually, leaving Jesus until Christmas Eve.

- At *Hannukah* children are given one present every night, rather than an entire sack or stocking on the one day. This is one way of avoiding a sickly surfeit of materialism.

- Use sparklers as a symbol of light in the darkness. Write your hopes and prayers in the air with them.

- Have a Christmas Day treasure hunt. (Admittedly, this suggestion came from South Africa, where it is full summer.)

Judith and Julian Campbell, who are heavily involved in their church at Christmas, suggested having a full Christmas dinner on Christmas Eve, with lamb rather than turkey, 'providing us with an opportunity to talk about the Lamb of God.' Dinner lasts two to three hours and no TV is allowed. After it is over the youngest child places Jesus in the family crib and the musical instruments come out. Each child receives a Christmas tree ornament that is theirs to keep – they will have a full set when they leave home, as a reminder of their family life together. The evening finishes with a Christmas story around the fire.

On Christmas Day before church, dad and the older children make pasta for the evening meal and hang it to dry on a clothes-rack. (Have a look at the celebration cannelloni recipe in the last section.) The sauce is already in the freezer. The pizza dough (for lunch) goes in the bread-maker before leaving for church and is ready when they get back. Each child or visitor chooses their own lunchtime pizza topping. Everyone shares in making both meals, creating a real sense of team spirit and thankfulness.

Christmas Day doesn't have to follow any rules!

Ideas for New Year's Eve

- Have a party with a difference, where there is a chance for everyone to give a short overview of their past year, and share their hopes, dreams and prayers for the coming year. Use the New Year liturgy on page 113 if it seems appropriate.

- As a family, share a record of the past year – in videotape, photographs, a scrapbook, or in any special symbols that have been collected.

Ideas for New Year's Day

- Treat your family or home group to a sumptuous brunch – eggs Benedict (poached eggs on a bed of steamed spinach, smothered in cheese sauce), pancakes served the American way with maple syrup, blueberries and crispy bacon, fish kedgeree (see the recipe in the final section of the book), and croissants
- Take a New Year walk. Find stones, or flowers that can be pressed, to keep and share the following New Year's Eve.

An Epiphany Idea

In the Coptic Church in Egypt, Christmas is celebrated on 6 and 7 January – Epiphany, the day designated as the visit of the Magi to the stable at Bethlehem. Churches are decorated with special lamps and candles, representing the candles Joseph used to protect Mary the night that Jesus was born. Coptic Christians go to the church for midnight mass on 6 January and eat their Christmas dinner when they get home.

The story of the visit by the Gentile Magi, recounted by Matthew the Jew, is an example of the fulfilment of God's promise to Abraham – that all the nations would be blessed through him.

Over Epiphany Sunday lunch, write down as many biblical promises as you can remember. Divide them into columns – those that have been fulfilled, and those that still await their fulfilment. There are more than you could ever imagine.

Valentine's Day ideas

Valentine's Day may well appear to be a pagan festival, but it is now so accepted in the West that it can be given spiritual significance. After all, Valentine was a Roman who was killed for refusing to give up his Christian faith. He died on 14 February 269, a day devoted to love lotteries. Legend also has it that he left a farewell note for the jailer's daughter, who had become his friend, signing it, 'From Your Valentine'. He was canonized in 496 and gradually St Valentine became the patron saint of lovers everywhere.

- Design a special love card for each member of the family, filled with words of encouragement and affirmation.

- Create a red-heart mobile. To make the mobile, cut out a number of red hearts and write on each, 'Jesus loves' with the name of the family member or friend. Each heart also has a 'love' text from the Bible, which the respective person reads out over dinner in the evening.

- Hold a home-group celebration of marital romance and commitment. If the children are old enough, get them to cook dinner for several couples and serve it by candlelight. Alternatively, buy it from a good, upmarket store and share the costs. Have some smooth music available for smoochy dancing afterwards.

The Feast of Esther

There is nothing like a communal letting-your-hair-down every once in a while. It's such an antidote to the sober, stressful, grown-up world most of us are forced to inhabit in our working lives. The Jews do it in March at the Feast of Esther, or *Purim*,[30] which celebrates the way an evil genocide was foiled by the courage of a little Jewish girl who became Queen of Persia. It's an occasion for total mayhem – both in the synagogue and out of it. But I can't think of a single contemporary Christian equivalent, certainly not one that encourages this kind of boisterousness in church. That's why it's worth taking a quick look at this colourful festival to see what ideas Christians can appropriate and use to enhance our own celebrations.

Interactive story-telling

The tale of Esther is a cliff-hanger, full of court intrigue, deception, miscommunication, drunken parties, assassination plots, a foolish king, a delinquent queen, a villain, and a beautiful heroine. And some people think the Old Testament is dull?

Anyone who stands outside the synagogue at *Purim* and listens in could be forgiven for thinking they have come to a football match. As the familiar story is read aloud, the children clap and cheer for Mordecai, the hero, and for Esther, his adopted daughter, and hiss and boo and stamp their feet whenever that villain Haman's name is mentioned. They wave rattles and blow any instrument or home-made contraption that will make a rude belching sound. It's about the only time the congregation hangs on the Rabbi's every word. It would be wonderful to see this kind of congregational participation in church – every once in a while at least. We can take ourselves far too seriously.

Interactive story-telling engages an audience. It makes the point memorable. It can be used to great effect on virtually any occasion, but especially if it involves a great deal of noise, for example at Pentecost, when there is the roar of wind, worship in every language, laughter and commotion. The parables, Paul's shipwreck, the Book of Revelation, the stories in Genesis such as Noah's Ark, all lend themselves to this technique. Bob Hartman has published several books full of ideas that he is happy for people to use, but it isn't difficult to make up your own.

Musical instrument accompaniment

Make your own musical instruments. Fill empty tins, jamjars or boxes with small bells or pulses such as chick-peas or lentils. Different-sized pulses will make different sounds – so you could end up with the entire percussion section of a band. Experiment and see how many ordinary household items have the potential to make music. Every Sabbath our children loved to see how many notes they could get by tapping a kitchen knife against glasses containing different quantities of water.

Fancy dress and carnival

Esther's story is very satisfying. Haman is hanged on his own gallows. Wickedness is turned on its head. The joy of it spills out onto the streets – in carnivals and masquerades that may owe more to the Catholic tradition of Mardi Gras than to the Old Testament. Children and adults wear fancy dress, funny costumes, or masks. They perform plays and pantomimes – rather like the tradition for nativity plays, only children end up playing bloodthirsty Persian soldiers with swords, rather than benign little angels with wings. There is inevitably a huge, celebratory meal, and the wine can flow a little too freely. Food baskets are taken to anyone who can't afford a celebration. The joy of *Purim* is so great that the sages say it will be celebrated throughout the Messianic era.

Ever since medieval times, people have enjoyed dramatic re-enactments of Bible stories. The York Mystery Plays were hugely significant in my own understanding of faith. Have a fete or festival in your local community where everyone dresses up as a well-known or little-known Bible character. All Saints' Day is one possibility. If full fancy dress proves too stretching, try simply making a mask to represent that character. One year, during Christmas week, one or two members of the congregation put on a 'pantivity' – a hilarious conglomeration of some of the misconceptions people have about the Christmas story. It was very salutary for visitors to see us laughing at ourselves.

- If children are present, begin home group with charades – where people have to improvise a mime based on a Bible story or character, while the rest guess who it is.

- Make simple masks and act out a Bible story.

- If you have the time and the inclination, lay on a grand carnival or pageant for your community. Easter is the ideal time. We have twice staged an Easter pageant in Lancaster. It takes a huge amount of time and commitment, and needs generous funding. It is imperative to have an excellent sound system, so that everyone can hear what's happening. Anyone who has ever taken the risk of staging such an event says it can be a bit of a nightmare, but well worth it in the end.

Writing in *The Guardian*, Theo Hobson laid down this challenge for the church:

Our Christian culture...needs to learn from the boom in festival culture. The popularity of festivals and carnivals is one of the most important trends of the last decade... More and more of us want to attend events with a carnival feel. It's as if we have discovered that we are party animals; we yearn to join a crowd that is celebrating. Christian culture must learn from this. Christianity is meant to be a religion of celebration.

We should celebrate Easter...and by celebrate I do not mean a few songs and smiles at church and then back home to watch the golf. I mean something that our wider culture notices. Christians ought to venture out from their stony shells and stage a public demonstration. Their event ought to put pagan carnivals in the shade: larger, noisier, more unpredictable and dangerous...where there will be drumming, dancing and parades. Let's have two million of you out there.[31]

Useful books

Bob Hartman, *Anyone Can Tell a Story: Bob Hartman's Guide to Storytelling*, Lion Hudson, 2002

Bob Hartman, *The Lion Storyteller Christmas Book*, Lion Hudson

Bob Hartman, *Telling the Bible*, Monarch, 2006

Spring

It took me a long time to discover Easter. I am always amazed that the death and resurrection of Christ often seems to pass Christians by with the barest acknowledgment, when it seems the one festival we should celebrate above all others. But for many years the churches we attended appeared ambivalent about it, uncomfortable with the welter of pagan bunnies and chickens in the world around them. Better to keep our Christian heads down. What recognition there was – an extra service on Good Friday, some rousing hymns on Easter Sunday – certainly didn't put it in the Christmas league.

As a Jew, Lent always left me cold – once the pancakes were eaten. My schoolfriends all gave up chocolate, and I just couldn't see the point. It didn't appear to make them any nicer, or have any other reasonable purpose. Once I became a Christian I can't say I was much the wiser. And I was continually amazed at how much of the Easter story was lost without an understanding of Passover. Now, however, the whole Easter season is the richest time in my spiritual life.

The seeds of what our Easter is now were sown when Peter became vicar of a church in Coventry that maintained several throwbacks from its Anglo-Catholic past, such as early meditations and communal breakfasts every morning of Holy Week. To my amazement, the children, aged eight and five, leapt out of bed and shot past me into church as I left for work at 8 a.m. It took me a while to realize the main attraction was cornflakes and white toast – mother denying such treats in the name of wholemeal healthiness. But church members loved their presence at breakfast, and this access to full membership of the community made Holy Week special for them.

We suggested a Passover meal, explaining that Easter would benefit from putting it into its historic context. The Passover, celebrating that moment when God intervenes and rescues his people from slavery, heralds Easter as the great freedom festival. 'I will bring you out', 'I will free you', 'I will redeem you', 'I will take you as my people', say the four symbolic cups of wine, drunk during a long service that tells the story of how God reveals his extraordinary love and longing for his people. It had a particularly poignant significance at the Last Supper, where Jesus called his disciples his friends and underlined the purpose of their relationship. This was his last opportunity to explain that he was the fulfilment of Messianic history, the ultimate sacrificial lamb. On this occasion, familiar symbolism became a set of audio-visual aids that would vividly make the point, year after year, every time the Passover was celebrated.

But the idea of having a Passover wasn't universally welcomed. A party? On the night the altar was stripped? A quiet Communion was far more appropriate. This ancient Christian ritual involved removing every decoration from the front of the church – flowers, tapestries, banners, any gold or silver ornaments – until all that remained, for the night-long vigil into Good Friday, was a solitary wooden cross. It was an important tradition, so we worked out a compromise.

That first Passover was a wonderful occasion, culminating in a magnificent candle-lit, bring-and-share supper beneath the roof-beams of the church in an area that was already conveniently called 'the upper room'. At the end of the evening, Peter explained that Jesus went out from this last party into the loneliness of Gethsemane to prepare for the heart-rending task of buying our eternal freedom. We walked down the stairs in complete silence and went into a darkened church. There stood a solitary, rough-hewn cross, illuminated by a single candle. Bleary-eyed children, who, a moment earlier, were slouched sleepily against parents, walked up to it, wide-eyed, as if they were seeing it for the first time, and, without a word, knelt. Adults sat motionless in the pews. The intense, profound silence, after so much noise, drove home the overwhelming desolation of Jesus, who, having said his goodbyes, now faced the cross alone. What started as compromise became a profoundly enriching experience as two great traditions were woven together.

When we moved to Lancaster, Peter introduced Holy Week meditations, morning and evening. I still told myself that going out to work meant I couldn't manage that commitment. What I meant was I couldn't get out of bed. But in the last few years, as colleagues have helped us establish a whole Easter experience, I began to realize that missing any part of it was my loss.

Two years ago, Sam, the Curate, introduced an intensive prayer rota throughout Lent in a small, specially decorated room, where children, juvenile geriatrics and all in between prayed alone or in groups, accompanied by Gospel Heavy Metal or Albinoni, whichever they chose, writing their heartaches, intercessions, visions and aspirations in graffiti on walls specially covered with paper for that purpose.

A team of volunteers from the congregation designed and led the morning and evening meditations. Some had never done it before. A hallowed space was created within the church, using black material, spotlights, and a few simple symbols such as a rough cross, hung with coloured pieces of fabric that were changed every day. Visual images were projected onto a white sheet, and classical music played quietly in the background. Each day of Holy Week I was taken a little further on my journey with Christ to the cross.

We moved Passover to the Wednesday evening, to avoid disturbing a more creative Maundy Thursday Communion, sometimes accompanied by footwashing. With the help of Debbie, our Assistant Vicar, Good Friday was transformed. The outer aisles of the church were divided into small 'prayer stations' by using black drapes to separate them into sections, each centring around the symbol or picture that was a theme in one of the meditations earlier in the week. During an hour or so of quiet reflection, people were free to wander from one to another. Then the drapes were removed and everyone gathered together in the centre for readings, reflections and monologues around the cross.

The year before last I finally made it to every meditation. The Good Friday service culminated with John 14:1–3: 'Trust in God, trust also in me. In my father's house are many rooms... I am going there to prepare a place for you...and take you to be with me that you also may be where I am.' Karl Jenkins' 'Sanctus' from *The Armed Man* was playing quietly in the background. Suddenly, I began to sob as if my heart would break – with a sorrow way beyond anything my mind could comprehend. I felt I was having a glimpse into the love of Christ for his disciples as I had never understood it before. I realized that up to that moment I had always fastened on his irritation. 'Get thee behind me, Satan', or 'How long have I to bear with you?' I had never seen those words from John's Gospel in the context of his last, tender farewell, or understood his immense sorrow at separation, and his pain at the bereavement and desolation his friends would feel. Of course he tried to prepare and comfort them.

Afterwards a dozen or so folk came back to our house for coffee and hot-cross buns – and every now and then I was caught, mid-mouthful, by an unexpected sob. My make-up was wrecked for the rest of the day.

By Easter Sunday, most of us are so emotionally wrung out that we're ready to let rip. At home, we decorate the sitting room and dining room after the children (no matter how big) have gone to bed. Everyone awakens to real coffee, hot croissants and the 'Hallelujah Chorus' blasted out through the house. In church we have experimented with blazing torches brought from the sunrise ecumenical event on a hill overlooking the city, tombs fronted with huge, rollaway, cardboard stone fronts, and helium-filled balloons that we let loose after the service. The sky is certainly the limit. And one thing I do know – this long commemoration of the most important event in the church's calendar makes Christmas pale by comparison.

Ideas for Lent

Shrove Tuesday

Shrove Tuesday is the last day before Lent. 'Shrove' comes from the old word 'shrive' which means 'to confess', because in the Middle Ages people used to confess their sins and receive absolution before the season of Lent began. But just as the Jews have a huge meal before the Day of Atonement to help them survive the fast, Shrove Tuesday was seen as a last chance for self-indulgence before the days of abstinence. Pancakes are supposed to use up the last remaining luxuries of fat, butter and eggs.

For French Catholics the day was known as Mardi Gras or 'Fat Tuesday', and was celebrated with a carnival. 'Carnival' comes from the Latin word meaning 'farewell to meat or flesh', and what probably started as a pre-Christian festival has now become a huge festival in post-Christian New Orleans in the USA.

- Have a pancake party with a difference. Use it as an opportunity for each person to share how they intend to make the most of Lent and prepare for Easter. Giving to the poor, acts of justice and mercy, are an essential part of any fast, so discuss how that can be done individually and as a group over the next forty days.

Ash Wednesday

Ash Wednesday is the first day of Lent. In many churches the priest burns the palm crosses kept from the previous year, then mixes the ashes with holy water to make a greyish paste. He then dips his thumb in the paste and smudges a cross on the forehead of everyone present at the Ash Wednesday service, as a sign of their identification in the suffering of Christ.

> • In a small group take a few minutes to meditate on what it means to
>   you to take up your cross and follow Christ. Then mark a cross on each
>   other's forehead, palms or feet, whichever they choose. Seal it by hold-
>   ing hands and saying, 'Today I receive the mark of the cross, a sign that
>   I want to serve my fellow human beings as Christ did.' The mark can
>   be washed off, but leaving it to fade naturally will give everyone a
>   chance to consider how they will keep this promise.[32]

The Hebraic time of penitence is the ten days between the New Year and the Day of Atonement, but since the fourth century Christians have always opted for Lent. Lent comes from the Middle English word *lente* or 'springtime', and can be seen to parallel Jesus' forty days in the wilderness following his baptism. As the Protestant Reformation spread, Lent was dismissed as a Roman Catholic institution, but today many people still adhere to some aspect of it, even if they're not sure why.

There is an essential difference between the Jewish Days of Awe and Lent, highlighting the dangers of a tendency to asceticism. Hebraic penitence looks for positive things to do, while Christians look at what they can give up. Putting relationships right benefits the community, but mortifying the poor old body benefits the individual. The Jewish attitude to religion in general is corporate and communal, while the Christian attitude tends to be private and personal, and that has led to a basic misunderstanding about the nature of fasting. Giving up chocolate, or cake, or alcohol, or sweets for Lent can be a useful spiritual dis-cipline, as long as it isn't done for the sake of it, or to lose weight, or as a sub-stitute for treating the family and the community with consideration. Real fasting, said the prophet Isaiah, is about actively fighting injustice, caring for the poor, behaving with integrity. That's why I warm to this Lent Love Project for any family or home group.

A Lent Love Project [33]

As a family or a home group, why not adopt a 'Love Project' for each of the six weeks leading up to Easter? Sometimes relationships can be a bit strained. Sometimes people don't know or realize how much they are appreciated. This is why the practical Lent Love Project, which is essentially a Mennonite idea, can be so enriching.

Week 1: 'The Hand of Love'

Write a letter to someone saying how much you appreciate them. This is far less ephemeral than an email, that can be easily or accidentally deleted.

Week 2: 'The Voice of Love'

Telephone someone each night with the express idea of encouraging them, thanking them, or expressing your appreciation.

Week 3: 'The Feet of Love'

Take a very simple gift, possibly hand-made, or some seasonal hand-picked flowers, to two or three people who would particularly benefit from the encouragement.

Week 4: 'The Heart of Love'

Make a list of around five people, friends and enemies, you want to pray for daily. Forgive them if they have wronged you. Ask their forgiveness if you know you have upset them.

Week 5: 'The Mind of Love'

Use this week to reflect on where you feel you are at. Praise God for his love, whether you are in the heights or the depths. Let go of those who annoy or frustrate you, and try to laugh at their foibles.

Week 6: 'A Life of Love'

Get outdoors if you can, enjoy a walk with friends and share God's new life in creation. As a treat, take friends, or someone younger, on an outing to a concert, museum, exhibition, or the theatre and give thanks for the creativity God has shared with human beings.

A Lenten prayer space

To emphasize the Lenten concept of 'turning aside', create a special space for prayer and reflection (it can be just part of a room). It will need to be a restful place where people of all ages can find peace and quiet, as well as a variety of resources to help them concentrate. Cover at least one of the walls in lining paper to create a large graffiti area where people can write out their prayers and comments. You can include:

- rugs and scatter cushions
- at least one comfortable armchair for older folk
- a CD player with a wide variety of CDs – classical, rock gospel, hymns
- candles and matches
- a cross
- songbooks
- Bibles
- children's storybooks
- paper, pens and coloured crayons
- Blu Tak, drawing-pins and sticky tape
- testimony books where people can write down what they believe God is saying to them
- string, stones, shells and other potential symbols
- a map of the world and one of the local neighbourhood

Provide a selection of meditations. These books are a useful start:

- Henri J. M. Nouwen, *Show me the Way: Readings for Each Day of Lent*, Darton, Longman & Todd
- Vanessa Herrick, *Take Up Your Cross: Daily Readings for Lent*, Darton, Longman & Todd
- Robert Warren and Sue Mayfield, *Life Balance – A Five Session Course on Rest, Work and Play for Lent*, Church House Publishing
- Students of Ridley Hall Theological College, Cambridge, *I Desire Justice – Daily reflections from Ash Wednesday to Easter Day*, SCM–Canterbury Press

- Neil Paynter (ed.), *Iona Dawn: Through Holy Week with the Iona Community*, Wild Goose Publications
- John Pritchard, *Living Easter Through the Year*, SPCK

Lenten fasting and abstaining (see 'A Time of Repentance' in the Autumn section, p. 116)

If you are abstaining from food, remember that the command to rejoice on your festival supersedes it, so if someone is celebrating a birthday or you take Mother out for dinner on her day, you may, in fact should, accept cake, chocolate, alcohol, or whatever you have given up for Lent, on that occasion.

Mothering Sunday

Mothering Sunday was originally known as 'Refreshment Sunday' because the fasting rules for Lent were relaxed in honour of the feeding of the five thousand.

The idea of Mothering Sunday probably began about 400 years ago when, on Refreshment Sunday, village folk made a point of going not to their local church but to the nearest big or 'mother' church, and were said to have gone 'a-mothering'. Gradually it became a tradition for young English girls and boys 'in service' to be given this one day every year to bake a cake and take it home for mother. The favourite was simnel cake – a fruit cake covered in marzipan. The 'Guinness fruit cake' in the recipe section of this book should do just as well if you're treating Mother to afternoon tea. Although, if you can afford it, she may prefer to be taken out!

Ideas for Holy Week

With the will and a little imagination, the week leading up to Good Friday and Easter Day can be a very special time for families and small neighbourhood groups. The Passover service can be used for the whole church, or shortened for home groups and families.

Holy Week reflections for small groups

- Encourage a small group to meet every night for just an hour. If the children are older, they may enjoy participating in this preparation for Easter.
- Darken the room and light it with a single spotlight or candle.
- Choose some quiet, reflective background music and play it as people arrive, to start the session, and during the session if you wish.
- Choose a theme that can be divided into five or six segments, and short Bible readings for each. Invite a different person to lead a meditation each night, bringing their own prayers and reflections to share.
- Create a visual focal point with a cross or some other symbols. You can also drape the cross with different coloured fabrics each night, or hang different symbols on it to match the theme.
- Try to maintain silence, other than having the meditation, throughout. It's amazing how deeply you will in fact communicate with each other.

Possible themes include:

- The head, eyes, hands, feet, heart of Jesus.
- The stages of his journey to the cross.
- Aspects of his last conversation with his disciples in John's Gospel (John 13–17).
- The crucifixion story told by several different witnesses.
- Readings from men and women who have walked the way of the cross: Amy Carmichael, Brother Roger, Henri Nouwen, Corrie Ten Boom, Dietrich Bonhoeffer, Mother Theresa, Martin Luther King.
- The books listed under 'A Lenten prayer space' above may provide food for thought.
- Follow a Holy Week book.

An alternative would be to share breakfast and a short meditation every morning of Holy Week. It may or may not be appropriate to invite children. If a home is being used, they could join in the meal.

Passover (See Haggadah Appendix)

The Passover should be shared as a celebration rather than done as a demonstration.

Jesus said he was really looking forward to this one last party with his disciples. It is a time for storytelling, laughter, jokes, singing and eating. At our church we manage a *hora* or two round the room, since Miriam led the people in a dance of joy after the Red Sea parted, but dancing at Passover is not essential. As a living demonstration of how the sacred and secular can be integrated fully, the service works brilliantly in churches, home groups or families, and really does involve and engage children. Don't open or close in prayer. The whole evening is an integrated act of worship.

It is possible to do a greatly reduced version for smaller groups or families. Simply use the four questions and the reply, the four cups and the major symbols (unleavened bread, and bitter herbs).

Maundy Thursday

At that final supper Jesus took a bowl of water and a towel and began to wash his disciples' feet. At a time when feet were dusty, it was a common courtesy for a servant to wash the guests' feet when they arrived at someone's home. (Today's equivalent would probably be their car.) This particular act of Jesus is remembered in many churches during a Maundy Thursday Communion. Rather than having a Passover service, you may prefer to celebrate Jesus' last meal with his friends in this simpler way:

For home groups

Lay out cushions or chairs in a circle in a room. Spread a cloth in the centre and place bread and wine, and a lit candle in the middle. Turn down the lights and have music playing quietly in the background. Fill a bowl with water and add some drops of essential oil. Lavender is very soothing. Read the story of how Jesus washed the disciples' feet, then round the circle, in turn, gently wash each other's hands or feet, or instead, massage them with a little neat essential oil. Then share the bread and wine, saying some simple words of offering as you pass them round, such as, 'The body of Jesus Christ, our Passover Lamb, given for you, to make you whole', and 'The blood of Jesus Christ, keep you in eternal life'.

For churches

In the Anglican Church it is traditional to renew baptismal vows during the Maundy Thursday service. At the end of the service, the minister and leaders of the church form a tunnel. The congregation is invited to walk through the tunnel, one at a time, receiving the laying on of hands or anointing with oil for rededication from each member of 'the tunnel'. It is then the turn of members of the congregation to form a tunnel, so that ministers and leaders can receive prayer and ministry too.

Good Friday

1. Create a giant-sized Easter garden in a corner of your home, using scrunched-up green crepe paper, branches and twigs, pebbles, flowers etc. Tell the story of the crucifixion and make sure you leave Jesus in the tomb.

2. Make unleavened bread:

- 200g/8oz pl flour,
- half a teaspoon of salt
- 142ml/5fl oz water

Combine the ingredients. Knead the dough well, then cover and allow it to sit for 30 minutes. Cut off pieces of dough a little larger than the size of your thumb. Sprinkle flour on the counter and roll the small pieces of dough into 20cm/8in discs. Place the discs of bread on well-oiled baking sheets, prick all over with a fork, then bake at gas mark 5/190°C for 20 minutes or so until golden. Your bread will look more like chapatties than the unleavened bread you can buy in boxes – but take heart, it's probably more authentic.

3. Tell the Good Friday story, dramatizing the events. The great storm and the emptying of the graves always goes down well!

4. Tell the stories of some of the characters who might have been involved in the Good Friday story. Each person present could be one of those characters, and write a monologue, describing the event. Discuss how they might have felt as events unfurled:

- Martha and Mary
- Mary, the mother of Jesus

- The centurion
- Pilate (or his wife)
- The thief on the cross
- Barabbas
- John, Thomas or any other of the disciples
- Mary Magdalen

These two monologues were written by the Revd Debbie Peatman, Assistant Vicar of St Thomas, Lancaster. They are an excellent example of how powerful imaginative story-telling can be and how well it can work during Holy Week.

Miriam's story

I couldn't wait to get to Jerusalem. Couldn't wait to be part of this crowd; to feel the heat, the excitement, the thrill of it all. To be here for Passover – the years I've longed for it! The years I've wept as the village has emptied itself and I've been left with the silence. There's been no Passover for me this last eighteen years; no celebration of freedom, no glimpse of the Promised Land. Just an excruciating ache running up and down my spine like a sword, and an ache in my heart to match.

It was just after Reuben died that it started. Maybe there's a connection, maybe there isn't, I don't know. I know that part of me died when he did; that's certainly true. He was everything to me. My beautiful strong boy, so tall, so good looking! I used to love just watching him. I couldn't believe my body had given birth to something so perfect. And when he died...it was as if someone, something just hollowed me out and bent me over. For weeks, all I wanted to do was curl up, curl over on myself, curl round this awful aching hole in my belly. And then I found it was all I *could* do. In a few short weeks I turned from a woman in the prime of her life to a dried-up bent old hag. I could hardly hobble to the synagogue, let alone make the trek to Jerusalem every year. And so for eighteen years, Passover has passed me by. Until this year, that is.

It all started a few months ago – is it really only a few months? I arrived at the synagogue and there was all this fuss going on – everyone talking about this Jesus, some prophet from Nazareth who was staying in the village. Can't say I was very bothered, really. It's hard to get excited about much when all you can see is the floor. I was just bracing myself to get down into my seat, when it happened. This voice – this amazing voice – called out my name. 'Miriam!' I froze. Nobody calls my name like that any more. Nobody even talks to me unless they have to. 'Miriam, don't sit down. Come here, to me.' And I must have gone – I don't know how, I just followed the voice until I knew I was standing in front of him. He bent down and looked into my face. So long since anyone has done that! He had a look of Reuben about him, that same kind smile... 'It's all right,' he said, 'it's all right. You're free now.' And then he touched me. I thought, I'm going to cry, I'm going to cry, and this great sob welled up inside me until I couldn't hold it any longer and it exploded through my body and...it pushed me straight. Straight as I am now. No pain, no crushing pain on my back and my shoulders any more. Just tears, and laughter, and freedom.

So I couldn't wait to get to Jerusalem this year. To join the crowds. And the joy when he rode into the city! I threw my cloak in his path and I shouted 'Hosanna!' till I had no voice left. Something amazing was about to happen. I just knew it. I followed him every day to the Temple. I wanted to find a chance to thank him for what he'd done, for giving me my life back, but there was always a crowd round him and the moment never seemed right. Anyway, words weren't enough; I wanted to do something. So I took my little purse with all my savings in and dropped it all into the treasury. Not that he even saw me; but somehow that didn't matter. I knew and God knew. And then I waited.

I can't believe that this was what I waited for. I can't believe that we could do this to him. I can't bear to see his strong straight back crushed under that hideous thing, as bent as mine used to be. And now it's me calling out his name, but he can't come to me; and I can't look into his face and my love can't make him free; and I can't touch him. I wish I could touch him. I wish Reuben was here. Oh God, I hope his mother isn't here to see this.

Joseph of Arimathea's story

I don't know what to do. I really don't. I can't believe that this is happening. I can't believe that one night can turn everything upside down.

I trusted Caiaphas. He couldn't stand Jesus, of course, I knew that. And it grieved me. But I hadn't given up hope that, in the end, he would get down off his high horse and give Jesus a hearing. Because, I thought, he was basically a good man, a just man. I was proud to be a part of the Council under his leadership.

I'm not proud now. It was just before dawn when they came and dragged me out of my bed – emergency meeting of the Council, they said, you've got to come at once. They hardly even gave me time to dress. I felt like I was the one under arrest – I was bewildered, my wife was distressed, it was like some horrible torchlit nightmare. Little did I know that the nightmare was only just beginning. I still don't know what shocked me more – seeing Jesus so bruised and beaten and – small, somehow; or seeing Caiaphas' face so distorted with lust and hate. It was hideous. I still don't know the full story of what went on through the night, but I know that by the time I got there any facade of a fair trial had long since been dropped. It was just torture and humiliation, just for fun, just for the hell of it. And the one I have trusted as a father looking drunk with the pleasure of it all.

What could I have said, what could I have done? I don't know. But it torments me that I did nothing. I did nothing today – I just watched as they tied him up and led him out like an animal. And I did nothing weeks ago, months ago, when I should have seen all this coming. Nicodemus and I have talked – oh, how we've talked – about whether we should take a stand in the Council. Whether we should make it clear that we believed this Jesus was the One; whether we should at least try to make them give him a fair hearing. But we're not men who rock the boat, either of us. We decided to hang on and play the long game. What we didn't realize was how fast the clock was ticking. Suddenly the game's over, and it's too late to do anything.

Oh God, Joseph of Arimathea, what have you become! The man who stands by and does nothing. The man who is too afraid to open his mouth. The man who wants to stay safely lost in the crowd. But the crowd has become a crowd of monsters, and there is no safe place to hide any more. Oh Jesus. I cannot bear to look at you and think that I did nothing.

There is still one thing that I could do. I never dared to ask you to my home, Jesus – too afraid of what others would say to let you under my roof. But perhaps it isn't too late. My tomb – it's a beautiful one, I paid a great deal for it – in the most lovely garden, just minutes away. Would you rest there, Jesus? Would you let me do now what I should have done long ago?

I will ask Pilate for you when this is all over, and I will wash you and anoint you and see you laid to rest. Is it risky? Oh yes. Do I care? Not any more. If this now is the only thing I do, I will ask you to take my place in death. And I pray God will have mercy on my soul.

Easter Day

- Take Jesus out of the tomb overnight when any children are in bed and hide him! They can hunt for him in the morning.

- Decorate the house – it can be expensive to use fresh flowers, so have just a few in key places, while the rest could be made of fabric or paper and taken out from year to year. Use yellow and green ribbons, streamers, balloons.

- Have a communal breakfast (Use the Kedgeree (p. 218) or muesli (p. 233) recipes at the end of the book.

- After the main meal, hold an Easter egg hunt – mini eggs hidden with a Bible verse on each.

- Make Easter baskets – one for each person. Line each basket with moss, and fill them with small goodies the night before. Hide them somewhere in the house, to be found after Easter breakfast or dinner.

Useful websites

www.lifewords.info/easter/ for the liturgy for a 'Tenebrae service'. Traditionally the Tenebrae service was held on Easter Friday evening, with a series of candles being snuffed out between readings until it ends in darkness. The final extinguishing of the Christ candle symbolizes both Jesus' death and the hopelessness of a world without God, and is often accompanied by the slamming of a door or the closing of a book to symbolize the closing of the tomb. The service ends without another word, leaving the congregation to reflect on the darkness of a Godless world, until they return on the Sunday to celebrate the resurrection.

Useful books

Em Coley, *Mothering Sunday*, Grove Booklets, Worship series 185.
Various authors, music by Adrian Snell, *Seven Words for Three Hours: A Good Friday Meditation in Words and Music*, Darton Longman & Todd
Bob Hartman, *The Lion Storyteller Easter Book*, Lion
Christian Leadership magazine is full of useful resources: to subscribe, go to www.cpas.org.uk

Summer

Pentecost

Summer is Pentecost. There is no other major celebration in this season, so it's a great opportunity to concentrate on a much neglected festival.

When my husband Peter was a lad in Ashton under Lyme, the festival was known as Whit. All the faithful poured out of their back-to-back terraced houses in the narrow cobbled streets, and processed through the town behind the church banners and the vicar – Peter's father – dressed in full ecclesiastical regalia. As he marched along, the girls in white dresses, the boys in white shirts, would fill his cassock pockets with coppers in the hope that it would become so heavy that he couldn't get up the next hill, but Peter's father was a big man and all they ever succeeded in doing was filling the church's coffers. Nor did they have any idea where the word 'Whit' came from.

Oy, it all goes to show what happens when people have no knowledge of their Jewish roots.

Shavuot (The Feast of Weeks)

When you enter the land I am going to give you and reap its harvest, bring the priest a sheaf of the first grain [barley] you harvest...the priest is to wave it on the day after the Sabbath [after Passover]... From the day after the Sabbath...count off fifty days up to the day after the seventh Sabbath and then present an offering of new grain [wheat] to the Lord. Leviticus 23:10–11, 16

Firstfruits

The Jewish festival of Pentecost has three names: the Festival of Weeks (*Shavuot*), the Festival of the Harvest (*Hag HaKatzir*) and the Day of the Firstfruits (*Yom HaBikkurim*).

'Pentecost' is in fact the Greek word for 'fifty', but ask most practising Christians what 'fifty' has to do with the coming of the Holy Spirit, and they would be hard pressed to tell you. In the Book of Leviticus there are two first-fruit festivals – one for barley, harvested on the day after the first Sabbath after Passover, and one for wheat fifty days later. The Jews were actually told to count the fifty days from Passover to Pentecost – a ritual they do to this day. Since the barley offering was called an 'omer' – a weight of around 43 ounces or half a gallon, this became known as 'counting the omer': 50, 49, 48, 47... It created a tremendous sense of anticipation, especially since the wheat harvest celebration was worth waiting for.

By May the skies of the Holy Land were usually a gentle blue and the weather caressingly, pleasantly warm, before the temperatures soared uncomfortably in the hotter summer months. A farmer would tie a red ribbon around the first of his crops, then gather these *Bikkurim* or firstfruits into baskets. The whole family would set off for the great Temple in Jerusalem, laden with fresh figs, dates, grapes and pomegranates, if you lived near enough for them to stay fresh, or with the dried version if you didn't. They would pitch camp just outside the city gates, and spend that first night in festive mood, sharing good company, good food, and plenty of new *kosher* wine. Somehow, despite the inevitable headache, when dawn streaked the sky and a voice cried out, 'Let's go up to Zion', they managed to hoist their baskets onto their shoulders, form themselves into as orderly a procession as Jews can manage, and march towards the city, singing 'I rejoiced when they said to me, let us go to the house of the Lord.'

The locals would appear on the city walls and herald their arrival on fifes, timbres and drums. When they heard the pilgrims singing, 'Our feet are standing in your gates, O Jerusalem. This is where the tribes go up to praise the name of the Lord,' the leaders of the Temple would go out to the city gate to meet them. As they marched into the city, calling out the name of each town represented, Jerusalem's craftsmen stood up and shouted, *'Shalom aleichem!'* The singing rose to a crescendo as the procession entered the Temple: 'Let everything that has breath praise the Lord.' And the choir of Levites in the outer court responded, 'I will praise you, O Lord, for you have not let my enemy triumph over me.'

Sinai

In AD 70 the fun stopped abruptly when the Temple was destroyed and it was impossible to bring firstfruits to a Temple that wasn't there. But the enterprising Jewish people with their love of biblical numbers kept the festival alive by ingeniously establishing that the Torah, the law of life, was given to them by God on Mount Sinai fifty days after their deliverance from slavery in Egypt.[34] So the festival became known primarily as *Shavuot* or 'weeks' – a celebration of that extraordinary day when they entered into a special covenant relationship with God. Rabbi Yonason Goldson writes:

> It was the Torah that provided the moral and legal foundation that has enabled the Jewish people to build a nation devoted to spiritual ideals, a nation that endured for nearly 1,500 years in its land and nearly 2,000 years scattered across the globe. It was the Torah that introduced the concepts of peace, of charity, of justice, and of collective responsibility to a world that knew no value other than might makes right. It was the Torah that formed the basis of Christianity and Islam, spreading monotheism throughout the world and fashioning the attitudes of modern progressivism.

The law, of course, is pure, and purity is symbolized by the colour white, and this is what gave the British their 'Whit' holiday.

The Book of Ruth

There's a tradition for reading the Book of Ruth at *Shavuot* – partly because instructions for leaving some grain behind for the poor (known as gleaning) immediately follow the commandment to offer God the firstfruits, and partly because Ruth's story is a celebration of commitment – both to God, and to a nation. The rabbis of old hoped that just as Ruth made a firm commitment to the Jewish people, so, every year on *Shavuot*, the people themselves would renew their own personal commitment to keep the faith.

The story of Ruth is also an object lesson in the importance of welcoming the outsider. Ruth was a Moabite, an Arab and an enemy of the Children of Israel since the exodus from Egypt, yet she became part of the family that produced King David and the Jewish Messianic line.

Shavuot is the designated birth and death day of King David. Many Jews stay up all night the first night, reading the Psalms in their entirety, which is no easy feat. It's seen as a penance for the negligence of their forefathers who over-slept and missed God's arrival on Sinai.

The Day of Pentecost

At the time of Jesus the Second Temple was, of course, still standing. On that first *Shavuot* after the crucifixion and the ascension, the disciples gathered in Jerusalem as they always did, all the more so because just before his ascension to heaven he had told this cowering, frightened bunch to wait for power from on high.

Waiting, as we have seen, is what they always did at this time of year. They must have been pencilling off the days – ten, nine, eight, seven... Something had to happen at *Shavuot*, the wheat harvest. It stood to reason. After all, Jesus had risen on the barley harvest. For fifty days they had discussed what Jesus might actually be planning to do this time. What was power from on high? They vaguely remembered something he said seven months earlier at Tabernacles about rivers of living water flowing from their guts. But it still didn't make any sense.

That particular Pentecost morning, they gathered in a fever of excitement and anticipation in what some seem to think was the tiny upstairs room where Jesus had first appeared to them. Could it hold 120 people? It hardly seems likely. How could thousands of people have seen the amazing events that were about to take place if they happened in private? Only if they were all carrying binoculars or portable telescopes! And where would 120 good Jews be on *Shavuot*? In the Temple, of course, as they were for every festival. The 'house' is also the Hebrew word for 'Temple', as in 'the glory of the latter house'. Get the geography right, and the historic events fall into place. They were in a room within the Temple colonnades where they could be seen by everyone – relatives, friends, out-of-town visitors, and the foreign traders who had all come to the festival to make a fast buck.

It's nine in the morning and silence descends in the vast, echoing porticoes for the traditional Pentecost readings. First from Deuteronomy, an account of the giving of the Torah. God descends in flames of fire; Sinai, wrapped in smoke, appears to quake; and all the while, the trumpet blast grows louder and louder. Then from Ezekiel, the prophet's vision, high above him, of a fiery figure on a throne, made from glowing metal and enfolded in flames from the waist up. Fire has always been the tangible sign of God's presence.

Suddenly, in the room in the colonnade, flames appear to hover over the heads of Jesus' followers. News of it spreads like wildfire amongst the congregation, and the hubbub gradually builds into a disturbance as people want to catch a sight of this extraordinary phenomenon. The priest, thinking he has had too much *kosher* wine the night before, tells the reader to continue as if nothing has happened, and so he reads, 'Then the Spirit lifted me up, and I heard behind me a loud rumbling sound...' At which point an unmistakable roar fills the entire building. Prayer shawls flap with the force of the sudden mighty gust of wind, head coverings are lifted and personal effects scattered. And then the disciples begin to worship in gobbledegook, and roll around on the floor as if they are drunk. It's total pandemonium, and the priest, having by now lost most of his congregation, knows when he is beaten and sits down.

Peter takes control of the situation. This is not sheer spontaneity on his part. He knows exactly what is happening. He has had seven weeks to think it out, and the sheer ingenuity of God's timing makes him laugh out loud. On this one glorious party occasion, rich with significance and symbolism, God is fulfilling all the promises he made to his people in the Book of Joel and the other prophets. The Holy Spirit is the down payment.

None of the disciples are thrown by events. In fact, they're completely fearless for a change, happily making complete idiots of themselves, laughing helplessly, falling around like clowns, holding onto each other for support, shouting out in languages they have never learnt to speak. It is total, unalloyed, uninhibited, unrestrained fun. A collection of Galilean oddballs make a complete exhibition of themselves and don't appear to care. What's more, the women join in.

Peter, that trembling, lily-livered coward, is turned into a mighty preacher overnight. Three thousand people of every nation commit themselves to Jesus the Messiah, the firstfruits of a mighty, worldwide, human harvest, and are baptized in the *mikvot*, the Temple ritual baths, which just happen to be handy and can process three thousand immersions in fifteen minutes. In Jerusalem itself, where fifty days earlier Jesus was rejected and crucified, the church is born. Thousands of Jews from all over the Diaspora celebrating the festival will now take the gospel home with them.

Two parallel festivals

Just as Easter fulfils Passover, Pentecost fulfils *Shavuot*. Each is a mirror image of the other. Each defines and completes the other. The giving of the law was accompanied by noise, smoke, fire and heavy drama. So was the coming of the Spirit. *Shavuot* was a festival of firstfruits. Pentecost is the guarantee of plenty more to come. Which is why we need to make more of this lovely season, the birthday of the church, so easily taken for granted and passed over.

Shavuot	Pentecost
Birthday of Judaism	Birthday of the church
Giving of the law	Giving of the Spirit
Laws on stone	The law on our hearts
Can't approach	See and touch the glory of God
Sign of belonging	Guarantee of inheritance
The people are wedded to God	The church is the bride of Christ
Righteousness/right relationships	The gift of unity and community (Acts 2)

Ideas to enliven your Pentecost

In your home or in small groups:

- Create a simple calendar (out of a drawing of Mount Sinai if you really want to be creative) and count down the fifty days from Easter Day to Pentecost with your family or home group, climbing ever nearer the summit. Use the seven weeks as an opportunity to discuss the seven key traditional themes: love, fear, unity, ambition, commitment, community and obedience.

- Have a pyjama party or a sleepover for the children the night before. Use it as a chance to study the book of Ruth as a story of commitment – to God, to a community, to relationships, to a church. There's too little of it around these days. Provide party hats, and at midnight bring in a large birthday cake.

- Adults could spend the evening and as much of the night as they want (not in pyjamas!), reading or singing the Psalms and studying the Book of Ruth.

- Make a Pentecost birthday cake. It could be covered in white icing, and have a large, central candle to represent Christ our Light, who promised to send the Holy Spirit. Since red is the traditional church colour for Pentecost, surround the cake with twelve red birthday candles, ideally ones that will not blow out, representing the apostles receiving the Holy Spirit as tongues of fire. Seven red ribbons radiating from the cake could represent the gifts of the Holy Spirit. Twelve strawberries (or red cherries), sitting on top, could represent the twelve fruits of the Holy Spirit. Before the cake is cut, let all the children blow out the candles, by making the sound of a 'mighty rushing wind'! Serve the cake with vanilla ice cream and strawberries or raspberries to maintain a red-and-white theme.

- Alternatively, the cake could well be cheesecake (there is a recipe at the end of the book, p. 237). Because the law given to Moses at Sinai was holy and pure, and because the Promised Land was called a 'land flowing with milk and honey', it's a Jewish custom to eat sweet, milky or white foods at Pentecost. A red-berry topping would add red to the white.

- Make a table centrepiece out of a dozen red roses on a white tablecloth. Surround the bouquet with twelve tea-lights, representing the twelve fruits of the Holy Spirit. Seven flame shapes cut out of red paper, each labelled as one of the seven gifts of the Holy Spirit, can also be arranged around the centrepiece.

- Share lunch on the day and encourage everyone to wear something red and white. Decorate the room or table with red and white flowers, and flame decorations. You may want to eat red food – Italian pasta with tomato sauce, Mexican dishes with red peppers and chillies, red wine, red cordial...and red ice lollies! Light red candles, sprinkle red rose petals on the table (an Italian tradition), and share testimonies of where the Holy Spirit is burning in your life.

- For smaller children: put a collection of weather vanes and windmills in the front yard or garden, so that they can see the effect of wind. Like the wind, the Spirit cannot be seen except in how he affects our surroundings.

In larger groups or in church:

- Decorate the space with red and white flags, banners, streamers, fabric or paper strips. Hang them from doorways or ceilings, placing a small fan in a strategic place to make them wave. A small fan mounted on the base of a large cylinder or tin can that has ribbons or strips of crepe paper attached to its upper rim can be very effective.

- Give people streamers and flags to wave so that when the well-known account of Pentecost in Acts 2 is read, they can make the sound of a mighty rush of wind.

- Attach a net across the ceiling, filled with either red and white balloons or paper doves, or flame shaped pieces of red netting. As the Pentecost story is read, or at the very end of the service, release the net and let them float down over the worship space.

- Construct a huge rainbow the width of the sanctuary made up of balloons and tissue paper.

- If you have *poi* swingers[35] in the congregation, the whirring sound they make when spun can be very effective. Real experts can light the ends, and spin the flames – but they must be highly experienced and know how to do it safely.

- Have a birthday celebration with a cake, and encourage people to bring gifts for the church – in wrapping paper of course. Perhaps candles or children's books or boxes of biscuits to share over coffee, small musical instruments or new flags.

- Encourage testimonies about the gifts God has given to people and how they have used them for ministry and spreading the gospel.

- Invite several different people scattered throughout the congregation to read the passage from Acts, or ask them to read the passage simultaneously in different languages – they will need to practise in advance!

- Have some sparklers to light during the reading or later in the service.

- Invite the children to cut out white doves and share them with members of the congregation during the peace. During a hymn or song, the doves are pinned to large red banners that flank each side of the worship centre or Communion table. The effect is stunning. The doves turn into flames reaching down from heaven and rising up to the skies.

- Alternatively, invite the children to cut out heart shapes and write one of the Ten Commandments on their heart. Explain that God's laws are written on our hearts when we receive the Holy Spirit. Mount them on a piece of board covered to represent the stone tablets, with the words 'The Ten Commandments' written across the top.

- Kites are great at Pentecost. You could try making one. Instructions can easily be found on the Net. Then have a flying time after morning worship, making the point that the Spirit blows where he will.

A Pentecost service

The service must begin quietly and gradually build to a crescendo.

Quiet song (played or sung): inviting the Holy Spirit to come.

Leader: Today we are going to try to recapture the atmosphere and events of that first Pentecost. Let's travel back 2,000 years in time to the land of Judea.

Rumours abound that Jesus of Nazareth, the man who claimed to be the Messiah, rose from the dead on that first Sabbath immediately after the Passover – the barley harvest. The disciples know he did. He has appeared to them repeatedly. They have walked and talked, even eaten with him. And all during this time they have been counting down the fifty days to the wheat harvest – *Shavuot*, the Day of the Firstfruits.

Just before he ascended into heaven (when, in their counting, they had arrived at day forty), Jesus said to them:

Reading: Luke 24:46–49.

Leader: What did he mean by 'power from on high'? What exactly were they waiting for, the disciples wondered, and they went on counting – ten, nine, eight, seven...and on day four, with real anticipation, they began the three-day journey on foot to Jerusalem for the festival.

Four, three, two, one...they were waiting for a blast-off, and they weren't disappointed.

Hymn or song.

Leader: The disciples marched in the grand and noisy procession up to the Temple for the festival, singing the familiar psalms, accompanied by an array of musical instruments, then gathered together in a room in the Temple courts to wait, as Jesus had told them to do.

As they waited they could hear the traditional chanting of the *Shavuot* Scripture readings, that described the glory of God when he revealed himself to Moses and to Ezekiel – in flashes of lightning, dazzling light and fire.

As the readings are read, gradually introduce a variety of audio-visual aids – the sound of wind, thunder, cymbals, flames on a screen, streamers wafted by fans – gradually increasing in crescendo (without drowning the readers) and continuing after the reading in Acts.

Readings: Deuteronomy 5:22–29; Ezekiel 1:4–9, 25–28; Acts 2:1–4.

Move from the sound and light effects into some form of dance. St Thomas, Lancaster created one that involved lifting children. Or you could adapt the maypole idea with streamers, or release balloons from a net, or use sparklers. Encourage congregational participation.

Hymns or songs.

Story: The story of Ruth.

Leader: The Sermon.

Prayers: It is a Hebraic tradition to read the story of Ruth at Pentecost. Her story celebrates commitment – both to God and to her community.

Today, Pentecost is a chance for us to recommit ourselves fully to God, and to his community, the church, whose birthday we celebrate.

A body without breath is a corpse, the church without the Spirit is dead. Pentecost is his way of deluging us with life – his life. It is:

- for those of us who have forgotten where we might be now if God had not intervened in our lives. Help us, Lord, to renew the vows we made when we first promised to follow and serve you. Anoint us to do whatever you call us to do, however difficult, and to share our stories wherever you send us.

- for those of us who have become stuck in our comfort zones and our materialism, and are no longer willing to take risks. Write your word on our hearts, Lord. Help us in every circumstance to hear your voice and obey, whatever the cost.

- for those of us so caught up in the stress and strain of the daily grind, so burdened by pressures and commitments, that we are too busy or too exhausted to dream dreams any more. Lord, renew our vision. Help us to see and welcome the signs of your eternal kingdom breaking through.

- for those of us who have lost the joy of knowing you, now that those early years of faith and excitement have faded and gone, or who now feel a failure, jaded, and cynical. Lord, let us know and feel your love for us again, and as we do, rekindle our love for you with your holy fire.

- for those of us, who, like Peter, are full of determination to serve – but quickly discover that it takes a great deal more than just willpower. Fill us with power from on high and make us prophetic voices, challenging our world with words of justice and mercy.

An opportunity for any who would like to rededicate themselves formally, or receive prayer, to do so. 'The tunnel' idea (see the 'Maundy Thursday' section, p. 169) would be very effective.

Hymns and songs.

Leader: The Blessing.

Part 4

Celebration Recipes

All celebrations, whether they commemorate a religious holiday, an episode of Jewish history, or a moment in the cycle of life – a birth, a circumcision, a first tooth, a coming of age, a marriage, the inauguration of a new home, pregnancy, death – were once, and in some cases still are, ruled by tradition, and special foods were part of these traditions. The dishes chosen to celebrate these occasions became part of festive rituals and acquired embellishments as they acquired symbolic significance. They were glamorised to glorify the occasions, and that meant colouring with saffron or turmeric, sprinkling with raisins or chopped nuts, stuffing, enclosing in a pie crust, and pressing into a mould.

Claudia Rodin, *The Book of Jewish Food* [36]

*I*t's amazing what you can concoct out of very little. The Jews in the Diaspora, particularly in Eastern Europe, were not allowed to own land or enter the professions and had no money to spare. But that only made them more, not less, imaginative with food – especially party food.

There is a story in a completely different, Christian context that has always captured my imagination because it reveals the same determination of the human spirit to celebrate in the least congenial of circumstances, with the minimum of resources. Circumstances can crush our celebratory spirit – or drive it to breathtaking ingenuity.

In 1942, when the Japanese invaded the China Inland Mission School at Chefoo in north-east China, and took all the staff and pupils to the Weihsien Concentration Camp, the teachers did their best to protect the children from the worst of the trauma, disease, and misery of their surroundings. Normalizing the next best thing to hell itself involved creating an atmosphere of celebration when the occasion demanded it –such as the wedding of two of the staff. Beatrice Lack, the school cook, decided to make them a cake – and everyone joined in creating what they felt should be 'a professional job'. She recorded in her diary how they collected apricot stones which they ground, manually, into 'lovely almonds'. Bits of orange and pumelo skin, some nearly two years old, added a little flavour. A quarter of the two pounds of sugar, meticulously gathered from tiny allowances throughout the camp, went into the mixture, while the rest was reserved for

the icing. Once they had added a few real sultanas from Red Cross parcels, a little dripping from one of the kitchens, plus oddments of spice and cinnamon,
and lots of sweet Chinese dates, everyone set about stirring the ingredients. The
tins were created from powdered-milk cans. The baking took five hours in a
kerosene tin oven. Someone happened to have a cake-icing outfit, and with
some persistence Mrs Lack managed to make a workable boiled icing. The ornament on the cake, a Gothic arch, was made from a strip of a milk tin. It was covered with white tape and lily-of-the-valley, adapted from a corsage she had worn
for five summers. That cake came to symbolize, not just the ability to celebrate
in the direst of circumstances, but also the irrepressible nature of the human
spirit and its trust in the God of the party.

It is this ability of food to do so much more than merely satisfy our
appetites that made me decide to include a recipe section in this book on celebration. Some may wonder why I've bothered. After all, not everyone enjoys
cooking. In our consumerist world, that's no barrier to throwing a party. We can
always eat out together, and if the budget won't run to it, most of the major
supermarkets offer passable and affordable versions of our latest favourites.
Better that than not eat together at all.

But cooking for an occasion really doesn't have to be difficult or time-consuming. Even the most reluctant and diffident cooks can be sparked into creativity. When I married Peter he was definitely remedial in the cookery
department. Despite sharing a bachelor flat for some years, a pale, rather greasy
roast chicken was about the sum of his culinary capabilities. After a term of
cookery classes at our local further education college, he managed a very passable lasagne, but it took him all day to make, and it took me all day to wash his
pans. What he lacked in the kitchen was not so much the ability, but the will.
Brilliant at DIY, at putting pipes, wires, boilers and furniture together, he simply did not enjoy putting a meal together. The logistics of having everything
ready at the same time seem to elude him.

But some months ago, stranded for several hours at the very end of the
world (Fleetwood, actually), he took himself off to the North Euston Hotel for
lunch. It's a bit dreary on the outside, but they have an excellent bistro. There
he had a spinach risotto that so delighted his taste-buds, it inspired him, to my
utter amazement, to have a go at recreating it at home. It was a huge success and
has become a firm favourite ever since. The recipe is below.

Another reason for devoting a section to food is that God didn't have to
make eating such a pleasurable experience. People who struggle with their

weight might wish he hadn't. But he could have designed us differently – imbibing what we need for survival through osmosis or by swallowing a tablet. Shovelling grub down our throats in front of the television set is the next best thing. If we give food time, the preparation of it can be a family or community experience, while the eating of it can evoke forgotten memories, fill us with warmth and pleasure, and create a sense of fellowship in a lonely, alien world. Fast food can never do that. It doesn't honour God's superabundant provision for our needs – in taste, texture, colour, and variety. It doesn't honour the long preparation process – the planting, growing, harvesting, transporting, converting, packaging, choosing, mixing and cooking. It only symbolizes the fact that 'I need feeding', and in that, I am no different from a cow chewing the cud. It doesn't make any contribution to family or community life, and should come with an emotional health warning: 'to be taken in moderation'.

While most people eat to live, the Jews live to eat. A traditional 'curse' invoked upon an ungrateful child by an embittered *Yiddishe mama* consists of a nice twist on a familiar blessing: 'May you, every day, eat chopped liver with onions, schmaltz-herring, chicken-soup with matzah dumplings, carp with horseradish, roast beef with tsimmes, pancakes and tea with lemon – and may you choke on every bite.' It's not that the Jews are the greatest gluttons or gourmands. They have simply learned that good food makes rest, relaxation, family, festival and community. That's why many of the recipes included here, though not necessarily Jewish, all contribute in some way or another to that end.

So here are my mother-in-law's Canadian cookie recipes that turned the Sunday afternoon teas of my husband's childhood into a proper family Sabbath treat; a South African pudding that fills me with memories of that wonderful country; French holiday food full of the magic of eating in the sun; Christmas and Easter recipes that have become part of the fabric of my extended family and are expected year on year; tray bakes for home groups that turn a Bible study into a night out; and suggestions for those bring-and-share community meals that test our culinary creativity to the limit.

None are particularly difficult, or time-consuming, except for the one or two that are specifically designated as being more complex. Life is too full and too busy for cooking to become an almost full-time preoccupation. And because I worked for years in the National Health Service, with a special responsibility for health promotion, most have been dressed in their healthiest possible disguise.

It was at the last meal he ate with his disciples that Jesus called them friends, despite the fact that he already knew that one would betray him, one would deny him, one would doubt him, and the rest would flee. But that meal was the ultimate symbol of forgiveness and reconciliation, as Jesus used it as an aide memoire, pointing to past history and future provision when he instituted the Communion. It is not simply coincidental that the two most important symbols of the Christian faith can be tasted, touched, seen, smelled and swallowed.

Some basic suggestions and tips

- The simplest of meals can be turned into something special if the table is set with care. For example, collect all your used pillar candles together, even if they are different heights, stand them on a pretty fireproof dish or tray and fill the spaces with pebbles or pot-pourri in colours that reflect the colours of the candles. This makes a really attractive table centre and is a great way to use up old candles. Pick up the same colours in placemats and serviettes.

- When margarine is a stated ingredient, always use a good-quality variety, one that does not contain hydrogenated oils, known as 'trans fats'. Hydrogenation is a process of turning liquid oil into a type of solid fat that raises cholesterol levels in the blood. This increases the risk of coronary heart disease. Evidence suggests that this type of 'trans fat' may have worse effects on the body than saturated fats. If in doubt, always check the ingredients. You could, of course, substitute best butter for margarine – and it may well improve the taste, but the jury is out on its effects on your cholesterol.

- Whenever creme fraiche or cream cheese is suggested, you can use a low-fat version – especially in desserts. Bear in mind that like yogurt, half-fat creme fraiche cannot stand up to being boiled and will curdle when used in casseroles unless you add a little thickener (flour or cornflour) first.

- Almost all the recipes below can be frozen, unless stated to the contrary. If you want to freeze a cheese sauce (for example, in some of the pasta dishes, such as cannelloni), thicken it with a mixture of cornflour and plain flour mixed to a paste in a little of the milk. This will prevent it 'cracking' when you defrost it.

- If many of the recipes below are prepared for four people, it's not that I have an average nuclear family in mind. It's simply that this is an easy figure to halve (for two), or double (for eight or sixteen).

- If the recipe suggests using stock, home-made is always the best. Pour juices of any roast meats, allow to grow cold in the fridge and skim off any fat. Or, for chicken stock, do the Jewish trick and boil up the carcass once the bird is eaten. But stock cubes or stock liquid make a very acceptable second best.

- I have a fan oven and it took me weeks after I first got it, to learn not to overcook everything. If you use a fan oven you will need to reduce the heat by around 20 to 30 degrees.

- Whatever the result of your cooking, and especially if ingredients disintegrate or puddings fall apart, they can almost always be repaired and always look tempting if decorated. For savoury food use sprigs of parsley, slices of tomato sprinkled with basil, grated cheese if appropriate and sliced lemon on fish. For desserts, try filling cracks with a little cream, creme fraiche, or Greek yogurt, sprinkle with icing sugar or decorate with lemon slices or shavings off a bar of chocolate, depending on the flavour of your dessert.

- If at all possible, use locally produced ingredients. Not only do they taste better, but they boost the local economy and keep your local producers in business. Many people prefer organically grown ingredients and there is some evidence that they are better for you – but they are more expensive, and you don't have to have them to eat healthily.

- Saying grace over a meal is important, not as a mere ritual, but because so many in our world are hungry. It also reminds us that we're not just animals satisfying a basic appetite. This is an opportunity for reflection (if you're alone), for savouring flavour, for building relationship, for acknowledging the presence of Reality himself as the important guest at the table. (See chapter on celebrating in the daily and ordinary, p. 77.)

Weights and measures – an easy conversion chart

British (and Canadian)	American (and Australian)
1lb/500g butter or margarine (shortening)	2 cups
1lb/500g flour	4 cups
1lb/500g granulated or castor sugar	2 cups
1lb/500g icing (confectioner's) sugar	$3^1/2$ cups
1lb/500g soft brown sugar	2 cups
12oz (or tablespoons) golden (corn) syrup or treacle	1 cup
1lb/500g dried fruit	3 cups
2oz/50g soft breadcrumbs	1 cup
20fl oz liquid	$2^1/2$ cups

Green Pea Soup –
a colourful and hearty starter.

elgian Chicken Liver Pate and Carrot
d Cashew Nut Pate –
good as chopped liver, with a tasty vege-
rian alternative.

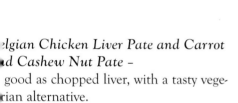

Smoked Mackerel Rillettes – artery-loving omega fish oils in a scrummy spread.

Main Courses

Festive Orange-Glazed Lamb – makes Easter as special as Christmas – if not more so!

Lamb Shanks in Red Wine (Lamb Henry) – a favourite with the guys.

Healthy Eastern Lamb Hotpot (with a vegetarian option) – a meal with Middle Eastern appeal.

Sweet and Spicy Lamb – a casserole with attitude and sweet potatoes.

Guinness Beef Pie – the pie with a kick.

Mother-in-Law's Meat Loaf – an economical dish that could almost pass itself off as a roast.

Mega Celebration Cannelloni – takes a while to make, but worth every minute.

Stir Fry Pork with Noodles – a fast dish with the veg thrown in, ideal for Alpha suppers.

Stuffed Turkey Breasts with Cranberry Gravy – a quiet Christmas for two, or an impressive, all-year-round celebration dinner for a crowd.

Ultra Quick Chicken and Apricots – a no-preparation fall-back for a quickly-prepared delicious meal.

Ground Nut Stew – a fun dish for sharing, all the way from Africa.

Spicy Turkey Cous-Cous – a tasty way to use leftovers for a light supper dish.

Tarragon Chicken – try hot in the winter, or cold on a summer's evening.

Sausage and Apple Turnover – a welcome Jacob's Join alternative to the inevitable quiche.

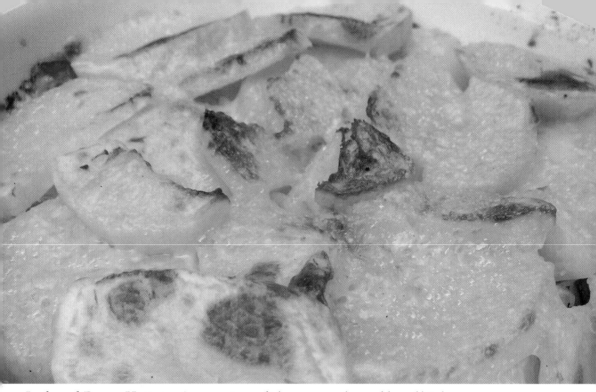

Leek and Bacon Hotpot – A tasty winter dish to warm the cockles of his heart.
Sausage Pasta – the easiest meal since the sausage was invented.

Boston Bean Bake – the Americans certainly knew how to dress up baked beans.
Salmon en Croute – a "knock-em-out" gourmet meal that's so much easier than it looks.

Salmon Lasagne – the salmon and pasta coupling is a hard combination to resist.

Hot Smoky Mackerel with Tangy Tomato Sauce and Chive Mash – one way to convert the most resistant of fish haters.

Tuna Bake – it's amazing what you can do with a few packets of crisps.

Kedgeree – a posh breakfast, tasty festival brunch, or simple supper.

Spinach Risotto – my husband's favourite vegetarian dish and one he designed himself.

Cranberry Cashew Nut Roast – it stands alone or gives a roast joint real flair.

Accompaniments

Lockschen Kugel – a pasta accompaniment that comes in savoury or sweet disguise.

Celebration Salads

Salade Paysanne – bacon and eggs the irresistible French way.

Smoked Salmon Terrine Salad – a gourmet salad for ladies who like to lunch.

Hot Puddings

Upside Down Butterscotch Pear Pudding – you'll be tempted to eat the lot.

Sticky Toffee Pudding – easy to make and would keep an army happy.

Chocolate Pear Crumble – the truly decadent variety.

Rhubarb Brown Betty – an economical pudding for expensive tastes.

Apple and Mincemeat Conde – the queen of rice puddings.

Malva Pudding – the South African celebration pudding to end all puddings.

Cold Desserts

Honey Cheesecake Apple Pie – an apple pie with conviction.

Real Muesli – you'll never want the sawdust variety once you've tasted this authentic dessert.

Hazelnut Strawberry Torte – melt-in-the-mouth, praline shortbread makes a strawberry cake deluxe.

Tiramisu Gateau – a grand celebration version of the famous Italian trifle.

Great Grandma's Baked Cheesecake – from Russia with love, an ancient Jewish recipe.

Quick Fresh Fruit Cheese Flan – use whatever fruit you can find to make the fastest and healthiest of cheesecake quiches.

Cakes

Grandma's Squidgy Lemon Cake – a moist and tangy cake that melts in the mouth.

No Fail Almond Cake (gluten free) – a treat with summer fruits.

Mrs Guinness' Fruit Cake – it's the beer that gives it the *je ne sais quoi*.

Extra Fruity Flapjack – the old, childhood favourite, with fuller flavour and fibre.

Tangy Lemon Slice – an easy, tray bake version of the irresistible French lemon tart.

Millionaire's Shortbread – a luxury treat that makes the bought variety look like a poor relation.

Spicy Cranberry Shortbread – the smell and taste of Christmas all year round.

Chocolate Tiffin – this no-bake crunchy biscuit is strictly for chocoholics.

Date and Nut Bars – chewy Canadian cookies. No one ever stops at one.

Squidgy Chocolate Truffles – no mass-produced variety can match these, but be warned, you'll be making them forever more.

Starters

Green pea soup

There's nothing as heartening on a winter evening (or a winter lunch, if work allows you) as a home-made soup, served with crusty bread. Some can be a bit fiddly to make, but my sister-in-law found this simple, nourishing and ingenious recipe for green pea soup. Let's face it, it may be difficult to encourage children to eat their greens, but most manage to eat peas! Being Jewish, of course, my sister-in-law wouldn't add the chopped ham – that was my addition, but I have to admit, it does give it an extra je ne sais quoi.

- 2 large onions – fried in a little olive oil
- 1 1kg/2.2 lb bag frozen peas
- 1 litre/just under 2 pints of water
- 2 teaspoons or two cubes vegetable stock
- salt, ground black pepper
- optional extra: some cubed pieces of ham or bacon

Fry the onions until golden, then add the bag of peas and the stock and the seasoning. Bring to the boil and simmer for around 30 minutes. Liquidize in a machine or with a hand-held blender. It's easier to leave some nice big pieces of pea when you use the latter.

Belgian chicken liver pâté

This isn't the famous Jewish chopped liver, which you can make with this recipe simply by adding two chopped hard-boiled eggs. This one came from Belgium with a friend who spent a year there.

- 450g/1lb chicken livers
- 100g/4oz good-quality margarine or butter
- 3–4 bay leaves
- 2 medium chopped onions
- salt, ground black pepper and a good sprinkling of garlic
- 1 tablespoon brandy (optional)
- 1 teaspoon tomato puree

Soak the livers for an hour in salted water, drain them. Fry the onion in a little of the margarine until golden, then add the liver, the herbs and seasoning and the rest of the margarine and simmer for around 30 minutes. Pour off any excess liquid, then liquidize the liver and onions with the brandy and a teaspoon of tomato puree. Pour into small pots and leave to cool. The pâté freezes well.

Carrot and cashew nut pâté (vegetarian)

This makes a good pâté alternative for vegetarians – and is delicious with a few cherry tomatoes.

- 2 large carrots – shredded in a mixer
- 225g/8oz roasted cashew nuts – ground in a mixer
- 450g/1lb cream cheese (half-fat if preferred)
- salt, ground black pepper

Shred the carrots in the mixer, then add the remaining ingredients and grind till fairly smooth. Keeps in the fridge 3–5 days, but can also be frozen.

Smoked mackerel rillettes

Rillettes *is the French word for a coarse pâté. I used to make mackerel pâté in a food processor, whizzing it smooth, but I learned in France that simply mashing all the ingredients together with a fork gives a much more interesting texture.*

- 2 fillets smoked mackerel
- 1 teaspoon Dijon mustard
- 1 200g carton low-fat cream cheese
- a sprinkling of season-all or ground black pepper
- 1 teaspoon lemon juice

Serve on a bed of Chinese leaves and rocket, with a twist of lemon to decorate and with crusty bread and tangy tomato chutney.

Main Courses

Festive orange glazed lamb – an Easter celebration lunch

Easter deserves as special a meal as Christmas, and this one, with its glaze, its sauce, and its chestnut accompaniment is certainly special. Why not have lamb with all its symbolic significance? As an added bonus, despite being truly celebratory, it isn't particularly complex.

- 1 boneless leg joint – around 2kg/4lbs for 6–8 people

For the glaze:

- juice of an orange
- 3 tablespoons redcurrant jelly
- 2 tablespoons honey

Roast the lamb joint in a roaster bag. You know your oven. Mine is fan-assisted and fierce, so I allow only 10–15 minutes per lb on 190 degrees. Then I cut open the bag, drain off the juices into the sauce, pour over several spoonfuls of the glaze and return to the oven uncovered for 15 mins extra. With a gentler cooker, allow 20 mins per lb (for example, on gas mark 5/190°C), and at least 20 mins to glaze. Pour over extra glaze as required. Place joint on a roasting dish and serve with stuffing and sauce.

For the special stuffing:

- 1 large onion, chopped finely and fried to golden in a dash of olive oil
- 25g/1oz melted butter or good-quality margarine
- 200g/8oz white or wholemeal breadcrumbs
- 1 vacuum pack of chestnuts – chopped

- 50g/2oz dried cranberries – thrown in whole
- freshly chopped rosemary
- salt, ground black pepper

Mix all the ingredients together and bake, uncovered, in the same oven as the meat for 30 mins until golden on top.

For the sauce:

- 2 tablespoons flour – mixed to a paste with water. Then add:
- 1 teaspoon mustard
- 142ml/5fl oz red wine
- 142ml/5fl oz water
- 284ml/10fl oz bottled or carton orange juice
- 3 tablespoons redcurrant jelly
- 1 stock cube or a few sprinkles of bottled red meat stock
- salt and ground black pepper

Bring the mixture slowly to the boil, stirring all the while until it thickens, then pour in any remaining juices from the meat or glaze and serve.

Lamb shanks in red wine (also known as Lamb Henry)

I picked up this recipe in South Africa, where it was served at a celebration Sunday lunch. Ask your butcher to make the shanks as lean as possible, or you may have a lot of extraneous fat to pour away. Serves 6.

- 2 tablespoons plain, seasoned flour (mixed with salt, black pepper)
- 6 lamb shanks – around 200g/8oz each
- 3 tablespoons olive oil
- 1 large onion finely chopped
- 3–4 carrots finely chopped
- 2–3 celery sticks finely chopped

- 400g can tomatoes
- 1 small tin tomato puree
- 300ml/10fl oz red meat stock
- 200ml/7fl oz red wine
- 100ml/3fl oz sherry
- 3 tablespoons sugar
- garlic to taste
- salt, ground black pepper
- 4–5 sprigs rosemary and thyme, finely chopped

Preheat oven to gas mark 1/130°C (110°C for a fan oven). On a plate mix together the flour, salt and pepper. Dip the lamb shanks in the mixture, and coat well. Heat the olive oil in a large heavy-based frying pan till hot. Add the lamb and cook over a medium heat, turning frequently until well browned. Transfer the shanks to an oven-proof casserole and pour away any excess fat.

Heat the remaining oil in the pan and add the onion, carrots and celery and cook over a low heat for 4–5 mins until soft. Add the remaining ingredients and stir. Pour over the lamb shanks. Cover and bake for 3 hours, turning the lamb shanks occasionally. Turn up the oven a little and cook for a further hour. This would work equally well in a slow-cook pot. Serve on a bed of mashed potato with sprigs of rosemary for garnish.

Healthy Eastern lamb hotpot (with a vegetarian option)

Pulses, peppers and vegetables – what healthier combination of ingredients could there be in a casserole that relies on the mix of spices to give it its Middle Eastern appeal? And, when there are lots of vegetables in the pot, the meal goes much further. Serves 8.

- 1kg/2lbs lean casserole lamb
- 1 large onion, chopped
- 3 medium carrots, peeled and cut into matchsticks
- 3 medium courgettes (zucchini), chopped into cubes

- 1 red pepper, sliced
- 1 tin chick-peas, drained
- 110g/4oz sultanas
- 1 teaspoon each of ground cumin, coriander, turmeric and ginger
- 1 half teaspoon each of salt, ground black pepper
- 1 tablespoon flour
- 1 tablespoon lime or lemon juice
- 300ml/10fl oz brown stock
- creme fraiche or natural yogurt

Fry the chopped onion in a little extra-virgin olive oil until brown, then add the carrots for a few minutes. While the pan is very hot, put in the lamb and brown. Then add the pepper and courgettes until they start to soften. Sprinkle in the flour and toss until all the ingredients are coated. Add the remaining ingredients and stir until the casserole thickens, adding a little more water if necessary.

Cook on gas mark 2, or 150°C, for around 45 mins. Just before serving, stir in a little low-fat creme fraiche or natural yogurt.

Vegetarians can leave out the meat and add presoaked brown lentils instead.

Served with couscous, or, if you prefer, add some parboiled potato chunks to the casserole just before putting it in the oven.

Sweet and spicy lamb

When a friend served this particular casserole for dinner, I loved it so much I have been making it ever since – sometimes with turkey chunks for economy, or with soya pieces for vegetarians. Serves 4.

- 1kg/2lbs good-quality stewing lamb
- 1 large onion, chopped
- 2 large sweet potatoes, cut into chunks
- 400g can chopped tomatoes
- 1 teaspoon ground ginger

- 1 teaspoon paprika
- 2 tablespoons mild curry paste
- 3 tablespoons mango chutney
- salt and freshly ground black pepper
- 150ml/5fl oz dry white wine
- 100g/4oz bag baby spinach leaves

Fry the lamb in a little olive oil until brown, and set aside. Fry the chopped onion in a little oil till golden, then add the chunks of sweet potato and the ginger and stir for around 3–4 mins. Add the browned lamb and all the other ingredients, except the spinach.

Cover and cook in a moderate oven, gas mark 3, 170°C (150°C in a fan oven), for around one hour, until the lamb is tender.

Just before serving, stir in the spinach, and serve as soon as the leaves melt into the casserole.

Guinness beef stew or pie

I couldn't miss the chance of sharing with you my son's favourite, dark, rich Guinness stew. For those of us who fail to understand its charms in the glass (even if my husband is great great grandson to the man whose name is on the bottle), Guinness can't fail to please in the pot. Don't be tempted to add more than the recipe says, however – or it will be bitter. Serves 4.

- 750g/1½lb lean beef braising steak, cut into pieces
- 2 tablespoons olive oil
- 1 large onion, chopped
- 225g/8oz button mushrooms (or you may prefer to use a tin of vacuum-packed chestnuts)
- 2 rashers of bacon, chopped (optional)
- half a 440ml can of Guinness
- 2 tablespoons Worcestershire sauce
- 2 tablespoons plain flour

- 1 400g tin chopped tomatoes
- 1 teaspoon dried bay leaves
- 1 brown stock cube
- salt, ground black pepper, garlic and a pinch of sugar

Marinade the meat in half the Guinness, 1 tablespoon oil, the black pepper, garlic, bay leaf and Worcestershire sauce for around 3–4 hours.

Heat one tablespoon olive oil in a pan, lift the steak out of the marinade and brown quickly. Set aside. Heat the remaining oil and cook the chopped onion until golden. Add the chopped bacon, the mushrooms, garlic and fry for another 2 mins. Add the flour and stir it in well to coat the bacon, onion and mushrooms. Add all the remaining ingredients, including the steak and cook until the sauce thickens. Place in a casserole and cook on gas mark 3/170°C for around an hour and a half.

To make a pie:
Simply roll out a sheet of ready-made puff pastry. 30 mins before the end of the cooking time, bring the casserole out of the oven (it should be a low-sided rectangular casserole for the pie) and cover the meat with the pastry. Raise the temperature to gas mark 4/180°C for the last 30 mins, until the pastry is risen and golden.

Mother-in-law's meat loaf roast alternative

(Suitable for bring-and-share meals, picnics and home-group suppers.) Peter loves to tell our children of his financially stretched childhood in a clergy home in Ashton Under Lyme, and they always mock up sad violin music to accompany his tales of deprivation. His mother used to make meat loaf as an alternative to a Sunday roast. I have layered it to make it more special, and personally, I think it's good enough for any occasion, hot, or cold with salads for a picnic treat. Serves 6.

- 500g/1lb good-quality, lean, minced beef
- 2 large onions minced

- 50g/4oz wholemeal or white breadcrumbs
- 2 teaspoons tomato puree
- half a red pepper, chopped
- 1 crumbled beef stock cube
- 1 beaten egg
- 2 teaspoons Worcestershire sauce
- a sprinkling of garlic
- 1 teaspoon chopped fresh or dried herbs
- salt, ground black pepper

Mix the ingredients for the meat loaf and press into a lightly oiled loaf tin. Cover with the filling mixture, then spread the rest of the meat loaf on top. Bake at gas mark 5/190°C for around 60 mins. Either serve hot, or allow to cool and slice.

Mega celebration cannelloni

When I was trying to come up with an ultra-special, yet more economical meal for Boxing Day one year, I hit upon the notion of cannelloni and set off with huge enthusiasm to prepare a mega-sized offering. I didn't realize, until I had launched out, that I really needed four separate sauces. Not only that, but stuffing the cannelloni took an entire BBC Radio 4 afternoon play and documentary. So this is no quick, simple meal – but it was such a success, as good if not better than any served at an Italian restaurant, I was told, that I have made it again and again. For a vegetarian option, simply omit the Bolognese sauce and double the amount of ricotta and spinach filling. Serves 8.

- 32 (2 boxes) cannelloni pasta shells (use either the 'no-cook' dried variety, or fresh pasta lasagne sheets and roll them around the mixture; the latter are slightly thicker)

For the tomato sauce:

- 2 onions chopped and fried until golden
- 2 large (400g) tins chopped tomatoes
- 2 tablespoons tomato puree
- 2 teaspoons soft brown sugar

- salt, ground black pepper, garlic and a good sprinkling of fresh or dried oregano

Mix all the ingredients together. You could, of course, cheat to save time and buy two jars of tomato ragu.

For the bolognese sauce:

- 1k/2lbs good-quality minced beef
- 2 onions, chopped
- salt, ground black pepper, garlic
- 1 egg
- 4 teaspoons green pesto

Fry the chopped onions, then add the beef until well browned. Season and bind together with the egg and pesto. Leave to cool.

For the ricotta and spinach sauce:

- 1 tablespoon olive oil
- 2 450g/1lb tubs ricotta cheese
- 2 200g/8oz bags of baby spinach leaves
- salt, ground black pepper
- half a teaspoon of ground nutmeg

Heat the olive oil in the pan and add the spinach. It will quickly dissolve into a much smaller amount than you thought you had. Cook for 2 mins, and then cool by placing the pan base into a few inches of cold water. Add the ricotta and seasoning and set aside.

For the bechamel sauce:

- 1 litre/2 pints whole milk
- 2 tablespoons plain flour
- 2 tablespoons cornflour
- 100g/4oz butter
- 150g/6oz grated Parmesan cheese
- salt, ground black pepper and a large pinch of nutmeg
- 4 tablespoons of creme fraiche

Mix the flours and add enough milk to form a runny paste in a heavy, non-stick pan. Keep adding the milk slowly, then put the butter, cheese and seasoning into the pan too. Bring slowly to the boil, whisking all the time, until the mixture thickens substantially. Then add the creme fraiche.

To put the entire meal together:
Cover the base of a large casserole dish with the tomato sauce. Fill half the cannelloni with the bolognese sauce, half with the ricotta and spinach mixture. You may have to use a small teaspoon, the handle of a wooden spoon or even your fingers. Place a layer of bolognese-filled cannelloni onto the tomato sauce, and then a layer of the ricotta and spinach cannelloni on top. Pour over the bechamel sauce. Sprinkle some additional Parmesan cheese on top to cover, then bake on gas mark 4/180°C for around 40-45 minutes. Serve when really golden on top with a crisp green salad, topped with chopped avocado slices.

Stir fry pork with noodles

(Suitable for a home group or an Alpha supper.) Here is a fast, throw-together, fairly economical, mild and spicy dish that goes down a treat, and has the veg thrown in. The secret is to cook your meat in small batches in a hot wok (not only does it cook better, you can keep on adding more as you need it.) And don't tell my family that I'm giving you pork recipes! Serves 8.

- 1 kg/2lbs diced lean pork
- 1 egg white
- 1 tablespoonful cornflour
- 2 bunches sliced spring onions (using the green part too)
- 2 large red peppers cut into strips
- 300g/10oz carrots, sliced thinly
- 300g/10oz sliced mushrooms and/or halved sugar snap peas, and/or broccoli florets as desired
- 4 tablespoons soy sauce
- 4 tablespoons dry sherry
- 2 tins coconut milk or 250g creamed coconut

- 2 teaspoons or 2 cubes of chicken stock powder (add around 450ml/15fl oz water if using creamed coconut, or there will not be enough sauce)
- 2 teaspoons ground ginger
- 2 teaspoons Thai spices or Thai curry paste
- salt, ground black pepper and garlic
- 2 boxes/approx 800g of 'Straight to Wok' stir fry noodles

Season the pork with salt and pepper and soy sauce, and toss in the egg white and cornflour. This will prevent the pork from losing its tenderness, but you will need to stir hard to stop it catching on the bottom of the wok. Heat a little olive oil in a wok and fry in batches on a high heat for around 5 mins a batch. Remove and set aside.

In a large casserole, gently fry the spring onions, carrots and peppers in a little olive oil for around 2-3 mins. Then add any other vegetables as chosen, and cook for around 5 mins. Add the pork and all the sauce ingredients, and allow to simmer gently until the vegetables can be bitten into comfortably (but are still just crisp). 2 mins before the stir fry is ready, add the contents of the two boxes of noodles. Stir for 2 mins and serve.

Individual stuffed turkey breasts with cranberry gravy

This impressive-looking celebration meal can be served as an alternative Christmas dinner for one or two people, for those who prefer a quiet day and may not want to buy an entire joint. But it is equally good at other times of the year. For a bigger crowd – perhaps at New Year, Easter or Pentecost – simply make more. Serves 2.

- 2 thickly cut turkey steaks
- quarter onion chopped very finely
- 100g/4oz mushrooms chopped finely (or half a tin of vacuum-packed chestnuts, chopped)
- 100g/4oz cream cheese
- 4 rashers lean smoky bacon

- salt and ground black pepper

For the gravy:

- 150ml bought gravy with 2 tablespoons cranberry sauce and 2 table-spoons red wine added

With a very sharp knife cut a slit down the side of each turkey steak lengthways to form a pocket. Fry the finely chopped onion until golden, then add the mush-rooms and cook quickly on a high heat for around 1 min. (If using chestnuts, remove the onions from the heat, and simply stir in.) Allow to cool, then drain off any liquid, and bind together with the cream cheese. Fill both steak pockets with the mixture, then wrap the steaks securely in two bacon rashers each, to hold them together.

Cover and bake in a casserole on gas mark 4/180°C or 160°C in a fan oven for around 30 mins. Remove the cover and allow to brown in the oven for a further 10 mins. There may well be a little liquid in the bottom of the casse-role – the meat juices – but simply pour it into the cranberry gravy, and serve.

Ultra-quick chicken and apricots

This is the one recipe I said I'd never share with anyone – my pièce de resistance, the one that takes no preparation, that I throw together in an emergency or when I can't be bothered to cook, and it still makes me look like a real culinary diva. It is a luxury din-ner party meal for busy people in a hurry, who want to have something special with min-imum effort. Serves 4.

- 4 chicken pieces (can be breasts for lower calories)
- 1 packet French onion soup (for 600ml/1 pint)
- 1 tin apricot halves in fruit juice (412g net weight)
- a few sliced almonds to decorate

Lay the raw chicken pieces in a lightly oiled dish. Sprinkle the packet soup over them. Reserve four apricot halves from the tin, then pour the rest of the con-tents over the chicken pieces and dried soup. Cover and place in the oven on gas mark 4/180°C, for around 45 mins. Remove from the oven and check the chicken is cooked (if the juice flows clear when you poke it with a knife, rather than pink).

With a fork, mash the apricots roughly into the juices (the sauce should be fairly thick – but if it is too thick, add a little water). Place a reserved apricot on each piece of chicken and sprinkle with almonds. Return to the oven uncovered, cook for a further 15–20 mins to brown, and serve.

Ground nut stew

(Suitable for a bring-and-share meal, or a home-group or Alpha supper.) I am indebted to Simon Barrington-Ward, a former Bishop of Coventry, for this unusual recipe, which I imagine he discovered in Africa, when he was Director of Christian Aid. It appeared in the 1988 Lambeth Conference Bishops' cookbook, sold to raise money for the Church Urban Fund, and became a huge favourite with my children and their friends.

But then, they always adored peanut butter and this recipe, that uses up all my turkey or chicken leftovers, was a pleasant change from the peanut-butter and jam sandwiches they always took for school dinners. (They have American relatives!) And since it was one of the quickest and easiest dishes in the world to make, I was happy to oblige.

I have to say, I cannot abide peanut butter – but find this dish (which can also be made with any cooked poultry, or even Quorn for the vegetarians) really tasty. It's the nearest thing to an oriental satay, and the little extras that go with it and can be served in the middle of the table on a revolving lazy susan, easily turn a meal into an event. Serves 8.

- 500g/2lbs cooked chicken or turkey (to make from fresh, simply grill 8 chicken breasts and chop into pieces)
- 1 100g/4oz tin tomato puree
- 3–4 tablespoons peanut butter
- 568ml/20fl oz chicken stock (can be made with 2 stock cubes)
- salt, ground black pepper
- 1 teaspoon chilli powder
- 1 teaspoon sugar
- 3–4 tablespoons roast peanuts

Mix the stock with the peanut butter, tomato puree, sugar, roast peanuts and seasoning. When it is hot, add the chicken pieces and heat through. Do not over-stir, as the chicken will become stringy! (If the chicken does disintegrate, it doesn't really matter). Serve immediately with rice, a mixed salad and a selection of the following side dishes:

- sliced bananas
- sliced oranges
- sultanas
- sliced red and green peppers
- pineapple chunks or slices
- sliced tomatoes
- roasted nuts
- desiccated coconut

Spicy turkey/chicken couscous

When simplicity and speed is required, and you don't want to spend a lot of time in the kitchen, here is an ingenious way of using up leftovers that turns them into something a bit more special. Serves 4.

- 450g/1lb leftover cooked turkey or chicken
- 2 tablespoons medium curry powder
- 2 tablespoons paprika
- 1 teaspoon cinnamon
- salt, ground black pepper and garlic
- 375g/14oz couscous
- 100g/4oz chopped apricots, dates or sultanas
- 2 tablespoons olive oil
- 75g butter
- 600ml/1 pint chicken stock (use cube or powder if you have no fresh)

N.B.: When you roast a turkey, pour off any fat and juices in the roasting tin into a bowl and refrigerate. By the next day, the fat will have solidified on the top and can be scraped off and thrown away. The remaining stock on the bottom can be used in this recipe. It will keep in the fridge for 3–4 days.

Put the couscous into an oven-proof dish, cover with the stock and 1 teaspoon salt. Leave for 6–7 minutes to absorb the liquid. Stir in the cooked turkey or chicken, the olive oil, the dried fruit and the spices, dot generously with butter, cover with foil and warm through in a low oven for around 15–20 mins at gas mark 2/150°C (130°C fan oven). Decorate with chopped coriander and serve with a mixed salad or fresh vegetables.

Tarragon chicken

For my passion for dinner-party cooking and for one or two of my favourite recipes, I'm indebted to retired consultant surgeon, Frank Little, and his wife, Susan, a retired GP. For the past fifteen years or so they have opened their home twice a year to seven of us – three vicars and spouses, and a single woman minister – who meet in a cell group. The aim, through listening, is to support, encourage and challenge each other. The Littles, in return for a small offering to their church, make that possible and spoil us rotten with their fine food and wines. Understanding the loneliness of ministry, they also understand how to make us feel loved, cosseted and valued. I can never serve this particular chicken dish without giving grateful thanks for the way they have so generously and selflessly served us, contributing so much to our ministries and, by the by, to the lives of our churches.

This meal can be served hot as a dinner-party recipe, or cold with a nice green salad when friends come round and you want to eat in the garden. Serves 4.

- 4 chicken portions or breasts
- a bunch chopped fresh tarragon or 2 teaspoons dried tarragon
- 284mls/10fl oz chicken stock (can be made with chicken stock cube or powder)
- 1 250g pot of creme fraiche (half or low fat if preferred)
- 1 tablespoon brandy (optional)
- 1 tablespoon flour
- 2 tablespoons Madeira (or sweet sherry)

- 1 teaspoon olive oil
- salt and ground black pepper

Put the olive oil in a frying pan. Coat the chicken pieces in the tarragon and brown in the oil. Sprinkle with the flour and turn the breasts over until they are well coated. Pour over the brandy, then set it all alight with a match (stand well back). Add the stock and Madeira, and cook until the sauce thickens. Add the creme fraiche and season to taste with salt and pepper. Place in a casserole, cover and cook slowly on gas mark 4/180°C (fan oven 150°C) for around 45 minutes and serve. Alternatively, allow to cool and serve.

Sausage and apple turnover

(Suitable for a bring-and-share meal.) As well as being an easy supper dish for family and friends, this savoury sausage and apple turnover is an excellent fallback for a shared meal – possibly for that Harvest Supper. Ever since Christian quiche became a cliché (it was asking for it), thinking up savoury food to share that isn't a variation on the pizza theme has been a real brain teaser. But a word of caution – never, never allow it to be served cold. Churches do have cookers, and cold pastry is about as appetising as corrugated cardboard. Serves around 4–6.

- 1 sheet ready-made puff pastry
- 452g/1lb low-fat sausage-meat
- 1 small red onion – chopped finely
- 1 tart eating apple – chopped finely
- salt, ground black pepper and a sprinkling of dried or fresh sage

Roll the puff pastry sheet, adding around an extra 5 cm to the rectangle on all sides. Mix the sausage-meat with the salt, pepper, sage and chopped onion. Spread it over the raw pastry, leaving a border of around 4 cm. Sprinkle the chopped apple over the top. Brush the pastry border with cold milk, then fold the shorter sides over the mixture. Pull up the longer sides and nip them together, or fold one over the other to form a long parcel. Alternatively, you can make diagonal slashes in the longer sides and overlap the strips to form a plait.

Bake in a hot oven – gas mark 6/200°C – for around 25–30 mins, until golden and crisp. Some apple juice may leak out – but this adds to the charm.

The roll can be cooked before the event, then reheated and re-crisped when needed.

For a vegetarian option: substitute the sausage-meat with 350g/12oz grated, melting cheese.

Leek and bacon hotpot

There is no more comforting winter food than the humble leek. 'Oh the leeks, onions and garlic', the Children of Israel said when they were lamenting the cuisine they'd enjoyed back in Egypt. I have a certain sympathy, I must confess, though I don't think I could exchange my freedom for them. When cooking with leeks, make sure you discard any round, hard centres, especially when spring is in the air and they are almost finished.

Courgettes (zucchini) should be sweet. If they are bitter, either your supplier or you have kept them too long. They may still look all right, but they may not taste all right. Always try a small raw chunk to ensure they're not past their best.

For a low-fat, non-bacon option, turkey rashers are quite passable. Serves 4.

- 3–4 large leeks, chopped finely
- 3 small courgettes (zucchini) chopped into chunks
- 200g/8oz bacon, cut into strips
- 2 teaspoons chicken stock powder (or one cube)
- 1 tub of low-fat creme fraiche
- salt and ground black pepper
- 4 large potatoes cut into slices
- 50g/4oz grated cheddar cheese
- 2 tablespoons olive oil

Place the potato slices into a pan of water, and boil for around 15–20 mins, until just soft. Meanwhile, fry the finely chopped leeks in 2 tablespoonfuls of olive oil until they begin to go soft and golden. As they do, add the courgette pieces. They too should be slightly golden, soft enough to eat, but still retain their bite. Finally, add the strips of bacon and continue to cook for a further 4–5 mins (less if using turkey rashers). Stir in the creme fraiche and stock, and season with salt and pepper.

Drain the potato slices and layer them over the leek and bacon mixture. Top with the grated cheese and bake in the oven for 20 mins, gas mark 4/180°C (160°C in a fan oven), or microwave for 6 mins on high. If the cheese hasn't started to bubble and turn golden, put the casserole dish under the grill for a few moments.

Sausage pasta

The following two recipes can be thrown together quickly with whatever ingredients you have at hand. And that means no thinking ahead, no need to stop at the shops on the way home from work, no digging in the freezer and defrosting at the last minute. They are a lifeline when those long-lost friends turn up unexpectedly – or, as I've done, you actually invite folk round, then forget to put it in the diary. When you find them on the doorstep, take a deep breath, smile sweetly, give them a drink and rush for one of these fast, no-fuss, no-fail recipes. I guarantee it will be cooked in ten minutes.

Serves 2–3. For 4–6, simply double the quantity or add some bacon or other preferred ingredients such as a can of sweetcorn or some broccoli florets or some sliced mangetouts.

- 1 (227g) large, pre-cooked sausage, sliced (either smoked or non-smoked, as you prefer)
- 1 onion, chopped
- 1 red pepper, chopped
- 2 small courgettes (zucchini), chopped
- 2 carrots, peeled and chopped
- 1 400g tin chopped tomatoes
- 1 tablespoon tomato puree
- 1 tablespoon pesto (or 1 teaspoon dried basil, if you have no pesto)
- garlic (either a squirt from a tube or a good sprinkling of the powdered variety)
- salt, ground black pepper

- 1 teaspoon olive oil
- 170g/6oz dried pasta
- freshly grated Parmesan cheese to serve

Put the pasta in salted boiling water (my son tells me it should taste like the Mediterranean), and bring to the boil. Simmer according to the instructions on the packet. Meanwhile, fry the chopped onion and the carrots in a teaspoon of olive oil in a wok or large frying-pan, and when the onion is golden, add the red pepper and the courgettes. When the vegetables appear just cooked, but still crisp (around 5 mins), add the sliced sausage, and the tinned tomatoes, then stir in all the other ingredients.

Serve the sausage sauce on a bed of pasta, sprinkled with freshly or ready grated Parmesan cheese, and a sprig of basil if you have any sitting in a pot on a kitchen shelf.

Boston bean bake

My children's favourite, cheap to make and a real heart-warmer in the winter. Beware the after-effects – all those beans! But they are nourishing if not sociable. Once again, you can use any variety of canned beans you have available at the time. Leave out the sausage or the bacon for a vegetarian option. Serves 4.

- 200g/8oz of bacon (at least 2 slices per person), chopped into pieces, or 2 tins of hot-dog sausages
- 1 onion chopped and fried
- 1 tin red kidney beans, drained
- 1 tin Borlotti (or other) beans, drained
- 1 tin chick-peas, drained
- 1400g tin chopped tomatoes
- 1 teaspoon French mustard
- 2 teaspoons tomato puree
- 1 tablespoon black treacle
- 2 tablespoons Worcester sauce

- 1 teaspoon ground bay leaves
- salt, pepper

Simply fry the onion and the bacon pieces in a saucepan until golden, then add all the other ingredients. Stir well and serve with baked or mashed potato, or crusty bread, and some green vegetables.

Salmon en croute

(Lovely for a special bring-and-share meal, e.g. at Tabernacles or Pentecost.) I make no bones about it – I love fish! Full of protein, low in fat, and fresh salmon is relatively affordable. What I love about serving salmon en croute (or steak for an even bigger treat), is that it looks impressive, stays wonderfully tender due to being steamed in the pastry, and goes down well with an interesting salad. Serves 4.

- 1kg/2lb whole fillet of salmon, skinned, or 4 fillet pieces
- 1 sheet puff pastry (there are two in a 425g pack)
- 200g/8oz herb and garlic cream cheese
- ground black pepper

Roll out the puff pastry sheet until it is big enough to wrap right around the whole fillet, or to wrap around each of the individual fillets when divided into 4 rectangles.

Wash and dry the salmon, then lay on the pastry and cover with the cream cheese, then sprinkle with a little black pepper. If using the whole fillet, brush the pastry on either side of the salmon with cold milk, then cut those edges horizontally into strips, fold the top and bottom pastry edges up over the salmon, then plait the strips over the top – until the salmon and the cheese are enclosed. If you prefer, or if you are making individual portions, simply fold the pastry over the salmon to make an envelope. Brush the top of the pastry with the milk to ensure it goes golden when cooked. The individual portions can be frozen at this stage, taken out, and baked as and when required.

Place on a baking sheet and cook in a fairly hot oven, gas mark 5/190°C for 25–30 mins (less in a fan oven), until the pastry is crisp, or a little longer if cooking from frozen.

For a different kind of treat, you can substitute the salmon with sirloin steak.

Serve with a rocket and avocado salad, and a hot new potato salad. For the hot potato salad simply boil the new potatoes, and when cooked, drain, return to the pan, add some chopped red pepper, black and green olives, 2 tablespoons lemon and honey dressing (p. 225) and toss together in the pan to warm through again.

Salmon lasagne

The first time our children show us how to cook, it feels as if the kitchen has revolved 180 degrees, but once I got over my initial shock and realized I had been preparing them for exactly that, I began to enjoy the benefits of saying, 'I've six coming for a meal tonight. Just rustle me something up, will you?'

My son Joel loved salmon, and loved pasta even more, and once he realized, from the menu in an Italian restaurant, that the two could be combined to great effect, he came up with an ingenious dinner-party recipe for salmon pasta all of his own. So what if his cooking sometimes makes Mama feel a veritable amateur these days? Maturity and experience means I still have a few tricks up my sleeve. I turned it into an alternative lasagne! Serves 4.

- 4 salmon fillet pieces
- half a 250g pack of fresh egg lasagne
- 300g bechamel sauce (see under the cannelloni recipe, p. 202 – make half the amount)
- small pack of asparagus spears
- 30g freshly grated Parmesan cheese

For the ricotta and leek sauce:
- 1 tablespoon olive oil
- 3–4 medium-sized leeks, chopped finely
- 1 450g/1lb tub ricotta cheese
- salt, ground black pepper
- half a teaspoon of ground nutmeg

Heat the olive oil in the pan and cook the leeks until soft and golden. Cool by placing the pan base into a few inches of cold water. Add the ricotta and seasoning and set aside.

To put the lasagne together:
Put the salmon pieces in a microwave-proof dish and cook for around 4 minutes on high. Remove from the microwave, flake with a fork and set aside.

Spread half the ricotta and leek sauce in the bottom of a well-greased, oven-proof dish, around 22cm by 13cm. Cover with a layer of the fresh lasagne. Spread with the rest of the ricotta and leek sauce, then scatter with half the salmon flakes. Put another layer of lasagne on top and cover with half the bechamel sauce, and the remainder of the salmon. Add another layer of lasagne, arrange the asparagus spears on top, then pour over the remaining bechamel sauce. Sprinkle the Parmesan cheese on top and bake in the oven, gas mark 4/180°C for around 30 mins.

If you prefer, you can replace the ricotta and leek sauce with the ricotta and spinach sauce from the cannelloni recipe – simply use half the ingredients. You can also replace the asparagus with some frozen sweetcorn.

Hot smoked mackerel with tangy tomato sauce and chive mash

My husband is not a great fish fan. I don't think many men are. After 30 years I've finally persuaded him that he loves fish pie (just when white fish has almost outpriced our pockets), but oily, heart-friendly varieties such as mackerel were another matter altogether – until, by experimenting, I found the perfect tangy sauce to set if off. Now it has almost reached his favourites list, and is certainly on mine. And if the children won't eat the fish, at least they're getting huge benefits from the tomatoes, which are actually more nutritious lightly cooked than raw, when they just release their lycopene – a great anti-cancer agent.

To serve four:
- 4 pieces smoked mackerel fillet
- 1 small punnet cherry tomatoes
- half teaspoon balsamic sauce (or vinegar – though sauce is preferable)

- a few dashes of Worcestershire sauce
- 2–3 teaspoons tomato puree
- 1 teaspoon brown sugar
- salt and black pepper to taste

For the chive mash:
Cook four floury potatoes, chopped in pieces, in salted water, drain and mash with a large knob of good-quality margarine or butter. Beat till smooth with one large tablespoon of low-fat creme fraiche and a good amount of chopped fresh chives.

For the tomato sauce:
Halve the tomatoes and cook in a heavy pan until the liquid is just beginning to ooze out, then add the other ingredients, and stir gently, so that the half tomatoes can still be seen!

Cook the smoked mackerel fillets in the microwave on high for 2–3 mins, till piping hot, then serve covered in the sauce, with the chive mash and green vegetables.

Tuna bake

It's a great idea – in principle – to invite strangers to a meal, and think we could be entertaining angels unaware, but in practice, when you haven't even managed to get a lunch hour, or any thinking time about menus, and you know, as you battle your way home from work, with that sinking feeling that both larder and freezer seemed very bare when last you had time to look – even finding food to put before potential angels can test creative ingenuity to the very limit.

On the other hand, not having friends and strangers round to eat would be sad. So relax. This tuna bake can be prepared in minutes. The secret is always having a supply of tinned tuna and beans in the pantry, and bags of frozen veg in the freezer, so that you can throw something together at the very last minute.

- 1 packet of unsalted, low-fat potato crisps per person
- 1 small tin of tuna for 2, or a large tin of tuna for 4 – drained
- 1 egg per person, beaten

- 140ml/5fl oz milk per person
- a little chopped raw onion per person (or some dried onion flakes if preferred)
- a few chopped mushrooms per person – optional
- salt (unless the crisps are the ready-salted variety), and ground black pepper
- also a mixture of frozen vegetables (pre-cooked for a couple of minutes) such as peas, sweetcorn, green beans

Topping:
- 50g/2oz grated cheese
- sliced tomatoes

Pour the bags of potato crisps into a deep, well-greased, oven-proof bowl. Add the drained tuna and the pre-cooked vegetables, and the chopped raw mushrooms and onion. Mix in the pre-cooked vegetables very gently. Beat the eggs and milk together and pour over. The mixture should be almost covered. Sprinkle on the grated cheese and add the sliced tomatoes.

Bake on gas mark 4/180°C for around 30 mins, until there is no evidence of any liquid, and the egg mixture is fully absorbed. Serve with green vegetables or salad.

Kedgeree

Want a special breakfast or brunch that's not too heavy – on New Year's Day, for example? This could well be what you're looking for. Serves 4.

- 200g/8oz risotto rice
- 1 teaspoon olive oil
- 426ml/15fl oz stock (using a vegetable cube)
- 500g/8oz yellow smoked cod or haddock
- 1 large onion, chopped
- 50g/2oz butter
- 2 hard-boiled eggs cut into slices or 100g/4oz mushrooms

- ground black pepper and a sprinkling of ground parsley

Fry the onion in a little olive oil until golden, then add the rice and cook for around 2 mins. Meanwhile dot the fish with 25g/1oz butter and cook (with the mushrooms, if being used) in the microwave on high for 5 mins. Use any juices that come off the fish to make up the 426ml of stock and add it to the onions and rice.

Cook until the stock is absorbed, then add the fish and mushrooms, pepper and parsley, and 25g of butter, and serve when piping hot. If eggs, rather than mushrooms, are being used, simply add the hard-boiled slices just before serving.

Spinach risotto

This healthy vegetarian recipe that Peter created, having discovered something like it in a hotel bistro, is proof that you don't have to be an expert to make a celebration meal. This is not the original recipe – we never had it. But I will credit the North Euston Hotel in Fleetwood, near Blackpool, for the idea, and for building my husband's confidence in the cookery department! Serves 2.

- 1 medium red onion, finely chopped
- 150g/5oz risotto rice
- around a litre of vegetable stock (use vegetable cubes or powder)
- 50g/2oz stringy cheese, grated
- 125g/4oz fresh spinach leaves
- black pepper

Also a combination of:

- broccoli florets
- chopped carrots
- chopped courgettes (zucchini)
- half a red pepper
- several cherry tomatoes

Fry the finely chopped red onion in a little olive oil, then add the rice and stir for a while. Add the stock as you go. Begin with around a quarter litre, and when the stock is absorbed, add another quarter litre. Simmer for around 5-6 minutes, and slowly add another quarter litre of stock as necessary, until the rice is just cooked (it will be creamy, but not stodgy).

Add the spinach and stir in well. At first it will appear as if there is far too much greenery, but as you stir it in, the spinach will soften and melt into the risotto. Stir in the grated cheese.

Meanwhile, stir fry your choice of other vegetables in a little olive oil (adding the tomatoes last, so that they don't disappear altogether). Finally, serve the risotto with the stir fry vegetables around the dish.

Cranberry cashew nut loaf

This is a lovely vegetarian celebration option, but it can also double as stuffing alongside roast turkey or chicken. Serves 4.

- 25g/1oz butter
- 1 small red onion, chopped finely
- 225g/8oz chopped roasted cashew nuts
- 125g/4oz fresh wholemeal breadcrumbs
- 1 tablespoon chopped sage
- garlic, salt and ground black pepper
- 2 medium eggs, beaten
- 75g/3oz crumbled Stilton cheese
- 75g/3oz fresh or dried cranberries

Melt the butter in a saucepan and fry the finely chopped red onion until soft. Add all the other ingredients, except the cranberries.

Grease a 700g loaf tin, and line the base with baking parchment and sprinkle with dried cranberries. Spoon half the mixture into the tin, level the surface, then make another layer of cranberries. Spoon over the rest of the nut mixture and level again. Bake on gas mark 4/180°C (160°C for a fan oven) for 45 mins or until golden brown. Leave to cool slightly, then turn out and slice.

Accompaniments

Jewish savoury stuffing

When we married my husband warned me he never ate stuffing – but that was because he'd only ever tried the packet, 'cardboard'-tasting variety. The Jews claim they alone know how to roast poultry – and this is due predominantly to their stuffing the bird to make it special. The majority of traditional recipes suggest boiling the onions. Don't ever. Make it the Jewish way – that makes their poultry the tastiest in the world. Serves 4.

- 1 large onion – chopped and fried in 1 teaspoon of olive oil until golden, then add the liver of the bird until it is thoroughly cooked
- 125g/6oz wholemeal breadcrumbs
- salt, ground black pepper and 1 teaspoon of fresh or dried ground sage

Add the fried onion and liver to the breadcrumbs in a food processor and whirr for a few seconds – till just blended, but still fairly dry and crumbly. Do *not* allow the mixture to go to mush! Pack into the cavity or neck end of the bird, or in a bowl and bake.

Alternatively (e.g. vegetarians) – leave out the liver, but add any of the following:

- 100g/4oz finely chopped, fried mushrooms
- or chopped, vacuum-packed chestnuts
- or finely chopped apples
- or dried apricots.

Lokschen Kugel

At Shavuot (Pentecost), a spring harvest festival that commemorates the giving of the Ten Commandments to Moses on Mount Sinai, and the birth of the Jewish nation, it is a tradition to eat white food, as white reflects the purity of the law. That means lots of cream cheese in mouth-watering disguises. This lokschen kugel (Yiddish for 'noodle pudding') is a Sephardi recipe. Sephardi Jews were the first to arrive in the UK from Spain and Portugal in the fifteenth century. The pudding can be served either savoury or sweet. When I was a child I always fought with my brother for the crunchy top. Bearing in mind that the Jews never mix meat and milk, the savoury version is perfection with a fillet of salmon on top and some green vegetables. Serves 4.

- 300g/10oz ribbon egg noodles, such as tagliatelle, cooked until tender
- 4 tablespoons butter or good-quality margarine
- 2 eggs, beaten
- 250g/9oz curd or cream cheese
- 500ml sour cream or half-fat creme fraiche
- salt, pepper and a good pinch of nutmeg

Mix the warm noodles straight from the pan with the butter or margarine. In another bowl, beat the eggs, cream cheese and cream, then mix with the noodles and add the seasoning.

Pour into a baking dish and cook on gas mark 4/180°C/350°F without a lid until set and the top is brown and crunchy.

For the sweet alternative:
Do not add salt or pepper to the mixture. Instead, when it is complete, stir in 125g/5oz brown sugar, the zest of a lemon and a large cooking apple, peeled, cored and chopped very finely.

Celebration Salads

One of the many things you'll never hear a man say when he is dining out is, 'I'll just have a salad, thank you.' Men cannot believe that a few green leaves can fill the manly-sized hole in their middles, and turn to the steak or the chips instead, hastening their coronary at every meal by around five minutes. So a celebration salad has to be a very special meal to give it man-appeal. Here are two that might just do – with an easy, tangy dressing, tested on a variety of male guinea-pigs, who gave it the thumbs-up.

Salade Paysanne (hot bacon and egg salad)

Serves 2.

- 4 slices low-fat bacon, chopped into pieces
- 2 slices bread (wholemeal or white), cubed
- 1 teaspoon olive oil
- 2 eggs
- mixed salad leaves – my favourite combination is iceberg, Chinese leaves and finely chopped red cabbage
- 1 packet of rocket
- half a red pepper, finely chopped
- 8 cherry tomatoes, halved
- a sprinkling of grated Parmesan cheese

Arrange the salad leaves, rocket and red pepper on two plates. Fry the chopped bacon pieces in a little olive oil, then throw the cubed bread into the pan and fry quickly on both sides to make croutons. Meanwhile, poach the two eggs until firm. Tip the warm bacon and croutons onto the salad plates, then arrange a poached egg on top. Decorate with the cherry tomatoes and sprinkle with Parmesan cheese.

You can substitute the eggs with cooked chicken pieces to make a more traditional Caesar salad if you prefer.

Smoked salmon terrine salad

Gone are the boring old days when salad meant one lettuce leaf, two slices of cucumber, half a tasteless tomato, a hard-boiled egg and a slice of fatty ham, with a dollop of salad cream to turn it into a special treat. Yes, I do remember those days, except that in the Jewish household of my childhood, at Sabbath meals every Friday night, the ham was substituted with a piece of cold, fried fish. I wouldn't dream of giving you the recipe for that. Suffice it to say that since our clothes were hung up to dry in the kitchen, every Monday morning my brother and I went to school smelling worse than the Tyne quayside where the fish was bought. We were convinced it ruined any chance of a love life. So here is a fish salad that won't send your children to school covered in shame. The combination of the fish with avocado really is delicious. Serves 2 as a main course, 4 as a starter.

- 50g/2oz smoked salmon pieces
- a sprinkling of lemon juice
- 1 200g/7oz carton of cream cheese (low fat if preferred)
- ground black pepper
- mixed salad leaves
- several slices of cucumber
- 1 avocado

Reserving a couple of pieces of smoked salmon for decoration, whizz the rest in a blender until it is in tiny pieces. Add the lemon juice to help it along, but don't worry if it gets stuck. It simply needs to be in shreds. Fold the salmon carefully into the cream cheese with a sprinkling of black pepper. The reason for care is that the lower the fat content of the cream cheese, the more easily it can liquefy.

Arrange the mixed leaves down one side of a plate. Scoop the avocado out of its skin with a dessert spoon and slice. Arrange the slices down half the other side of the plate. Fill the space with several spoonfuls of the smoked salmon terrine. Decorate with the cucumber. Serve with fresh wholemeal bread.

You can substitute the smoked salmon with cooked fresh salmon if you prefer.

Honey lemon dressing

- 1 teaspoon Dijon mustard
- 1 teaspoon wholegrain mustard
- 1 teaspoon chopped chives (fresh are best, but dry will do)
- 1 tablespoon balsamic vinegar or liquid
- 4 tablespoons lemon juice
- 2 tablespoons runny honey
- cider vinegar
- groundnut oil (or olive oil if anyone in the family has a nut allergy)
- salt, ground black pepper
- sprinkling of garlic grains or powder

Mix all the ingredients together in a 450g jam jar, then fill it to half full with cider vinegar and shake. Fill to the top with groundnut oil or olive oil and shake again.

Hot Puddings

In the winter, there is nothing like a hot pudding to finish off a meal – the stickier the better, but they don't have to be totally devoid of goodness. Winter fruits are full of vitamins and often, like dates, create their very own stickiness. Of the five very special offerings below (the sweet version of the Lokschen pudding above makes six), only the South African pudding is pure indulgence. Keep the accompaniment to low-fat custard, creme fraiche, yoghurt or ice cream, and it will save on some extra calories.

Sticky upside down butterscotch pear pudding

This is a wonderfully gooey, no-fail, old-fashioned pud. You can replace the pears with one sliced Bramley apple if you prefer. Serves 6–8.

For the topping:

- 3 pears, each peeled and divided into four quarters with the core removed
- 25g/1oz melted butter or margarine
- 75g/3oz soft brown sugar

For the pudding:

- 50g/2oz good-quality, soft margarine
- 50g/2oz soft brown sugar
- 3 tablespoons golden syrup
- 100g/4oz plain or wholemeal flour
- 1 teaspoon bicarbonate of soda

- 1 egg, beaten
- half teaspoon of cinnamon
- quarter teaspoon of nutmeg
- 1 teaspoon ginger
- a pinch of salt

Melt the butter and 75g soft brown sugar, mix together and spread over the base of a deep (loose-bottomed if you have one), well-greased 18cm (7in) round cake tin. Place the pear quarters, radiating out from the centre, on top of the mixture in the tin.

To make the pudding:
Beat together the margarine, soft brown sugar and golden syrup, then stir in all the remaining ingredients and beat till smooth. Spread over the pears, and bake in a moderate oven, gas mark 4/180°C for around 45 mins, until the pudding is well risen and springy to the touch.

Turn out upside down onto a warm serving dish and serve with custard or low-fat creme fraiche.

Sticky toffee pudding

I have tried making a variety of sticky toffee puddings, but this recipe seems to be the best. Apart from which, a little goes a very long way – and it keeps forever (well, almost!). Serves 9–10.

- 110g/4oz soft butter or good-quality margarine
- 175g/6oz soft brown sugar
- 3 eggs, beaten
- 225g/8oz wholemeal or white self-raising flour
- 225g/8oz stoned and chopped dried dates
- 1 tablespoon coffee granules dissolved in 10fl oz/285ml boiling water
- 1 teaspoon bicarbonate of soda
- 1 teaspoon vanilla extract

The sauce:

- 225g/8oz soft brown sugar

- 175g/8oz butter or good-quality margarine

- a 285ml/10fl oz carton of single cream or a 200g carton of low-fat creme fraiche

To make the pudding:
Put the chopped dates into a bowl with the bicarb and the vanilla essence, cover with the boiling coffee. Set on one side and allow to cool.

Meanwhile, cream the butter/marge and the sugar, then add the beaten eggs and fold in the flour. It doesn't matter if the mixture curdles.

Add the dates and coffee to the mixture to form a runny batter, then pour it into a square 10in/25cm dish and bake on gas mark 4/180°C for around 45–50 mins.

To make the sauce:
Mix all the ingredients in a pan and heat until the sugar dissolves. Pour around half over the pudding and place under the grill until it bubbles.

Serve the pudding with the remainder of the sauce and some thick, half-fat creme fraiche, or Greek yoghurt or even vanilla ice cream.

Chocolate pear crumble

This is a recipe I learnt at our French church. It was made by Kathy Perry, an English woman, but I had already discovered that the French think they have improved on the humble English crumble by adding chocolate. Marlene, who runs my local supermarket, had waxed lyrical about crumble. 'Ah yes, I make it with strawberries. And then I put chocolate bits on top.' Personally, I don't think brown chocolate does anything for red fruit, so I'll stick with the pears. Serves 6–8.

- 6–8 ripe pears

- 1 100g bar of milk chocolate, chopped

- 100g/4oz margarine

- 225g/8oz white or wholemeal flour

- 150g/6oz soft brown sugar

Peel and core the pears and place the pieces in a pan of boiling water for around 2 mins. Drain and lay in a pudding bowl. Cover with the chopped chocolate bar.

Rub the margarine, flour and sugar together, or whizz them together in a food processor, then spread over the pears and chocolate. Bake on gas mark 4/180°C for around 25 mins, until golden on top. Serve with low-fat vanilla ice cream.

Rhubarb Brown Betty

(Suitable for a bring-and-share meal, or a home-group or Alpha supper.) Rhubarb grows prolifically in most gardens – except mine! What to do with it all once the freezer is already bursting? I use it at the beginning of a new academic year, when I invite as many new students as I can. They're all feeling a bit homesick and longing for creature comforts. The beauty of this recipe is that it's no-fail, and delicious hot or cold. Serves 8.

- 1kg/2lbs rhubarb, chopped
- rind of 2 oranges and juice of 1
- 50g/2oz dark brown sugar
- 100g/4oz good-quality margarine
- 220g/8oz wholemeal or granary breadcrumbs
- 100g/4oz demerara sugar
- 1 teaspoon ginger powder
- half teaspoon nutmeg
- half teaspoon cinnamon

Gently stew the rhubarb with the orange rind and juice and the dark brown sugar until it is soft. This can be done in a microwave. Remove and pour off the excess juice.

Meanwhile fry the breadcrumbs in the margarine and demerara sugar until toasted. Stir in the spices.

Put a layer of the crumbs in the bottom of a large, greased, oven-proof dish (to mop up the rhubarb juice). Cover in the stewed rhubarb, then finish with a deep layer of breadcrumbs. Bake uncovered for 20 mins or so on gas mark 6/200°C – until the top is really crisp.

Alternatively, no need to cook at all. Simply layer the fruit and toasted crumbs in a see-through dish.

Serve with vanilla yoghurt – delicious!

Apple and mincemeat conde (gluten free)

You need a sweet tooth for this one! Serves 4.

- 1 624g can low-fat rice pudding

- 2 eggs

- 50g/2oz castor sugar

- 1 370g jar mincemeat

- apple puree made from 2 Bramley apples (or a 400g jar)

Mix the egg yolks with the rice pudding in a deep, oven-proof bowl and bake on gas mark 2/150°C for around 20 mins until the top is firm to the touch like baked custard. Spread with a layer of mincemeat and then a layer of apple puree. Whisk the egg whites until stiff, then fold in the castor sugar, and pile on top of the mincemeat and apple. Return to the oven for a further 10–15 mins until the meringue is golden, then serve.

Malva pudding

This traditional South African festival pudding of Dutch origin has a spongy caramelized texture and is often found on the dessert menu of South African restaurants. It is extraordinarily simple and economical to make, considering the special regard in which it's held, and makes a very pleasant alternative to sticky toffee pudding. Serves 6.

For the pudding:

- 1 egg

- 200g/8oz castor sugar

- 1 tablespoon apricot jam
- 150g/6oz self-raising flour
- 1 teaspoon bicarbonate of soda
- pinch of salt
- 20g (just under 1oz) butter
- 1 teaspoon white vinegar
- 250ml (9fl oz) milk

For the sauce:

- 125ml/4–5fl oz single cream
- 100ml/3fl oz milk
- 150g/6oz demerara sugar
- 100ml/3fl oz hot water
- 100g/4oz butter

To make the pudding:

Beat the egg and sugar well in a mixer and add the apricot jam. Melt the butter and the vinegar together, and cool slightly, then add them and the milk to the egg mixture, alternating with the flour, salt and bicarbonate of soda. Beat well, then bake in a greased dish at gas mark 4/180°C for around 45–55 mins.

To make the sauce:

Melt all the ingredients together and pour over the pudding as soon as it's removed from the oven. The sauce will be runny and there will be a lot of it, but the pudding needs it. Serve with creme fraiche.

Cold Desserts

The beauty of a cold dessert is that it can be made in advance and there's no need to worry about it on the day. Once again, apart from the Tiramisu gateau, which goes down a wow on Easter Day, dessert does not have to mean no vitamins or goodness. And there's no doubt about it, an impressive-looking pud certainly does create a party mood.

Honey cheesecake apple pie

For the base:
- 125g/3oz good-quality margarine
- 250g/6oz crushed shortcake or ginger biscuits (crackers or cookies)

For the cheesecake:
- 300g/11oz low-fat cream cheese
- 100g low-fat creme fraiche
- 1 teaspoon vanilla essence
- rind of 1 lemon
- 50g/2oz castor sugar

For the topping:
- 900g/2lbs Cox's Pippins or other eating apples, peeled, cored and sliced
- 50g/2oz good-quality margarine
- 1 large lemon
- 3 tablespoons runny honey

Grind the biscuits into crumbs, mix with the margarine and press into a 27cm (10in) quiche dish, and leave to cool. Beat the cheese with the vanilla, sugar, lemon rind and creme fraiche, and smooth over the base. Melt the marge in a frying pan, add the apple and the lemon rind and juice, and fry till translucent (about 4 mins). Add the honey and lemon juice, and cook at high heat until apples are caramelized. Cool, then tip onto the cheesecake mixture and serve.

Real muesli

(Suitable for a bring-and-share meal or an Alpha supper.) Away with the idea that muesli is only for breakfast! This version of the original Swiss recipe by Mr Bircher is not only more authentic, but it turns a supermarket travesty into a fabulous dinner-party dessert. You can double and triple the quantities, simply by adding whatever fresh fruit you have to hand to feed the hungry hordes. Serves 6.

- 1 large pot of low-fat Greek-style or thick yoghurt
- 2–3 tablespoons of half-fat creme fraiche
- 2 peeled and grated tart eating apples
- the grated rind and juice of a lemon
- the grated rind and juice of an orange or 108ml/4fl oz of orange juice with bits
- 1 large cup of porridge oats
- 1 large cup of brown sugar
- 1 cup of sultanas – or better still, a generous amount of fresh green and black grapes
- 1 chopped banana (optional)
- a few blueberries, raspberries, chopped strawberries or fresh pineapple
- a few toasted nuts
- a sprinkling of grape nuts (optional)

Mix all the ingredients – except the fresh fruit – together. If the mixture is too runny, add a few more oats; if too thick, add a little fresh bottled orange juice. Add more lemon juice if you prefer a predominantly tangy lemon taste. Place in a shallow bowl and decorate with whatever fresh fruit is available: raspberries, strawberries, nectarines, chopped pineapple, blueberries and grapes are all excellent. Sprinkle a few toasted chopped nuts over the top, and just before eating, some grape nuts.

Hazelnut strawberry torte

This is a favourite old recipe that never fails to delight. What makes this so different is the crispy, nutty shortcake, that sets off the delicious new English or Scottish strawberries and creamy cheese filling so well. Serves 6–8.

- 100g/4oz good-quality margarine
- 100g/4oz castor sugar
- 175g/7oz plain flour
- 50g/2oz chopped, toasted hazelnuts
- 300g carton of low-fat cream cheese
- several drops of vanilla essence
- a large punnet of strawberries

Beat the margarine, flour, hazelnuts, and 75g of the sugar together until the mixture is firm enough to press into a tin. Add a little more flour if necessary.

Divide the mixture in two and press into two, 20cm/8in greased tins, lined with baking parchment. Cook them on gas mark 4/180°C for 12 mins, or until just golden.

Allow to cool a little, then turn out onto a rack to become completely cold and crisp.

Mix the cream cheese with the vanilla essence and 25g of sugar and spread over both pieces of shortcake. Halve the strawberries and place on top of each. Sandwich both together and serve.

Tiramisu gateau

This is one of my Easter favourites and can be decorated with chocolate eggs. I know this involves a lot of bowls, but believe me, it's worth it. I make my own Victoria sponges, but you can buy sponge rounds that fit a 21cm/8in, round, loose-bottomed tin.

For the 3 sponges:
Whisk 4 large eggs with 175g/6oz sugar until white, thick and creamy. Fold in 125g/4oz of plain flour. Pour the mixture into three shallow 21cm/8in cake tins, lined with greased baking parchment, and bake for 10–15 mins on gas mark 4/180°C until pale golden and firm to the touch. Turn out and leave to cool.

For the filling:

- 100 ml/4fl oz strong coffee (dissolve 4 heaped teaspoons in boiling water)
- 100 ml/4fl oz Tia Maria liqueur (make 200ml/8fl oz coffee if alcohol-free version preferred)
- 2 eggs
- 25g/1oz castor sugar
- 142ml/5fl oz whipping cream
- 500g marscapone cheese
- 1 teaspoon vanilla essence
- 6 chocolate flakes, or 2 100g bars of milk chocolate, grated

Separate the eggs and whisk the yolks with the castor sugar until creamy. Add the marscapone cheese and vanilla essence. Whisk the egg whites until stiff in a separate bowl. Beat the cream until thick in another. Fold the marscapone mixture, stiff egg whites and cream together.

Line the bottom of a deep 21cm/8in tin with greaseproof paper. Put in one of the sponges. Pour over a third of the coffee liquid, then cover with half the marscapone mixture. Sprinkle heavily with grated chocolate. Place another sponge on top and press down gently. Pour over one third of the coffee, then cover with the remaining marscapone mixture and grated chocolate as before. Place the last sponge on top (it may stand above the edge of the tin), pour over the remainder of the coffee and let it soak into the sponges.

Leave for at least 24 hours. Decorate with cream and the remaining chocolate.

Summer fruits trifle

This is quick and easy, and nothing compares with its amazing bitter-sweet taste. But be warned – it isn't cheap to make and you may want to keep it in reserve, as I do, for special occasions like church Passovers. (Though, if you intend to serve it to Jewish people at Passover, you'll have to substitute the amaretti cookies with special, no-yeast Passover biscuits!) Serves 10–12.

For the base:

- 200g cantuccini or amaretti biscuits (or cookies)
- 4 tablespoons sweet wine, or *creme de cassis* (or blackcurrant juice)
- about 1kg/2–3lb fresh or frozen summer fruits – cherries, blackberries, blackcurrants, raspberries and blueberries
- 50g/2oz castor sugar

For the topping:

- 450ml double cream
- 500g carton best-quality fresh egg custard
- 200g/7oz bar white chocolate
- 500g carton low-fat creme fraiche
- several drops of vanilla essence
- 2 teaspoons castor sugar

Place the biscuits in a trifle bowl. Moisten with the wine or liqueur. Bring the summer fruits up to the boil in a heavy saucepan, then strain off the fruit, allow to cool a little, then place over the biscuits. Add 50g/2oz castor sugar to the liquid in the pan and boil for around 5–8 mins until it becomes a thick syrup. Cool slightly and pour over the biscuits and the fruit, then leave to cool completely.

Melt the chocolate in a bowl over a panful of simmering water, then leave it to cool slightly. Meanwhile, whisk the cream and set half of it aside. Add the melted chocolate to the custard and fold in half the cream. Spoon it over the fruit trifle base, and allow to set in the fridge. Once it is set, mix the remaining whipped cream with the creme fraiche, vanilla essence and 2 teaspoons sugar, and cover the trifle with it.

Decorate with a few pieces of fresh red or black fruits, or some toasted chopped almonds. Make it the night before for the best results. Once you have cut into this trifle, be warned, it liquefies quickly, so try to finish it in one sitting – or enjoy it in a runny state the next day.

Great Grandma's baked cheesecake

My great grandmother's secret recipe for baked cheesecake (don't share it with anyone!) is decidedly Ashkenazi and came with her from Lithuania at the turn of the century. Once she was widowed and lived alone, she made it as a tray bake, cut it into squares and served it on her best plates with cake-forks at afternoon tea on the Sabbath. Any leftover squares can be frozen and kept for future celebrations. Serves 8–10.

For the pastry crust:

- 100g/4oz self-raising flour
- 60g/2–3oz butter or good-quality margarine
- 50g/2oz icing sugar
- 1 egg yolk

Mix all the ingredients together, and press onto the base of a 21cm/8in loose-bottomed sandwich tin.

For the filling:

- 200g/8oz curd or cream cheese
- 25g/1oz ground almonds
- 50g/2oz castor sugar
- 2 eggs separated and 1 egg white
- 2 tablespoons sultanas (plumped in boiling water for 5 mins, then drained)
- 1 small teaspoon vanilla essence
- grated rind and juice of a lemon
- a large knob of butter or good margarine

Blend all the ingredients together except the egg whites. Whisk the 3 egg whites (including the white left over from the pastry) till stiff, and fold into the mixture. Spoon over the unbaked pastry case and level with a knife.

Bake on gas mark 4/180°C for around 40 mins, until the top is golden and the whole feels firm to the touch. (It will spring back.) Once it is removed from the oven it may crack, but the crevices will shrink as it sinks a little while cooling. Cool, push gently out of the tin, and dust lavishly with icing sugar to serve.

Quick fresh fruit cheese flan

There's nothing like having an impressive-looking dessert in your repertoire that's really easy, tastes wonderful, and can be made fairly quickly, or at least, at the last minute. This pud is one of my favourites – mainly because the sweetness and tartness work so well together. And not only that – it is loaded with fruit, so is relatively healthy, if the other ingredients are low or reduced fat.

- 250g/6oz shortbread biscuits
- 60g/2oz good-quality margarine, melted
- 2 200g/7oz tubs low-fat cream cheese
- 50g/2oz castor sugar
- a few drops of vanilla essence
- around 1kg/2lb fresh fruit
- 150ml/5fl oz orange or other fruit juice
- 1 heaped teaspoon cornflour (cornstarch)

Grind the shortbread biscuits, mix with the melted margarine and press into a 28cm/11in flan dish. Allow to cool. Beat the castor sugar and vanilla essence into the cream cheese and spread over the base. Cover the cream cheese in a variety of sliced and chopped fresh fruits – pineapple, nectarines, grapes, and strawberries all work well. Dissolve the cornflour in a little of the juice, then add the rest and bring to the boil to thicken. Allow to cool and pour over the fruit as a glaze. Refrigerate to set.

Cakes

Because of the pressure of our busy lives, baking isn't something we do very much these days, and that's sad. I fear that many children will grow up never knowing what it's like to lick out a mixing bowl, or get their fingers stuck in the dough, or be greeted at the front door by the most mouth-watering of smells. Nothing is as satisfying for a child, or ensures their future dedication to the culinary arts as seeing family and friends wolf down the results of their efforts – however basic.

My grandmother was a wonderful baker. I'll never forget the sight of her stirring and kneading with the skill, dedication and determination of an artist at work, puffing a Woodbine out of the corner of her mouth. I used to think it was the ash that made her baking taste so good. My mother never managed to make her cakes rise or taste like my grandmother's. Neither can I, I have to say, and it's one of the greatest laments of my life.

Grandma's squidgy lemon cake

My grandmother, who loved the tanginess of lemons, was one of the first to try pouring a lemon syrup over the cake after it had cooked, rather than adding the juice to the raw mixture. I have worked at her basic recipe for around thirty years to make it even more special.

- 110g/4oz good-quality margarine
- 200g/8oz sugar
- 2 eggs
- 170g/6oz self-raising flour
- 1 teaspoon baking powder
- juice and rind of two lemons

For the filling/topping:

- 200g low-fat cream cheese
- 2 tablespoons good-quality lemon cheese
- 1 teaspoon castor sugar

Beat together the margarine and 125g of the sugar, then add the self-raising flour, the egg yolks and the rind and juice of a lemon. Whisk the egg whites until stiff and fold in. Pour into 2 18cm well-greased tins, the bases lined with baking parchment. Bake for 20 mins on gas mark 4/180°C (150°C in a fan oven) or until it springs back in the centre.

Meanwhile, boil the rind and juice of the remaining lemon with 75g castor sugar until it thickens very slightly. Remove the cake tins from the oven and pour the syrup over each half immediately. Leave to cool and turn out.

To fill and top the cake:
Mix the cream cheese with the lemon cheese and a little castor sugar, spread it over each half, and sandwich together.

Easy no-fail almond cake (gluten free)

This almond cake is a tribute to anyone who is on a wheat-free diet and is always passed over when cake comes out. It is a delicious treat for anyone, possibly as a dessert, with lovely summer fruits – strawberries, raspberries, stewed gooseberries, and especially with stewed pink rhubarb. It also freezes well and keeps for at least a week, if you want a dessert to last. In fact, it just becomes more moist.

- 3 eggs
- 160g/5^1/$_2$oz ground almonds
- 150g/5oz castor sugar
- rind and juice of a lemon or an orange (depending on preferred flavour)

Separate the egg yolks from the whites. Beat the yolks with the sugar until pale and creamy, then add the almonds. Add the rind and juice of the lemon or orange. Whisk the whites till firm, then fold carefully into the mixture.

Transfer to a 17.5cm round or square tin, lined with greaseproof paper.

Cook on gas mark 4/180°C (150°C for fan ovens) for 35 mins. Cool, then sprinkle with icing sugar, cut into slices and serve – alone or with stewed fruit, or thick Greek yoghurt, or low-fat creme fraiche.

Mrs Guinness' rich fruit cake

When I married Peter, great great grandson of Arthur Guinness of Dublin, brewer, I became rather fond of the rich black stuff – in recipes, I have to say, rather than drunk from the bottle. It's full of healthy stuff like iron, and if it makes a mean stew, it makes an even meaner fruit cake. What better to have on your tea trolley on a Sunday afternoon? It can even make a pleasing alternative to Christmas cake for those who can't abide marzipan or icing sugar, but it does benefit from being sliced and buttered.

- 250g/9oz butter
- 175g/5oz dark muscovado sugar
- 350g/12oz plain flour
- 600g/1lb 5oz dried fruit
- 4 eggs
- 1 teaspoon mixed spice
- 1 teaspoon bicarb dissolved in 256ml/9fl oz Guinness (heated to boiling)

Beat together the butter and sugar, then add the remaining ingredients. Grease a 23cm-square tin and line with baking parchment. Pour in the mixture, cover and bake on gas mark 3/170°C for 2 hours or until firm in the centre. Remove from the oven, cool completely, then turn out. This cake will improve with keeping for a few days in a cool place. If it dries out, pour a little brandy over it and leave it to soak in for 24 hours. It is wonderful buttered, with a slice of Lancashire or Wensleydale cheese.

Tray Bakes and Cookies

I never have as much unalloyed fun as in all-female company, so for my last birthday I decided to invite the 'girls' round – none under forty, and some I didn't know too well, but I sensed they'd enjoy it. We laughed ourselves senseless. A full meal is a bit daunting when you don't get in from work until 7 p.m. – so it was coffee (or wine) and tray bakes, made the night before. Tray bakes are a good way of turning a home group, coffee morning or afternoon tea into a treat. There's no rolling out individual biscuits and they go a great deal further than a cake.

Tangy lemon slice

- 125g/4oz margarine
- 30g/1oz icing sugar
- 185g/6oz plain flour
- 2 teaspoons cornflour
- 4 eggs
- 120g/4oz castor sugar
- rind and juice of 2 lemons

Beat the margarine, icing sugar, cornflour and 150g/50oz of flour together till smooth and press into a 23cm slab tin, lined with greaseproof paper. Bake for 10 mins in a moderate oven – gas mark 4/180°C – till lightly browned.

Whisk the cornflour and the remaining 25g/1oz of flour with the lemon rind and juice, then add the remaining ingredients together – the eggs and castor sugar – and pour over the base. Bake in a moderate oven (temperature as above) for 15–20 mins until firm.

Cool, cut into slices, and serve well dusted with icing sugar.

Extra fruity flapjack

Here's an even healthier version of the ever popular, cholesterol-reducing flapjack (it's the oats that do it), put together when I had a fruit bowl full of leftover, browning bananas (why do my family always leave them to over-ripen then complain they're over-ripe?). But they do give it a special tang.

- 125g/4 oz good-quality margarine
- 350g/12oz porridge oats
- 125g/4oz desiccated coconut
- 75g/3oz chopped pecans (optional)
- 175g/6oz honey
- 125g/4oz dark brown sugar
- 1 teaspoon cinnamon
- $1/2$ teaspoon ground nutmeg
- 200g/7oz chopped dried dates
- 75g/3oz chopped dried apricots
- 4 bananas
- juice of a lemon

Heat the margarine in a saucepan with the honey and brown sugar until it is melted, and then add the oats, coconut, and nuts. Press half of the oat mixture into a greased 25cm by 35cm tin (at least 2.5cm deep). Mix the dates, apricots and chopped bananas with the lemon juice and spread over the mixture. Press the remaining mixture evenly over the top.

Bake at gas mark 4/180°C for 25–30 mins, until the top is golden and feels firm. Leave to cool in the tin, then cut into squares.

Millionaire's shortbread

Although this can be bought at most bakeries, their offering doesn't really compare with this home-made version. And it really isn't difficult or time consuming.

For the base:

- 75g/3oz sugar
- 150g/5oz margarine
- 250g/9oz plain flour

Rub all the ingredients together, then press them into a 20cm by 29cm Swiss roll tin. Bake on gas mark 3/170°C for 15 mins or so, till firm. Remove from oven and cool.

For the toffee filling:

- 100g/4oz margarine
- 100g/4oz sugar
- 2 tablespoons golden syrup
- 1 can condensed milk

Melt the butter, syrup and sugar in a heavy-based pan, then add the condensed milk. Bring to the boil and simmer gently for 7 mins, stirring all the time to prevent it catching on the bottom. Pour over the shortbread and allow to set.

For the chocolate topping:

- 1 175g/7oz bar good-quality plain or milk chocolate

Finally, melt the chocolate in a bowl over a pan of boiling water and spread over the mixture.

Chocolate tiffin

By the time she was eight, my daughter, Abby, was making tiffin for tea parties, family birthdays, presents and any or every special occasion. This is in fact her recipe. I have no idea where she first found it, but now that she is no longer at home, I have to make it myself – and think of her with love as I do so.

- 125g/4oz margarine
- 4 tablespoons golden syrup
- 2 tablespoons cocoa powder

- 200g/8oz biscuit (cookie or cracker) crumbs (Nice biscuits, shortbread or digestive)
- 50g/2oz sultanas, raisins or chopped dates
- 100g/4oz crunched cornflakes

For the topping:

- 175g/7oz good-quality cooking chocolate – milk or plain to taste

Melt the margarine, golden syrup and cocoa powder in a pan, then add the biscuit crumbs, crushed cornflakes and dried fruit, and stir. Press into a greased 30cm by 20cm (12in by 8in) tin and allow to cool. Melt the topping chocolate in a bowl over a pan of boiling water, or in the microwave on full power for approximately 30 seconds, then spread over the tiffin. Cool and slice.

Spicy cranberry shortbread

This is easy-to-make, Christmas shortbread with a difference. At other times of the year, simply substitute sultanas for the cranberries.

- 225g/9oz plain flour
- 150g/6oz butter or good-quality margarine
- 100g/4oz light, soft brown sugar
- 2 tablespoons clear honey
- 1 teaspoon ground ginger
- 1 teaspoon ground cinnamon
- 75g/3oz dried cranberries

Rub the butter, flour and spices together until they resemble fine breadcrumbs, then add all the remaining ingredients, and press the mixture down firmly into an 18cm shallow tin (round or square). Sprinkle with castor sugar and bake on gas mark 3/160°C for 20 mins. Remove from the oven and cut into squares, triangles or fingers.

Date (and nut) bars

My mother-in-law was Canadian and made the most amazing cookies. When I married Peter, we had one of those 'You will bake like my mother' moments that many couples have when they first tie the knot. And since I was hopelessly in love, I said yes, and acquired the recipes. So here is her turn-of-the-century, simple date-cookie mix that is one of the best date cookies I have ever tasted. It never turns out the same twice, so don't worry about it. Just go easy with the bicarbonate of soda (or the mixture will end up on the oven floor), and surprise your home group with a North American toffee-like treat.

- 50g/2oz melted butter or good-quality margarine
- 200g/8oz sugar
- 100g/4oz pl flour
- half teaspoon bicarb of soda
- 125g/5oz chopped dates
- 50g/2oz chopped hazelnuts (optional)
- 1 beaten egg
- pinch of salt

Melt the butter in a heavy pan, then mix in the remaining ingredients. Pour into a 20cm by 29cm well-greased Swiss roll pan, lined with baking parchment (this is a must!). Bake on gas mark 4/180°C for 12–15 mins, until firm. Cool and cut into squares.

Sweet Endings and Presents

I end with my *pièce de resistance* – one final triumph after any meal, and a lovely give-away in a pretty box, but the recipe has a story.

When I was first married, the late Linda Nicholls, who lived down the street, was my adopted mum. She was one of those wonderful old saints who had had a difficult life nursing a sick husband, and who was left widowed to raise three children on her own. But she never complained of loneliness. How could she, when so many surrogate children like me relied on her wisdom, warmth and support?

This is her unique recipe for chocolate truffles. I have never seen it in print, never found another to match it, and never found another with quite their soft, melting centres. I tried not making them last Christmas, to see if anyone would notice. There was an outcry!

Squidgy chocolate truffles

- 100g/4oz marshmallows
- 200g/8oz good-quality chocolate – plain or milk, as preferred
- 4 egg yolks
- 100g/4oz butter
- 4 tablespoons of icing sugar
- 1 or 2 teaspoons Baileys (optional)

Melt the mallows, chocolate and butter in a bowl over a pan of boiling water. (Watch they don't overheat or the mallows will solidify.) When the mixture has melted, remove from the heat and beat in the icing sugar and egg yolks – one at a time. (It may curdle a little initially – but don't despair, it will become the consistency of melted chocolate.) Cool in the fridge until firm enough to handle. Roll into balls with cold hands – and toss in some drinking chocolate. Keep in the fridge, as they will soften at room temperature. The truffles keep for around a fortnight, and can be frozen.

And finally

When I was a teenager, I remember going to a home where an old copper plaque with the words, 'Christ is the Unseen Visitor in this home, the Unseen Guest at every meal', hung above the dining-room table. It seemed rather lugubrious, and I suspected it was there to encourage children to mind their manners. Not surprisingly, it threw a dampener and solemnity on the occasion, rather than filling us with the merriment that his actual presence would certainly have done.

In the Talmud, one of the ancient sages, Rabbi Shimon, offered these similar, yet life-enhancing words of wisdom on eating 'with attention':

> *Three who eat together idly*
> *attending to neither friends nor food*
> *and sharing no words of Torah or Truth –*
> *it is as if they have eaten sacrifices to the dead.*
> *Without attention, there is no life.*
>
> *But three who eat together mindfully*
> *attending to talk and taste*
> *and sharing words of Torah and Truth –*
> *it is as if they have dined with God,*
> *for God is Reality and Reality is ever present.*
> *All we need do is attend.*[37]

At its best, sharing food is about recognizing taste, colour, creation, creativity, and conversation, and God's part in all of it. Every meal can be a celebration, a party in miniature.

Our most memorable Sabbath meals when the children were young always ended up in deep theological discussion, from 'Where is heaven?' when they were little, to 'Where is God?' as they got older. And Reality himself seemed to draw very close as our special guest. Their friends loved it. Perhaps that's why

Joel decided to recreate the experience in his university bedroom. He has just bought his first home, and become a dad. Our gift to him on these life-changing occasions was a pair of candlesticks for his dinner table.

One final after-dinner grace

Praise the Lord, O my soul
>*and forget not all his benefits –*
who forgives all your sins
>*and heals all your diseases,*
who redeems your life from the pit
>*and crowns you with love and compassion,*
who satisfies your desires with good things
>*so that your youth is renewed like the eagle's.*   Psalm 103:2–5

May our experience of eating and being satisfied liberate us from the illusion that resources are scarce and that we have to hoard.

May what we drank help us to be fluid and flexible, and bring healing to our world.

May what we have left behind – the leftovers on our plates, the words we have exchanged, the ideas we've shared, the openness and intimacy we've created, the space we made for God to make himself known – be a blessing to each and every one at this table, that we may go out and be a blessing to others.

An Abridged Passover Haggadah in English

For use at home or in a church

Some General Instructions

For use at home, follow these instructions but make the 'top table' your only table, and of course use your own cutlery and best crockery.

For the hand washing, somewhere accessible from the top table, you will need:

- a jug of water

- a hand towel

- a bowl

On the top table:

- a 3-tier *matzah* holder. You can buy or make one. It is often simply a flat cloth bag, decorated with embroidery, into which 3 *matzahs* (unleavened bread 'slices') are placed, one on top of the other.

- Elijah's Cup. A small glass left ready for a guest who never arrives!

- Communion chalice(s)

- 2 candlesticks, candles and matches

- serviettes in which to wrap the *Afikomen*

- prize(s) to redeem the *Afikomen*

- a cushion to lean on

- a Seder dish. A large ordinary, or decorative plate or platter will suffice, on which is placed:

  Charoseth (recipe to follow)

  a baked egg (a token of grief for the destruction of the Temple, and a symbol of resurrection)

  parsley or watercress (representing the hyssop)

  shankbone of a lamb (to represent the lamb sacrificed at Passover when there was a Temple). It is best for someone to buy a leg of lamb some weeks before and keep a part of the bone in the freezer until you need it.

  horseradish (the bitter herbs, symbolic of the suffering in Egypt)

So that the team arranging the event know everything that is required, we usually give them instruction sheets (see below). They look a bit daunting, but in fact it is hardly more complicated than a harvest supper, or church fellowship meal. If helpers know the ethos of the event, they are more likely to prepare the room appropriately and have the required items to hand.

From experience, we have found that congregations tend not to know what to expect, and therefore in the advertising we always quote the first paragraph of the team instructions given below, to encourage families, single people, the elderly and the very young to come.

A microphone and simple amplifier is essential for the leader of the evening because he or she will need to be heard above the general noise. At most family occasions, the family does not always listen in awed silence to the head of the household each time they open their mouths! In our experience, when the meaningful moments come, such as remembering what Jesus did at the Last Supper, a profound silence descends upon even the smallest children. The music group will add to the atmosphere with worship songs, while everyone shares in the Communion. If of course you are celebrating at home in a smaller group of say 12 people, then it is all much simpler. You can do without microphones and music groups and sing unaccompanied, but you will still need to read the liturgy out loud if other members of the family group are chattering, asking questions or causing a distraction.

Instructions for the Organising Team

The Aim & Objective of the event you are organising

People are coming to an event that lasts about 3 hours, but passes very quickly. The Passover is essentially an extended family celebration at home, so we are keen for it to be a family occasion with both young and old present. Singing, worshipping, chatting and enjoying a good meal are all interwoven. A snack is not appropriate. Each person or group should bring enough food for a reasonable evening meal (first course and dessert) to share with others from a buffet – the meal is very much part of the occasion.

Arrangement of the room

Have one 'top table' for the service leader(s) and a group with them, which should be big enough for candlesticks and a few other items. Then have tables of 8–10 people so that each group can 'copy' what is being done. The leader(s) will be using microphones and amplification, so everyone will hear the instructions, teaching and liturgy.

Food and equipment

1. Transparent plastic 'glasses' for each person (for wine). Small, low ones are best.

2. Cutlery and crockery (see the summary list on page 288).

3. Table cloths. Paper catering rolls are quite acceptable.

4. Colourful paper napkins for each person.

5. Red wine (70cl bottles). Spread them around the room so people can help themselves. Buy one bottle per 4 or 5 adults plus 3 extra. (You can sell off excess bottles). The top table will need some extra wine for Communion.

6. Orange juice for the youngsters. Why not spoil them with real stuff, rather than squash; it is a special occasion!

7. Non-alcoholic wine for teetotallers.

8. Water (in jugs).

9. Coffee and tea, for after the meal.

10. Eggs. Hard-boiled, peeled and sliced. These will be eaten by everyone just before the meal begins. Prepare one egg for every three people. (One egg per person is more correct, but many find this a bit daunting as an appetizer!).

11. Unleavened bread (*Matzah*). To ensure it is in stock, purchase from your local supermarket as soon as possible. You will need one box per 10 people (at least one box per table). Buy a few extra boxes. They are made by Rakussens and are blue or red (they do not need to be 'kosher for Passover') and they keep for ages. On the day, open the box, tear off the lid and slit both inner packets along the top with a sharp knife. Leave the Matzah in the boxes on each table so people can help themselves. The boxes usually have some Hebrew on them, which adds to the occasion.

12. Fresh parsley. Order from your local grocer beforehand as they won't be expecting such a quantity. One small sprig is needed per person, failing that buy watercress instead.

13. Salt. Provide a bowl of salt water for every 10 persons.

14. Horseradish root. You need one root about 3/4" diameter and 6" long per 100 people. Cut it up into small pieces to look like half length matchsticks. This item creates a lot of interest, and some tears if it is too strong! In some areas of the country it is hard to find a supplier of horseradish root, so if you really can't get it use horseradish sauce, but it doesn't have the same visual impact. Perhaps you could ask a friend living in an area of the country where there are Jewish delicatessens to post you a root or two the week before.

16. *Charoseth.* The following recipe should serve approximately 20 people, but for a large group of up to 150, four times this amount is ample. A dessert spoonful will be sufficient for each group.

> You will need:
>
>> • 100g (4 oz) chopped walnuts
>>
>> • a large cooking apple, peeled, cored and sliced
>>
>> • 1 tsp sugar
>>
>> • 2 tsps cinnamon
>>
>> • Red wine to moisten
>
> Blend the dry ingredients in a mixer, then moisten with wine until it is the consistency of mortar.

17. Chalices for Communion will be required immediately after the meal, distributed from the top table.

18. Word-sheets – for those parts of the liturgy in which everyone shares, and the words of the songs.

19. Finally, do anything you can to help make the meal feel special – Passover is in the same league as Christmas. The only thing *not* to bring is leavened (i.e. ordinary) bread.

Summary of requirements

Each person will need:
- 1 transparent plastic 'glass' for wine/drink
- 1 side plate
- A knife, fork and spoon
- 1 napkin

Each group will need:
- 1 plate with the hard boiled egg ready-sliced and a spoon to serve it with.
- 1 medium sized plate with parsley, and a desert spoonful of *Charoseth*.
- 2 slivers of horseradish per person.
- 1 bottle of wine per 5 persons (opened!).
- 1 jug of water.
- 1 small bowl with salt water in it, and a teaspoon.
- 1 box of *matzah* (unleavened bread), which should stay in the box.
- A table decoration e.g. a small posy of flowers.

During the meal each person should serve themselves from the buffet. At the end of the meal, after tea and coffee, the service continues. Some clearing can be done during the coffee time, but full clearing will need to wait until the very end.

Timings

6.30pm. Start.

First part of service.

7.30pm. Eat

8.30pm. Tea/Coffee

Second part of service

9.30pm. Finish

Laying out the room

Make space so people can dance conga-style around the room. The buffet should have access on every side to speed people through.

Music

A strong lead from a music group makes a big difference. The choice of songs and hymns needs to be familiar, although there is opportunity to learn some folk melodies. Some of the songs we have used from time to time are inspired by the psalms used in the actual Passover service liturgy. Most modern hymn and chorus books have the words and music and copyright can be purchased through Christian Copyright Licensing Ltd (www.ccli.co.uk). Jewish folk songs are sung at the Passover; why not choose your own to give the event that special Hebraic flavour, examples are, *Hinei Ma Tov Umanaim, Chevet Achim Gam*

Yahad and *Hevenu Shalom Aleichem*. In addition, there are a number of new songs by Messianic Jews, notably, *Great and wonderful, are thy wondrous deeds* and *You shall go out with joy and be led forth in peace* by Stuart Dauermann. Obviously, you can choose hymns like, *Glory be to Jesus, who in bitter pain* and *When I survey the wondrous cross*, for when the chalice is being passed round, but choose livelier ones at other times, especially if you intend to dance. Encourage a few people to start a slow grapevine dance around the tables, like a long, circular conga and others will eventually join in.

Liturgy

Bold text in the service (see p. 268) indicates responses that all the participants should say together. There are eight such sections, all numbered on the congregational response sheet on p. 259. Only the first one, the blessing for the wine is repeated, (four times in all). The leader should announce the number (shown by the # symbol and a number) to prompt everyone to join in. You may also want to use the hash symbol to refer participants to the words of songs printed out on an additional songsheet of your own making.

Inventory

- a jug for water
- a hand towel
- a bowl for hand-washing
- *matzah*
- a *matzah* holder
- a *Seder* dish
- *Haroseth*
- a baked egg
- a shank-bone
- horseradish
- parsley
- lettuce
- Elijah's Cup
- chalices
- candlesticks
- candles
- matches
- a bowl (small)
- salt

- a cushion
- a serviette for the *Afikomen*
- chocolate eggs to redeem
- two orders of service
- song-sheets
- the four questions
- the three sons' words
- a few breadcrumbs
- a torch
- a dustpan & brush

Questions

Photocopy this page. Cut along the lines and give to each volunteer who will ask the questions or say the part in the service.

Question 1
Why is this night different from all other nights? Why can we eat leavened or unleavened bread on any other night, but tonight only unleavened bread?

....

Question 2
Why can we eat all kinds of vegetables on any other night, but tonight only bitter herbs?

....

Question 3
Why do we not normally dip our food, but tonight we dip it twice?

....

Question 4
Why can we eat sitting or leaning on any other night, but tonight everyone has to lean?

....

The wise son says:
What is the meaning of all the signs and rules which the Lord our God has commanded us? (Deuteronomy 6:v20).

....

The wicked son says:
What does this service mean to you? (say it a bit insolently).

....

The foolish son says:
What's this for ? (say it as if you're a bit stupid!).

....

Passover Congregational Responses

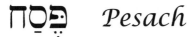 *Pesach*

1 Baruch ata Adonai
Elohenu melech ha'olam
baure peri hagafen.

Blessed are you, O Lord
our God, King of the Universe
who created the fruit of the vine.

2 Dom, Tsfardeyah, Kinim
Arov, Dever, Schechin,
Barah, Arbeh, Cheshech,
Makas Bechodos

Blood, Frogs, Lice,
Wild beasts, Pestilence, Boils,
Hail, Locusts, Darkness,
Death of the firstborn.

3 Da-yainu
Pesach
Matzah
Maror

It would have been enough for us
Passover (old adjective "Paschal")
Unleavened bread
Bitter herbs

4 Therefore it is our duty to thank, praise, glorify, exalt, honour, bless, extol, and adore him who performed all these miracles for us and for our forefathers. He brought us from slavery to freedom; from anguish to rejoicing; from mourning to feasting; from darkness to light; from bondage to redemption. Let us therefore sing a new song to him. Hallelujah!

5 Blessed are you O Lord our God, King of the Universe, who redeemed us and our forefathers and has kept us alive to eat *matzah* and *maror* tonight.

6 Blessed are you O Lord our God, King of the universe who in his goodness feeds the whole world. With grace, loving kindness and mercy he gives food to all flesh, for his mercy endures for ever. By his great goodness we have never been without food and never will be, because he does good to all and feeds the creatures he has created.

7 For you have redeemed us, freed us, fed us, delivered us, saved us and spared

us. Therefore, our limbs which you have made; the spirit and soul that you have breathed into our nostrils; the tongues that you put into our mouths, will thank, bless, praise, glorify, exalt, reverence, sanctify, and ascribe kingship to you, O Lord our King. For every mouth shall thank you, every tongue shall confess to you, every knee bow to you, and every being fall down before you.

8 Blessed are you Almighty God and King, great in praises, God of thanksgivings, Lord of wonders who enjoys our singing and our worship.

The Background to the Passover (to be used as appropriate)

The Seder

The Jewish festival is called, in Hebrew, *Pesach* (from which we get the word 'Paschal'), from the Hebrew verb, 'to pass over' or 'to spare'. *Pesach* is celebrated for seven days, and nothing with yeast in it may be eaten – bread, cakes, biscuits. Only unleavened bread is permitted. This is why it is also known as 'the Feast of Unleavened Bread'. On the first evening of Passover, the *Seder* ('the Service' or 'the Order') is read and chanted in Jewish homes. The father of the household leads, and the mother, in particular, has been preparing the home, the festival meal, special unleavened cakes and other recipes for many days. It is the night when Jews remember that they escaped to freedom from the tyrant in Egypt, the night when the angel of death passed over their homes, which had the blood of a lamb daubed on the doorposts. The *Torah* – the Old Testament Law, the books of Moses – instructs that the festival must be fulfilled with groups of friends and relatives. No one should be left on their own. It commands that this festival should be kept annually. The account of the first Passover is to be found in Exodus 12 – 15.

The Haggadah

The service liturgy is in a book called the *Haggadah* – 'the narration' or 'the telling'. Copies are often beautifully illustrated for children and adults. The service is in Hebrew and Aramaic, which means that for most Jews it is not in their everyday language, so children and many adults will not fully understand what they are saying. It is only fairly recently that Israeli Jews have had a service in their common language. The *Haggadah* we use here is our own much-abridged and adapted version. It has been paraphrased using the English translations from three *Haggadahs* which are given in the Bibliography below. Jewish groups have written their own adaptations. Most are for home use, but there are many for communal use, especially in *kibbutzim* in Israel, where the whole community takes part. In some ancient communities the rabbi would lead the *Seder*. The first part of the *Haggadah* is very old. Copies from the tenth century prove its antiquity, but hints about issues from the Second Temple period make it evident that parts predate the time of Jesus. The general form and the wording used for the first part and the blessings after the meal are very likely the same as would have been in use during the time of Jesus. Scholars believe the early parts are much older.

The Sages

Various rabbis are mentioned in the *Haggadah*: Rabbi Hillel, an old man when Jesus was young, and a very influential and respected Pharisee; Rabbi Gamaliel, a doctor of the law, a member of the Sanhedrin, and a teacher of the Apostle Paul; and Rabbi Akiba, born around AD 40, who attributed his greatness to the goodness of his wife, Rachel! He lived to a grand old age, but was martyred in AD 137 for his support of the revolt by Bar Kochba against the Romans.

The freedom theme

The theme of freedom and liberation from tyrants has inspired persecuted Jews in different ages, including this century. Christians could well benefit from a realization that they rejoice in a freedom obtained on that particular Passover around AD 29, but that they still wait with longing for the full freedom they will enjoy when they celebrate this feast within the kingdom of heaven.

On which night was the Last Supper?

The Gospel writers all assume we know about Passover. Jesus' parents went every year to Jerusalem for the Passover, and when Jesus was twelve he got into trouble for not going home with them. On the 14th day of the month of Nisan at midday, the slaughter of the lambs took place in the Temple precincts. In Jesus' last week, according to Matthew, Mark and Luke, this took place on the Thursday afternoon until sunset. 15th Nisan starts at nightfall on the Thursday, the evening when they celebrated the Passover – just the twelve disciples and Jesus. After the *Seder* – Jesus' Last Supper with his disciples – they sang hymns (as we will do) and went out to Gethsemane, having had a full meal, wine and a long service. In the night Jesus was arrested and tried, and by Friday midday the Roman authorities had crucified him. He died at 3 p.m. He therefore was crucified on the first day of Passover. Friday nightfall was the start of the

Sabbath, so Jesus' body was hurriedly placed in simple grave-clothes and laid in a new tomb nearby.

It is a little puzzling how so much travelling – from Gethsemane to Annas' house at night, then on to Caiaphas the High Priest's house, then to Pilate, then to Herod, then back to Pilate, and then to ill treatment by the soldiers and crucifixion – could all occur between midnight Thursday and midday Friday on a festival day. Some suggest that Jesus had this early Passover meal even on the Wednesday; consequently there was enough time for the trial and the travelling.

John, uniquely in his Gospel, keeps the same timing and sequence as the other Gospel writers, but has the proper Jewish Passover on the Friday night. He begins the account of the Last Supper with, 'Now *before* the feast of the Passover' (John 13:1). In John's Gospel, Jesus celebrates a Passover meal on Thursday evening, one day earlier than everyone else. Judas Iscariot is able to go out and do his betrayal. The events take place during Thursday night and Friday morning, so that Jesus is himself killed between midday and 3 p.m. – at the *same* time that the Passover lambs are being slaughtered in the Temple precincts. John ends his account with the need to get Jesus buried hurriedly because it was the Day of Preparation. They did not want to leave the bodies on the cross for the Sabbath, 'for that Sabbath was a high day' (John 19:31). It was the day of 'Preparation for the Sabbath' and the Passover.

The main significance for John is that Jesus **is** the Passover Lamb. For St Paul the paramount idea is: 'Christ our Passover has been sacrificed for us, so let us celebrate the feast, not with the old leaven of corruption and wickedness, but with the unleavened bread of sincerity and truth' (1 Corinthians 5:8). The chronology of the events is much discussed. Whichever view one takes, either John's view or the Synoptic Gospels' view, it is evident that Jesus celebrated a Passover meal with his disciples during that week, and died and was buried on Friday afternoon.

The Last Supper table arrangement

What was the possible arrangement of the guests that evening? Roman and Greek meals at the time were held at low tables, at which one lay down, leaning on one's elbow. A typical table is likely to have been in three sections, in the shape of a squared C. The disciples lying on their sides, Roman style, at right angles to the low table, would all have their feet pointing out to the walls of the room. A servant could supply food from inside the C shape, gaining access at the open end of the C. The servant could wash feet by going along the walls of the room, washing them one by one, whilst dinner was being eaten.

One can conjecture that Peter is at the extreme end of one of the branches of the C shape. John is at the other end of the C, across the gap. Jesus lies next to John, Judas next and the remaining disciples in turn round to Peter. At one point in the evening Peter cannot hear what Jesus has said, so he calls across to John to find out. John is lying 'close to Jesus' breast' (John 13:23–26). He can then ask Jesus, 'Who is it that will betray you?' Jesus replies that he will give a dipped morsel to that person. Judas must be within reach, possibly lying on the other side of Jesus from John, so that Jesus can supply him with this morsel. It is reckoned that this place is reserved for the honoured guest, right next to the host. If so, Jesus is giving Judas a sign of friendship.

Leaning

There are references to 'leaning' in the *Haggadah*, and it is traditional that who-ever is leading the service has a cushion at his back and slouches against it to make it appear as if he is leaning. It appears that traditionally, unlike the Romans, the Jews ate sitting upright. But since they had to be ready to get up and go at any moment, they ate this meal in haste, leaning in wait for the signal. This is another reason why John would be leaning against Jesus' breast.

The four cups

The Passover rules required that four cups of wine be drunk, because it was a feast and great celebration was encouraged. Normal meals would not have wine. Each cup has come to have symbolic significance, described in the text below.

A time to rejoice

The Jewish Passover is a time for laughter and plenty of jokes. Humour, partic-ularly the self-mocking variety, is a safety-valve for the Jewish people. It means they can laugh at themselves before others laugh at them. It enables them to take some of the sting out of persecution and hardship. They talk easily about the way many in the world have tried to destroy them – and they laugh about it. It is essentially a festival of freedom, and therefore the first night is one of rejoicing. It is followed by eight days without leaven of any kind, as a more sober reflection of life in the wilderness. The Passovers we have enjoyed with church groups of 60 to 150 have been wonderfully exciting and celebratory, with children sensing the power of the occasion. There is singing, laughing, dancing and plenty of noise. And yet it can move to a deep sense of reverence and awe.

The significance of Passover

Passover has great significance for the Christian. It is the source, inspiration and meaning within the Communion service. It is a celebration of freedom from the bondage of sin. It is a Eucharist – a thanksgiving – for our deliverance from the sting of death, and looks to the joy of Easter.

An introduction to the Jewish Passover

Passover is the great festival of freedom. Only a few generations have passed since Abraham became the founding father of the people of faith, but already they are subject to the lust for power that makes one group of human beings oppress another – they are slaves in Egypt, humiliated, beaten and abused, making bricks for the Pharaohs.

But this story is a picture of the eternal story of God's great rescue of his people. It takes ten horrendous natural disasters before the Egyptians make any connection between their own suffering and the suffering they are inflicting on their slaves. Finally, a terrible virus takes off their firstborn sons.

But the Hebrews have been told to daub the blood of sacrificial lambs on their doorposts. And when the Angel of Death sees it, he 'passes over' their homes, and they do not die.

Then there is another passing over. They flee from the Egyptians. There's no time to make sandwiches, no time for the bread to rise – so they grab the unleavened bread and make a dash for it, but can't go fast because of the children. And the Egyptians in their chariots catch up with them at the Red Sea.

But (this story is full of buts!) God parts the Red Sea and they cross over to safety, freedom and the Promised Land. In response to many commandments in Exodus, Leviticus, Numbers and Deuteronomy, the Jewish people have celebrated that key event in their history ever since.

It is a great celebration – a chance to rejoice, sing, laugh, joke,[38] and drink four glasses of wine – the very symbol of rejoicing. Even if you were too old, infirm or poor to travel the distance to the Temple in Jerusalem, you could convert your tithe into food and drink for the occasion and enjoy them at home.[39] And that is exactly what happened after the destruction of the Second Temple and throughout the Diaspora of the Jewish people.

But the idea is not simply to tell the tale. Tonight, we're going to live it. It must seem as if we were actually there. As a child I so well remember my grandfather saying, in the middle of the service, 'The Egyptians made us suffer – oy, it was terrible!', and I really thought he had been there, enduring slave labour.

Alternatively, you can imagine you have joined the hordes in Jerusalem to celebrate that fateful Passover when Jesus of Nazareth is crucified, and unwittingly, you find yourself caught up in the Holy Week events that will change the world.

Indeed, we were all in captivity. This celebration is a wonderful picture of what Easter is for Christians. Jesus submits to humiliation and abuse – so that death can pass over God's people, once and for all. It's at the very moment when he knows what's to come, that he chooses to enjoy this great historic celebration and have one last party with his friends. 'I have earnestly desired to eat this with you.' He is even looking forward to it as much, if not more, than ever.

The familiar Passover symbolism he knows so well now becomes an audiovisual aid, so that, whenever his disciples celebrate the Passover, as they will every year, they will remember what their freedom cost him.

The night before the Passover

It is imperative that not a trace of leaven (raising agent) should be found in the home once the Passover has begun. So the mother[40] will spend the entire day before the Passover cleaning the house from top to bottom.

It has become a tradition for the father, followed by all the children, to inspect the house, using a torch to look into every corner, every nook and cranny, to ensure the job has been done properly. Anyone who knows a Jewish woman will know that when it comes to housework, they are the real professionals and there is not a hope of him finding anything. So several bread or cake crumbs will be strategically placed for the children to find.

This is a fun way to begin the evening. The leader with a torch or candle to hand can lead the children in a hunt for a pile of crumbs – which must then be cleared away into a dustpan, or publicly burnt. Meanwhile, whoever is playing 'mother' can say:

> St Paul writes: 'Don't you know that a little bit of yeast works through the whole batch of dough (and makes it rise)? Get rid of the old yeast (of sin), so that you will be a new batch of dough without yeast, as I know you really are. For Christ, our Passover Lamb, has been sacrificed. Therefore, let us keep the festival, not with the old yeast, the yeast of malice and wickedness, but with bread without yeast, the bread of sincerity and truth.'   (1 Corinthians 5:6–8, paraphrased)

The Passover Haggadah

The lighting of the candles

The mother lights the candles as she says:

Blessed are you, O Lord our God, King of the Universe. We light these candles at the beginning of this festival, as a reminder that your word is a lamp for my feet and a light on my path.

Kiddush and the first cup

Everyone fills their glasses for the first cup. Whilst each holding it up all say together:

#1 Blessed are you, O Lord our God, King of the Universe, who created the fruit of the vine. [Baruch Ata Adonai, Elohenu Melech ha'olam, baure peri hagafen.]

Leader: Blessed are you, O Lord our God, King of the Universe, who has chosen us from among all peoples and made us special by giving us your commandments. In your love you have given us times for gladness, and seasons of rejoicing; you have given us this festival of unleavened bread as a celebration of the freedom you have given us and in memory of our departure from Egypt.

Blessed are you, O Lord our God, who has given us life and brought us safely to this time of our joy.

Now all drink (a sip will do) from the first cup, the Cup of Sanctification or Holiness ('I will bring you out').

The father washes his hands

The leader washes his hands: a young person pours some water over his wrists and hands, and then the leader dries them.

[This practice originates from the ritual washing before handling sacrifices in the Temple.]

Parsley dipped in salt water

This 'first dipping' is to be passed round and then before it is eaten, the leader says:

Blessed are you, O Lord our God, King of the Universe, who brings forth fruit from the earth.

[This is purely to arouse interest! The parsley reminds us that they used sprigs of hyssop to daub the doorposts with the blood of the lambs so that the Angel of Death would see it and pass over.]

The breaking of the middle matzah

The middle of the three matzot is taken out of the coverlet, and broken in half. One half is wrapped in a serviette and kept hidden by the father. This piece is called the Afikomen (the 'desert'). It will be the last thing to be eaten, and will represent the Passover lamb. The other half matzah is returned to lie amongst the other two.

[The *Afikomen* is in modern Judaism the symbol of the Passover lamb. The three loaves under one coverlet are called 'a unity' – for the Christian, a picture of the Trinity. The wrapped *Afikomen* could be seen as a picture of the death and burial of Christ. On all Sabbaths and festivals, two *matzot* are used because two portions of manna fell during the time of wandering in the wilderness when Moses took the people of Israel out of Egypt. The extra middle *matzah* commemorates the Exodus, and is also known as 'the bread of poverty'.]

The leader raises the three matzot and the Seder dish and says:

This is the bread of affliction which our fathers ate in the land of Egypt. Let all who are hungry for more than just physical food come and eat. Let all who are in need, who want something more in their lives, come and celebrate the Passover.

Fill the second cup.

The four questions

The service is designed to encourage questioning. Before the actual story of the Passover is told, four children, each in turn, ask a question that has been given to them before the service began (see p. 258).

(1) Why is this night different from all other nights? Why can we eat leavened bread or unleavened bread on any other night, but tonight only unleavened bread?

(2) Why can we eat all kinds of vegetables on any other night, but tonight only bitter herbs?

(3) Why, when we don't normally dip our food, do we have two special dippings tonight?

(4) Why can we eat our food sitting upright or leaning on any other night, but tonight we are all supposed to lean?

The reply given by the father

Leader: We perform these rituals to help us remember a very special story. Long ago we were slaves of Pharaoh, King of Egypt; but God brought us out with his mighty hand and an outstretched arm. It's a terrible thought, that if the Lord, blessed be his name, had not brought our forefathers out of that country of cruelty, we, our children and our children's children might still be slaves.

No matter how clever or comfortable we become, the more we talk about the escape from Egypt the better. We must talk about it all the days of our lives, even after the Messiah has come.

Three people have been chosen before the service to represent the wise child, naughty child and stupid child. Each reads on cue the comments given to them before the service began (see p. 258).

Leader: The Torah speaks of four kinds of children which the father must answer: a wise and diligent child, a naughty child who couldn't care less, a stupid child and one who never asks the right questions.

    (1) What does the wise child say? '**What is the meaning of all the signs and rules which the Lord our God has commanded us?**' (Deuteronomy 6:20).

Leader: The father's duty then is to explain all the rituals of the Passover to him.

    (2) The naughty child says, '**What does this service mean to you?**' (Exodus 12:26).

Leader: Now because he says, 'to you', it shows that he has no interest in the service. This is a very serious thing, for it means that he is separating himself from the rest of the people of Israel. The father should therefore give him a sharp answer and say, 'It is because of what the Lord did for me when I came out of Egypt' (Exodus 13:8). 'For me', the father should point out, and not for him; for if he had been in Egypt, God would not have thought him fit to become a free person.

(3) The stupid son says, **'What's this for?'**

Leader: 'This is to remind us of how God brought us out of Egypt and out of bondage by the power of his mighty hand' (Exodus 13:14).

Now since the fourth son cannot ask the right questions, the father has to answer what he hasn't been asked! He says:

Long, long ago, before the days of Abraham, our forefathers were worshippers of idols. But now, the Lord is our God and we serve only him.

Joshua told the people, 'The Lord God of Israel says, "I took Abraham your father out of the land East of the river Euphrates and led him into the land of Canaan. There I increased his family and gave him Isaac his son. Isaac had two sons, Jacob and Esau. To Esau I gave the country around Mount Seir, but Jacob went down into Egypt"' (Joshua 24:2-4).

Blessed be God, who keeps the promises he made to Israel. Blessed be he, for he calculated the exact number of years we should spend in slavery in Egypt so that he could fulfil what he had told to Abraham. He said, 'One day your children will be strangers in a land which isn't theirs. They will be slaves to the kings and peoples of that country and will live in misery for 400 years. But I will punish that cruel nation and they will come out with great wealth' (Genesis 15:13-14).

[Moses is not mentioned anywhere in the service because no one is to attract attention away from God who rescued the people himself.]

Everyone raises the second cup without drinking from it.

[This raising and setting down of the second cup without drinking it is sometimes humorously called 'the false alarm'.]

Leader: This is the promise which we and our forefathers have clung to. Pharaoh is not the only tyrant who has tried to destroy us. There have been Pharaohs in every generation, but the Holy One, blessed be he, delivers us from their hands.

At this point in the service the 6 million who died in the Holocaust are remembered in a short silence. You may want to encourage participants to reflect as well on other genocides caused by the tyranny of one human being to another.

Replace the cup.

Leader: My father, Jacob, was the original wandering Jew. He went down into Egypt as an immigrant, because of a famine in Canaan. There were only about seventy of us at the time, but we multiplied and became like the stars of heaven. We grew strong and powerful and the Egyptians became afraid of us. So they mistreated and abused us. They gave us hard work to do, they beat us and refused to pay us. They took away our newborn babies and drowned them in the Nile. Then we cried to the Lord, the God of our fathers, and he heard us and saw our suffering and oppression. He brought us out of Egypt – he alone in the power of his might – with terror, with signs and with wonders. He said:

'I shall pass through the land of Egypt, I – not an angel.

'I shall strike down every firstborn, I – not any seraph.

'I shall destroy all the Egyptian gods, I – not any messenger.

'I am the Lord, the one God; there is none beside me.'

And these are the ten signs which the Holy One, blessed be his name, brought upon the Egyptians, to prove that he alone is God:

Spill a drop of wine, by dipping your finger in your wine, and touching your plate, as each plague is mentioned.

[The wine is spilt to signify the spilling of blood, and to remember that we take no pleasure in the plagues inflicted upon the Egyptians. Each was a direct attack on a specific Egyptian deity, rather than on the people themselves – though they had to endure the awful consequences.]

#2 All say each plague slowly together:

Blood	Dom
Frogs	Tsfardeyah
Lice	Kinim
Wild beasts	Arov
Pestilence	Dever
Boils	Schechin
Hail	Barah
Locusts	Arbeh

| Darkness | Cheschech |
| Death of the firstborn | Makas Bechodos |

[Participants sometimes add to the list, 'mother-in-law, kids...'!]

Optional section

[This piece from the *Haggadah* is an example of some of the rather more contorted rabbinical arguments that should make us want to praise God even more.]

Father: Rabbi José the Galilean said he could prove that in addition to the ten plagues in Egypt, the Egyptians were also afflicted by fifty at the Red Sea.

Child: How did he do that?

Father: Well, the Torah says that when the plagues broke out, the magicians said to Pharaoh, 'This is the finger of God.' But when the Egyptians drowned in the sea, the people of Israel saw God's mighty hand. If one finger on God's hand caused ten plagues, then five fingers would produce fifty.

Child: So there were really sixty plagues.

Father: Rabbi Akiba reckoned on 240.

Child: Is that a record?

Father: No. Rabbi Akiba proved that every plague God brought really consisted of five plagues.

Child: Five plagues?

Father: Yes. Remember the verse that says, 'He sent forth against them the fierceness of his anger, wrath, fury, trouble and angels of destruction'? Well, anger is one, wrath is two, fury is three, trouble is four, and angels of destruction is five. That adds up to 250 plagues – 50 in Egypt and 200 at the Red Sea. How thankful we ought therefore to be to our God for his many acts of kindness.

[End of optional section.]

Da-yainu

[*Da-yainu* means, 'It would have been enough for us', or 'that would have been sufficient'.]

#3 The word 'da-yainu' is to be said or sung in response to each phrase said by the leader:
If he had only brought us from Egypt and not executed judgment on them.
   Da-yainu.
If he had only slain their firstborn and not given us their wealth. **Da-yainu.**
If he had only given us their wealth and not divided the sea for us. **Da-yainu.**
If he had only divided the sea for us and not caused us to pass through it on
   dry land. **Da-yainu.**
If he had only satisfied our needs in the wilderness and not fed us with
   manna. **Da-yainu.**
If he had only brought us to Sinai and not given us his law. *Da-yainu.*
If he had only brought us into the land of Israel and not built for us his
   Temple. **Da-yainu.**
In building the Temple for us, he gave us a place to atone for our sins.
   Therefore how much more must we go on thanking God for all his
   great mercies to us.

Rabbi Gamaliel used to say, 'He who does not explain the following three things on *Seder* night has not done his duty.'

The leader points to each item on the Passover dish and says:

(1) The Paschal Lamb – *Pesach* (the shankbone).

[Apart from the *Afikomen* (the half *Matzah*), this shankbone is the only reminder today of the lambs sacrificed in the Temple. A shankbone – a forearm or leg of lamb – is used because of the text, 'with outstretched arm he delivered us'.]

(2) The unleavened bread – *Matzah*.

[The bread is strictly made so that the dough does not rise. As a precaution, it is pierced, to prevent fermentation during baking. 'He was pierced for our transgressions' (Psalm 22; Isaiah 53).]

(3) The bitter herbs – *Maror*.

[The horseradish's bitter taste is to remind us of the harshness of the slavery in Egypt. The baked egg is an ancient symbol of mourning in the Middle East. It is burnt to remember that the Temple was burnt and destroyed. Without a Temple, no actual lamb sacrifices are possible. 'Messiah shall cause sacrifice to cease' (Daniel 9).]

The leader or others continue with the following questions and answers:

Leader: Why did our forefathers eat the Passover lamb when the Temple was standing?
All: Response: They ate it because God passed over and spared the homes of the people of Israel on the night when he smote the Egyptians.

Leader: Why do we eat unleavened bread?
All: Response: We eat it because at the time when God appeared in glory to rescue our forefathers, they were in such a hurry that there was no time for their dough to rise.

Leader: Leader: And why do we eat bitter herbs?
All: Response: We eat them because the Egyptians embittered the lives of our fathers in Egypt.

Leader: So you see, in every generation every Jew should feel as if he himself actually came out of Egypt.
All: #4 Therefore it is our duty to thank, praise and honour our God, to sing psalms of his highest power and glory, and to bless and adore him for performing all these miracles for us and for our forefathers.

He brought us from slavery to freedom, from sadness to gladness, from mourning to feasting, from darkness to light, from captivity to redemption.

Let us therefore sing a new song to him. Hallelujah!

Read or sing from the 'Little Hallel' (Psalms 113 & 114). Or sing other songs. Then lift the second cup and all say together:

#5 Blessed are you, O Lord our God, King of the Universe, who redeemed us and our forefathers and has kept us alive to eat matzah and maror tonight.

Leader: So, Lord our God, God of our fathers, grant us health and happiness so that we can enjoy many more anniversaries and festivals in the future.

Blessed are you, O Lord, who has redeemed Israel.

All: #1 Blessed are you, O Lord our God, King of the Universe, who created the fruit of the vine. [Baruch ata Adonai, Elohenu Melech ha'olam, baure peri hagafen.]

Drink the second cup – the Cup of Promise: 'I will free you.'

The men wash their hands with a small quantity of water poured over their hands and a towel to dry them, and say:

Blessed are you, O Lord our God, King of the Universe, who commanded us to wash our hands.

[The servant would wash the feet of all the guests at a feast in ancient times.]

Someone should read this text from John's Gospel whilst the men are washing their hands:

During supper Jesus...rose from [the table], laid aside his garments, and girded himself with a towel. Then he poured water into a basin and began to wash the disciples' feet, and to wipe them with the towel... 'Do you know what I have done to you? If I then, your Lord and Teacher, have washed your feet, you also ought to wash one another's feet' (John 13:2-5, 12-14).

Eating the Passover symbols

Each table should follow the example of the top table, wait for the leader to get each item ready, then say the blessing (Beracha) and eat.

Matzah
The leader breaks off a piece of matzah from one of the three matzot in the holder, then passes a smaller piece to each person, and says

Blessed are you, O Lord our God, King of the Universe, who brings bread from the earth and has commanded us to eat matzah.

Maror
The leader dips maror (horseradish) into the charoseth, gives a piece to each person and says:

Blessed are you, O Lord our God, King of the Universe, who has commanded us to eat bitter herbs.

[Charoseth although it is made from walnuts, apple, red wine, cinnamon has a brown, mud-like consistency. The tiny stick of horseradish looks like a piece of straw sticking out of the mud.]

Matzah, maror and charoseth

Each person receives a piece of horseradish dipped in charoseth, sandwiched between two small pieces of matzah, and the leader says:

We do this to remind us of what Hillel said when the Temple was still standing. He did it to fulfil the verse which says, 'With unleavened bread and bitter herbs they shall eat it' (Numbers 9:11).

[This reminds us of the mud-and-straw bricks that the Israelites had to make in Egypt.]

[Cutlery is a modern invention! Either of these 'dippings' is possibly the 'sop' – the 'morsel' dipped in food. It is a Middle Eastern custom for the host to give it to the most honoured guest.

Leader: John 13:26: 'So when he had dipped the morsel, Jesus gave it to Judas, the son of Simon Iscariot.' The second dipping has now taken place.

The meal is now served

Beginning with slices of hard-boiled eggs in salt water, eaten with matzah.

[The salt water reminds us of the Red Sea and the tears of the Israelites in Egypt.]

During the meal the 'father' hides the Afikomen. In large gatherings it's a good idea to hide several half pieces of matzah, each wrapped in a serviette (a different colour to the ones used with the meal or there will be forgeries!) After the meal the children will search for the Afikomen, and the 'father' will redeem them by exchanging them for a small prize such as a chocolate egg.(One for each child) They can then be shared after the meal as the "communion" bread.

The grace and thanksgivings after the meal

The pieces of Afikomen (representing the Passover lamb) are distributed by the leader among the tables and eaten after the following readings. Nothing more may now be eaten.

Leader: 'Jesus, on the night when he was betrayed, took bread and when he had given thanks, broke it, and said, "This is my body which is broken for you. Do this in remembrance of me"' (1 Corinthians 11:23–24).

Pause.

'...Christ our Passover lamb has been sacrificed for us. So let us celebrate the feast, not with the old leaven of corruption and wickedness, but with the unleavened bread of sincerity and truth' (1 Corinthians 5:7–8).

Fill the third cup – the Cup of Blessing: 'I will redeem you.'

At this point, chalices rather than individual cups can be used. They can be shared by everyone, children included, when the time comes to drink.

The third cup, the Cup of Blessing, is so called because it follows psalms and prayers giving thanks to God. To bless (in Hebrew, *baruch*) means 'to give thanks'. In Greek the word is *eucharisteo*, from which we get the title 'Eucharist' for our Communion service, as we give thanks for the bread and the wine.

Read or sing several psalms or songs, one or two can lead off in dancing a grapevine around the room.

All: #6 Blessed are you, O Lord our God, King of the Universe, who in his goodness feeds the whole world. With grace, loving-kindness and mercy he gives food to all flesh, for his mercy endures for ever. By his great goodness we have never been without food and never will be, because he does good to all and feeds the creatures he has created.

Various blessings that occur here can be turned into intercessions by the participants:

The All-merciful! He shall reign over us forever and ever.

The All-merciful! He shall be blessed in heaven and on earth.

The All-merciful! He shall bless... *(relations, friends, family, those who are ill or grieving).*

The All-merciful! He shall be praised through all generations. He shall be glorified among us and honoured for ever.

The All-merciful! He shall send Elijah the Prophet who will tell us when that great day is coming.

The All-merciful! He shall send abundant blessing on this house and table at which we have eaten. May we who celebrate this freedom meal tonight live as free people, challenging injustice and striving to bring reconciliation to the world.

The All-merciful! He shall one day break the yoke off the necks of all who suffer or are persecuted because of their love for you, and shall lead us all at last into eternal freedom.

The All-merciful! He shall make us worthy of the days of the Messiah and of the life of the world to come.

Leader: May the Lord, the maker of *Shalom* [peace], give *Shalom* to us, to the land of Israel and Palestine, to Iraq, to Afghanistan and to all those lands where there is war and conflict.

All: Blessed are you, O Lord our God, King of the Universe, who created the fruit of the vine.
[Baruch ata Adonai, Elohenu Melech ha'olam baure peri hagafen.]

The third cup (the Cup of Blessing) is passed around for all to share.

As we drink this Cup of Blessing, we read from the earliest written account of the Last Supper, and a commentary on it, both written by St Paul:

Leader: In the same way after supper, he took the cup and when he had given thanks, he gave it to them saying, 'Drink this all of you; this is my blood of the new covenant, which is shed for you and for many for the forgiveness of sins. Do this in remembrance of me' (1 Corinthians 11:25–26).

The cup of blessing which we bless, is it not a sharing in the blood of Christ? The bread which we break, is it not a sharing in the body of Christ? (1 Corinthians 10:16).

Sing various reflective songs during Communion. which can lead into a more party mood once the cup(s) have been returned to the leader.

Fill the fourth cup (the Cup of Wrath). People can now revert to using their own glasses for this cup. At the same time fill Elijah's Cup.

[Elijah's Cup is a spare goblet that has been on the table since the beginning. The Jews expect that Elijah will return before the Messiah comes. 'Jesus' disciples asked him, "Why do the scribes say that first Elijah must come?" Jesus replied, "Elijah does come, and he is to restore all things; but I tell you that Elijah has already come..." The disciples understood that he was speaking to them about John the Baptist' (Matthew 17:10–13).

The scriptures connected with the fourth cup refer to judgment on the enemies of God. It is sometimes called the Cup of Wrath. We remember that Jesus drank the Cup of Wrath, when on the cross he was forsaken by God for our sake. After the Passover meal, in Gethsemane he prayed, 'Father, if you are willing, let this cup pass from me; but not my will but yours be done.']

Place Elijah's Cup on the table. The 'mother', followed by some of the children, goes to open the front or back door of the house, while the leader says:

Pour out your wrath on the nations that do not know you and the kingdoms which do not honour your name, for they have devoured Jacob and laid waste his home. Pour out your fury on them, pursue them in anger and destroy them from under your heavens (Psalms 79:6–7; 69:24; Lamentations 3:66).

More worship songs with a prophetic ring such as "These are the Days of Elijah" may be sung here, with more dancing if people are still awake enough.

Leader: The soul of every living creature shall praise you, O Lord, and the spirit of all flesh shall glorify your memory. From everlasting to everlasting you are God. We have no king, redeemer or saviour to deliver and rescue us except you. For the Lord never slumbers or sleeps.

[The actual Passover service is much longer than this version. Children and others may be somewhat sleepy by now!]

He awakens the sleeper, rouses the slumberer, makes the dumb speak, frees the captive, supports the weak, and lifts the burdens from our shoulders.

Even if our mouths were filled with song like the sea, our tongues with joy like its mighty waves, our lips with praise like the breadth of the sky, if our eyes shone like the sun and the moon and our hands were spread out like the eagles of heaven, if our feet were as swift as the hind, we should still be incapable of thanking you adequately for one thousandth part of all the love you have shown us.

All: #7 For you have redeemed us, freed us, fed us, delivered us, saved us and spared us. Therefore, our limbs which you have made, the spirit and soul which

you have breathed into our nostrils, the tongues which you put into our mouths will thank, bless, praise, glorify, exalt, reverence, sanctify, and ascribe kingship to you, O Lord our King. For every mouth shall thank you, every tongue shall swear to you, every knee bow to you, and every being fall down before you.

Leader: Praise be to your name for ever, O our King. You, Lord God of our fathers, are worthy of song, adoration, hymn, psalm, might and dominion, eternity, greatness, strength, glory, holiness, kingship, blessings and thanksgivings now and for all eternity.

All: #8 Blessed are you, Almighty God and King, great in praises, God of thanksgivings, Lord of wonders, who enjoys our singing and our worship.

Some final songs of praise can be sung, with a last dance or two.

Leader: As we lift the final cup we'll shout together, 'Next Year in Jerusalem!' – the cry of hope of every Jew in the Diaspora – a great proclamation of the hope of eternal freedom for all humanity when we reach the final Jerusalem.

All: Next year in Jerusalem!
#1 Blessed are you, O Lord our God, King of the Universe, who created the fruit of the vine. [Baruch ata Adonai, Elohenu Melech ha'olam baure peri hagafen.]

Drink the fourth cup – 'I will take you as my people.'

Leader: Our *Seder* is now complete according to the laws and customs of our people. As we have observed it here, so may we fulfil it in our lives in the days to come.

Leader: Jesus went out from the Passover party into the darkness of Gethsemane, on the first stage of the journey that would take him to the cross. Please try to go out quietly, spending some time reflecting on what the end of this Passover celebration meant for him.

[If possible, have people go out through a darkened room or corridor, where a bare cross is standing, lit by a solitary spotlight.]

Bibliography

Scripture quotations from Revised Standard Version, 1946, 1952

Gordon Jessop, *Passover*, Olive Press, 1980. CMJ, 30c Clarence Road, St Albans

Mordell Klein, *Passover*, Popular Judaica Library, Keter Books, Jerusalem, 1973

J. Lehmann, *The Lehmann Haggadah*, 1969. Publishers: 20 Cambridge Terrace, Gateshead NE8 1RP

Cecil Roth, *The Haggadah with English translation & notes*, Soncino Press, London, 1959

Dr A. M. Silbermann, *Children's Haggadah*, illustrated by Erwin Singer, translation in prose and verse by Isidore Wartski and Arthur Saul Super, Routledge and Kegan Paul, London, 1974

Notes

1. There is no evidence of a gallery or of any segregation of the sexes in the excavated synagogue at Capernaum, or indeed, in any other pre-sixth-century synagogue. It would appear that segregation was introduced gradually in the post-Christian era, possibly under the influence of Islam.

2. Acts 2:44.

3. Samuel Wells, *God's Companions: Re-imagining Christian Ethics*, Blackwell Publishing, 2006, p. 202.

4. An average child laughs 400 times a day, an average adult 15 times a day, according to *USA Today*, quoted by Killy, John and Alie Stibbe, *Bursting at the Seams*, Monarch Books, 2004, p. 138.

5. John 15:11.

6. Matthew 25:23.

7. John 4:14 in Eugene H. Peterson, *The Message: The New Testament in Contemporary Language*, Navpress, 1993.

8. *House Churches Are More Satisfying to Attenders Than Are Conventional Churches*, www.barna.org

9. I am indebted for his ideas on church as a 'one-stop shop', and the way this has undermined the role of men, to Revd John Atkinson, formerly Associate Vicar of Christchurch, Kenilworth in Capetown, South Africa. He preached a whole sermon series on spirituality in the home, based on his knowledge of the Hebraic roots of Christianity, and graciously gave me access to his notes.

10. Henri J. M. Nouwen, *Creative Ministry*, Doubleday Image, 1971, p. 95.

11. Samuel Wells, *God's Companions: Re-imagining Christian Ethics*, Blackwell Publishing, 2006, p. 93.

12. Derek Kidner, *Ezra and Nehemiah: An introduction and commentary*, Tyndale Old Testament Commentaries, Inter-Varsity Press, 1979, p. 107.

13. *Matthew Henry's Commentary on the Whole Bible*, ed. Revd Leslie F. Church, Marshall, Morgan and Scott, 1960, p. 499.

14. Matthew 16:25; Henri J. M. Nouwen, *Creative Ministry*, Doubleday Image, 1971.

15. Hebrews 1:3.

16. Hebrews 12:22.

17. John 15:15.

18. From Robert Siegel, *A Pentecost of Finches*, © Robert Siegel. Used by permission of Paraclete Press (www.paracletepress.com) and of the author.

19. From *Praying With the Jewish Tradition*, introduction by Lionel Blue, Triangle, 1988; used by permission of SPCK/Sheldon Press, an imprint of SPCK.

20. Whether or not this grace was actually written by John Wesley, no one really knows. It can be sung to the tune of 'Praise God from whom all blessings flow'. The source is the Huron Hunger Fund of the Anglican Church of Canada.

21. 'And when you son asks you, "What does this mean?" you shall say to him, "By strength of hand the Lord brought us out of Egypt, from the house of bondage"' (Exodus 13:14).

22. 'In the future, when your children ask you, "What do these stones mean?" tell them that the flow of the Jordan was cut off before the ark of the covenant of the Lord' (Joshua 4:6–7).

23. *Judaism's Religions Vision and the Capiatalist Ethic*, Acton Institute, Religion and Liberty, Nov & Dec 2001, Vol II, Number 6.

24. Constantine probably moved it from Saturday to Sunday, not so much because Sunday was the day of the resurrection, but because he wanted to dejudaize it. Since he was highly syncretistic despite his conversion to Christianity, he maintained many of his pagan practices, including sun worship. Sunday was the day of the sun.

25. 1 Corinthians 15:20.

26. I have slightly adapted this lovely idea from Margot Hodson, *A Feast of Seasons*, Monarch Books and Olive Press, 2000, with her permission.

27. Adapted from an original idea by Walter Riggans, for the Church's Ministry Among Jewish People, reprinted with their permission.

28. Adapted from a liturgy written by the Australian Mothers' Union.

29. Adapted from Sara Wenger Shenk, *Why Not Celebrate*, Good Books, 1987. Copyright by Good Books (www.GoodBooks.com). Used by permission. All rights reserved.

30. In Hebrew the word *Purim* means 'lots', referring to the lots that were cast by Haman and the Persians to decide the day on which the Jews should be annihilated.

31. 'A Carnival of Christianity', *The Guardian*, 14.7.05. In 2006, thousands of Christians and members of other faiths and none filled Manchester city centre on Good Friday for the Manchester Oratorio – a promenade version of the day's historic events, performed and sung by professional actors. It was televised live by ITV.

32. From an idea by Olive M. Fleming Drane in *Spirituality To Go*, Darton Longman & Todd, 2005.

33. The Lenten Love Project is adapted from an idea in Sara Wenger Shenk, *Why Not Celebrate*, 1987. Copyright by Good Books (www.GoodBooks.com). Used by permission. All rights reserved.

34. Some of the Christian commentators, including Matthew Henry, find it hard to establish that Sinai did in fact happen 50 days after the flight from Egypt. The Bible says, however, it occurred in the third month. The third new moon was exactly 45 days after the great escape. On day 46 Moses goes up Sinai and comes down on day 47, when he tells the people they have three days in which to prepare to meet with God. Mathematically accurate or not, the link between the giving of the law and the coming of the Holy Spirit is too significant to be purely coincidental.

35. Originally native to the New Zealand Maori, swinging *poi* have recently become popular with jugglers and performers. The two weighted fabric balls suspended on long coloured ribbons are swung in a series of complex sequences. The ends can be lit, and watching the flames spinning through the air is very dramatic, but it must be done by an expert – and church insurance may not cover such an act of daring!

36. Penguin, 1996, p. 9. Used with the permission of David Higham Associates.

37. Rabbi Rami M. Shapiro, *Wisdom of the Jewish Sages*, a modern reading of the *Pirke Avot (The Talmud)*, Bell Tower, 1993, p. 47.

38. Q.: What kind of cheese can turn unleavened bread into a pizza? A.: Matzarella! This year we're having wholemeal-and-bran matzah – it's a new kind whose brand name is 'Let My People Go'!

39. Eat the tithe of your grain, new wine and oil... in the presence of the Lord your God, at the place he will choose as a dwelling for his Name... But if that place is too distant... then exchange your tithe for silver, take the silver with you to the place the Lord shall

choose. Use the silver to buy whatever you like: cattle, sheep, wine or other fermented drink, or anything you wish. Then you and your household shall eat there in the presence of the Lord and rejoice (Deuteronomy 14:23–25).

40. Gender roles are clearly differentiated in Jewish cultural history – but this does not mean there is a difference in status. Men take the lead in spiritual matters, in prayers and blessings, while women create the environment in which the rituals and traditions can best take place. The woman is the rational, practical member of the family, making many of the key decisions. It is a matriarchal society.